莎士比亚经典戏剧

中英文对照 （全译本）

哈 姆 莱 特

Hamlet

本丛书编委会◎编

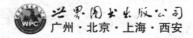
世界图书出版公司
广州·北京·上海·西安

图书在版编目（CIP）数据

哈姆莱特：汉英对照/《莎士比亚经典戏剧（中英对照）丛书》编委会编 . —广州：广东世界图书出版公司，2009.4（2024.2 重印）（莎士比亚经典戏剧（中英对照）丛书）

ISBN 978－7－5100－0596－1

Ⅰ. 哈… Ⅱ. 莎… Ⅲ.①英语—汉语—对照读物 ②悲剧—剧本—英国—中世纪 Ⅳ. H319.4：Ⅰ

中国版本图书馆 CIP 数据核字（2009）第 056103 号

书　　名	哈姆莱特
	HAMULAITE
编　　者	《莎士比亚经典戏剧（中英对照）丛书》编写组
责任编辑	韩海霞
装帧设计	三棵树设计工作组
出版发行	世界图书出版有限公司　世界图书出版广东有限公司
地　　址	广州市海珠区新港西路大江冲 25 号
邮　　编	510300
电　　话	020-84452179
网　　址	http://www.gdst.com.cn
邮　　箱	wpc_gdst@163.com
经　　销	新华书店
印　　刷	唐山富达印务有限公司
开　　本	787mm×1092mm　1/16
印　　张	19.5
字　　数	180 千字
版　　次	2009 年 4 月第 1 版　2024 年 2 月第 10 次印刷
国际书号	ISBN　978-7-5100-0596-1
定　　价	59.80 元

译者序

　　于世界文学史中，足以笼罩一世，凌越千古，卓然为词坛之宗匠，诗人之冠冕者，其唯希腊之荷马，意大利之但丁，英之莎士比亚，德之歌德乎，此四子者，各于其不同之时代及环境中，发其不朽之歌声。然荷马史诗中之英雄，即与吾人之现实生活相去太远；但丁之天堂地狱，又与近代思想诸多牴牾；歌德距吾人较近，实为近代精神之卓越的代表。但以超脱时空限制一点而论，则莎士比亚之成就，实远在三子之上。盖莎翁笔下之人物，虽多为古代之贵族阶级，然其所发掘者，实为古今中外贵贱贫富人人所同具之人性。故虽经三百余年以后，不仅其书为全世界文学之士所耽读，其剧本亦在各国舞台与银幕上历久搬演而不衰，盖由其作品中具有永久性与普遍性，故能深入人心如此耳。

　　中国读者耳闻莎翁大名已久，文坛知名之士，亦曾将其作品译出多种，然历观坊间各译本，失之于粗疏草率者尚少，失之于拘泥生硬者实繁有徒。拘泥字句之结果，不仅原作神味荡然无存，甚至艰深晦涩有若天书，令人不能阅读，此则译者之过，莎翁不能任其咎者也。

　　余笃嗜莎剧，曾首尾研诵全集至少十余遍，于原作精神，自觉颇有会心。廿四年春，得前辈同事詹先生之鼓励，始著手为翻译全集之尝试。越年战事发生，历年来辛苦搜集之各种莎集版本，及诸家注译考证批评之书，不下一二百册，全数毁于炮火，仓卒中只携出牛津版全集一册，及译稿数本而已，而后辗转流徙，为生活而奔波，更无暇晷，以续未竟之志。及卅一年春，目观世变日亟，闭户家居，摈绝外务，始得惠心一志，致力译事。虽贫穷疾病，变相煎迫，而埋头伏案，握管不辍。前后历十年而全稿完成，（案译者撰此文时，原拟在半年后可以译完。不料体力不支，厥功未就，而因病重辍笔仅余历史剧部分由虞尔昌先生续译完成）夫以译莎工作之艰巨，十年之功，不可云久，然毕生精力，殆已书注于兹矣。

余译此书之宗旨，第一在求最大可能之范围内，保持原作之神韵；必不得已而求其次，亦必以明白晓畅之字句，忠实传达原文之意趣；而于逐字逐句对照式之硬译，则未敢赞同。凡遇原文中与中国语法不合之处，往往再三咀嚼，不惜全部更易原文之结构，务使作者之命意豁然呈露，不为晦涩之字句所掩蔽。每译一段，必先自拟为读者，察阅译文中有无暧昧不明之处。又必自拟为舞台上之演员，审辨语调是否顺口，音节是否调和。一字一字之未惬，往往苦思累日。然才力所限，未能尽符理想；乡居僻陋，既无参考之书籍，又鲜质疑之师友。谬误之处，自知不免。所望海内学人，惠予纠正，幸甚幸甚！

原文全集在编次方面，不甚惬当，兹特依据各剧性质，分为"喜剧"、"悲剧"、"传奇剧"、"史剧"四辑，每辑各自成一系统。读者循是以求，不难获见莎翁作品之全貌。昔卡莱尔尝云："吾人宁失百印度，不愿失一莎士比亚"。夫莎士比亚为世界的诗人，固非一国所可独占；倘若此集之出版，使此大诗人之作品，得以普及中国读者之间，则译者之劳力，庶几不为虚掷矣。知我罪我，惟在读者。

生豪书于西元一九四四年四月

Contents

目 录

CHARACTERS IN THE PLAY

CLAUDIUS, *King of Denmark*

HAMLET, *Prince of Denmark*, *son to the late*, *and nephew to the present King*

FORTINBRAS, *Prince of Norway*

HORATIO, *friend to Hamlet*

POLONIUS, *Principal Secretary of State*

LAERTES, *son to Polonius*

VALTEMAND
CORNELIUS
ROSENCRANTZ }, *courtiers*
GUILDENSTERN
OSRIC

A Gentleman

A Priest

MARCELLUS
BARNARDO }, *officers*

FRANCISCO, *soldier*

REYNALDO, *servant to Polonius*

A Captain

English Ambassadors

The Players

Two Grave-diggers

GERTRUDE, *Queen of Denmark*, *mother to Hamlet*

OPHELIA, *daughter to Polonius*

剧 中 人 物

克 劳 狄 斯　　丹麦国王

哈 姆 莱 特　　前王之子，今王之侄

福 丁 布 拉 斯　挪威王子

霍 　 拉 　 旭　哈姆莱特之友

波 洛 涅 斯　　御前大臣

雷 欧 提 斯　　波洛涅斯之子

伏 提 曼 德 ⎤

考 尼 律 斯 ⎟

罗 森 格 兰 兹 ⎬　朝臣

吉 尔 登 斯 吞 ⎟

奥 斯 里 克 ⎦

侍 　 　 臣

教 　 　 士

马 西 勒 斯 ⎤

勃 那 多 ⎦　军官

弗 兰 西 斯 科　兵士

雷 奈 尔 多　　波洛涅斯之仆

队 　 　 长

英 国 使 臣

众 　 伶 　 人

二 　 小 　 丑　掘坟墓者

乔 特 鲁 德　　丹麦王后，哈姆莱特之母

奥 菲 利 娅　　波洛涅斯之女

Lords ,Ladies ,Soldieis ,Sailors ,Messenger ,and Attendants
The Ghost of Hamlet' s father

THE SCENE

Elsinore

哈姆莱特

Hamlet

贵族、贵妇、军官、兵士、教士、水手、使者及侍从等

哈姆莱特父亲的鬼魂

地　　点

艾尔西诺

ACT 1　SCENE 1

Elsinore. A platform before the castle

[*Francisco at his post. Enter to him Barnardo.*]

BARNARDO	Who's there?
FRANCISCO	Nay, answer me. Stand and unfold yourself.
BARNARDO	Long live the King!
FRANCISCO	Barnardo?
BARNARDO	He.
FRANCISCO	You come most carefully upon your hour.
BARNARDO	'Tis now struck twelve, get thee to bed, Francisco.
FRANCISCO	For this relief much thanks, 'tis bitter cold,
	And I am sick at heart.
BARNARDO	Have you had quiet guard?
FRANCISCO	Not a mouse stirring.
BARNARDO	Well, good night: If you do meet Horatio and Marcellus,
	The rivals of my watch, did them make haste.
FRANCISCO	I think I hear them. Stand ho, who is there?

[*Enter Horatio and Marcellus.*]

HORATIO	Friends to this ground.
MARCELLUS	And liegemen to the Dane.
FRANCISCO	Give you good night.
MARCELLUS	O, farewell honest soldier,
	Who hath relieved you?
FRANCISCO	Barnardo hath my place; give you good night.

[*Exit Francisco.*]

第 一 幕

第一场　艾尔西诺。城堡前的露台

（弗兰西斯科立台上守望。勃那多自对面上。）

勃 那 多　那边是谁？

弗兰西斯科　不，你先回答我；站住，告诉我你是什么人。

勃 那 多　国王万岁！

弗兰西斯科　勃那多吗？

勃 那 多　正是。

弗兰西斯科　你来得很准时。

勃 那 多　现在已经打过十二点钟；你去睡吧，弗兰西斯科。

弗兰西斯科　谢谢你来替我；天冷得厉害，我心里也老大不舒服。

勃 那 多　你守在这儿，一切都很安静吗？

弗兰西斯科　一只小老鼠也不见走动。

勃 那 多　好，晚安！要是你碰见霍拉旭和马西勒斯，我的守夜的伙伴们，就叫他们赶紧来。

弗兰西斯科　我想我听见了他们的声音。喂，站住！你是谁？

（霍拉旭及马西勒斯上。）

霍 拉 旭　都是自己人。

马 西 勒 斯　丹麦王的臣民。

弗兰西斯科　祝你们晚安！

马 西 勒 斯　啊！再会，正直的军人！谁替了你？

弗兰西斯科　勃那多接我的班。祝你们晚安！（下。）

MARCELLUS	Holla, Barnardo!
BARNARDO	Say——what, is Horatio there?
HORATIO	A piece of him.
BARNARDO	Welcome Horatio, welcome good Marcellus.
MARCELLUS	What, has this thing appeared again tonight?
BARNARDO	I have seen nothing.
MARCELLUS	Horatio says 'tis but our fantasy,
	And will not let belief take hold of him.
	Touching this dreaded sight twice seen of us,
	Therefore I have entreated him along
	With us to watch the minutes of this night,
	That if again this apparition come,
	He may approve our eyes and speak to it.
HORATIO	Tush, tush, 'twill not appear.
BARNARDO	Sit down awhile,
	And let us once again assail your ears,
	That are so fortified against our story,
	What we have two nights seen.
HORATIO	Well, sit we down,
	And let us hear Barnardo speak of this.
BARNARDO	Last night of all,
	When yond same star that's westward from the pole
	Had made his course t' illume that part of heaven
	Where now it burns, Marcellus and myself,
	The bell then beating one —
MARCELLUS	Peace, break thee off; look where it comes again!
	[*Enter Ghost.*]
BARNARDO	In the same figure like the King that's dead.

马 西 勒 斯	喂！勃那多！
勃 那 多	喂，——啊！霍拉旭也来了吗？
霍 拉 旭	有这么一个他。
勃 那 多	欢迎，霍拉旭！欢迎，好马西勒斯！
马 西 勒 斯	什么！这东西今晚又出现过了吗？
勃 那 多	我还没有瞧见什么。
马 西 勒 斯	霍拉旭说那不过是我们的幻想。我告诉他我们已经两次看见过这一个可怕的怪象，他总是不肯相信；所以我请他今晚也来陪我们守一夜，要是这鬼魂再出来，就可以证明我们并没有看错，还可以叫他和它说几句话。
霍 拉 旭	嘿，嘿，它不会出现的。
勃 那 多	先请坐下；虽然你一定不肯相信我们的故事，我们还是要把我们这两夜来所看见的情形再向你絮叨一遍。
霍 拉 旭	好，我们坐下来，听听勃那多怎么说。
勃 那 多	昨天晚上，北极星西面的那颗星已经移到了它现在吐射光辉的地方，时钟刚敲了一点，马西勒斯跟我两个人——
马 西 勒 斯	住声！不要说下去；瞧，它又来了！
	（鬼魂上。）
勃 那 多	正像已故的国王的模样。

MARCELLUS	Thou art a scholar, speak to it, Horatio.
BARNARDO	Looks'a not like the King? Mark it, Horatio.
HORATIO	Most like, it harrows me with fear and wonder.
BARNARDO	It would be spoke to.
MARCELLUS	Question it, Horatio.
HORATIO	What art thou that usurp'st this time of night,
	Together with that fair and warlike form
	In which the majesty of buried Denmark
	Did sometimes march? by heaven I charge thee speak.
MARCELLUS	It is offended.
BARNARDO	See, it stalks away.
HORATIO	Stay, speak, speak, I charge thee speak. [*Exit the Ghost.*]
MARCELLUS	'Tis gone and will not answer.
BARNARDO	How now Horatio, you tremble and look pale,
	Is not this something more than fantasy?
	What think you on't?
HORATIO	Before my God, I might not this believe
	Without the sensible and true avouch of mine own eyes.
MARCELLUS	Is it not like the King?
HORATIO	As thou art to thyself.
	Such was the very armour be had on,
	When he the ambitious Norway combated,
	So frowned he once, when in an angry parle
	He smote the sledded Polacks on the ice.
	'Tis strange.
MARCELLUS	Thus twice before, and jump at the dead hour,
	With martial stalk hath he gone by our watch.
HORATIO	In what particular thought to work I know not,

马 西 勒 斯	你是有学问的人,去和它说话,霍拉旭。
勃 那 多	它的样子不像已故的国王吗?看,霍拉旭。
霍 拉 旭	像得很;它使我心里充满了恐怖和惊奇。
勃 那 多	它希望我们对它说话。
马 西 勒 斯	你去问它,霍拉旭。
霍 拉 旭	你是什么鬼怪,胆敢僭窃丹麦先王出征时的神武的雄姿,在这样深夜的时分出现?凭着上天的名义,我命令你说话!
马 西 勒 斯	它生气了。
勃 那 多	瞧,它昂然不顾地走开了!
霍 拉 旭	不要走!说呀,说呀!我命令你,快说!(鬼魂下。)
马 西 勒 斯	它走了,不愿回答我们。
勃 那 多	怎么,霍拉旭!你在发抖,你的脸色这样惨白。这不是幻想吧?你有什么高见?
霍 拉 旭	凭上帝起誓,倘不是我自己的眼睛向我证明,我再也不会相信这样的怪事。
马 西 勒 斯	它不像我们的国王吗?
霍 拉 旭	正和你像你自己一样。它身上的那副战铠,就是它讨伐野心的挪威王的时候所穿的;它脸上的那副怒容,活像它有一次在谈判决裂以后把那些乘雪车的波兰人击溃在冰上的时候的神气。怪事怪事!
马 西 勒 斯	前两次它也是这样不先不后地在这个静寂的时辰,用军人的步态走过我们的眼前。
霍 拉 旭	我不知道究竟应该怎样想法;

But in the gross and scope of mine opinion,

This bodes some strange eruption to our state.

MARCELLUS   Good now sit down, and tell me he that knows,

Why this same strict and most observant watch

So nightly toils the subject of the land,

And why such daily cast of brazen cannon

And foreign mart for implements of war,

Why such impress of shipwrights, whose sore task

Does not divide the Sunday from the week,

What might be toward that this sweaty haste

Doth make the night joint-labourer with the day,

Who is't that can inform me?

HORATIO   That can I,

At least the whisper goes so; our last king,

Whose image even but now appeared to us,

Was as you know by Fortinbras of Norway,

Thereto pricked on by a most emulate pride,

Dared to the combat; in which our valiant Hamlet——

For so this side of our known world esteemed him——

Did say this Fortinbras, who by a sealed compact,

Well ratified by law and heraldry,

Did forfeit(with his life) all those his lands

Which he stood seized of, to the conqueror,

Against the which a moiety competent

Was gaged by our king, which had returned

To the inheritance of Fortinbras,

Had he been vanquisher; as by the same co-mart,

And carriage of the article designed,

可是大概推测起来，这恐怕预兆着我们国内将要有一番非常的变故。

马西勒斯　好吧，坐下来。谁要是知道的，请告诉我，为什么我们要有这样森严的戒备，使全国的军民每夜不得安息；为什么每天都在制造铜炮，还要向国外购买战具；为什么征集大批造船匠，连星期日也不停止工作；这样夜以继日地辛苦忙碌，究竟为了什么？谁能告诉我？

霍拉旭　我可以告诉你；至少一般人都是这样传说。刚才它的形象很像我们出现的那位已故的国王，你们知道，曾经接受骄矜好胜的挪威的福丁布拉斯的挑战；在那一次决斗中间，我们的勇武的哈姆莱特，——他的英名是举世称颂的——把福丁布拉斯杀死了；按照双方根据法律和骑士精神所订立的协定，福丁布拉斯要是战败了，除了他自己的生命以外，必须把他所有的一切土地拨归胜利的一方；同时我们的王上也提出相当的土地作为赌注，要是福丁布拉斯得胜了，那土地也就归他所有，正像在同一协定上所规定的，

His fell to Hamlet; now sir, young Fortinbras,

Of unimproved mettle hot and full,

Hath in the skirts of Norway here and there

Sharked up a list of lawless resolutes

For food and diet to some enterprise

That hath a stomach in' t, which is no other,

As it doth well appear unto our state,

But to recover of us by strong hand

And terms compulsatory, those foresaid lands

So by his father lost; and this, I take it,

Is the main motive of our preparations,

The source of this our watch, and the chief head

Of this post haste and romage in the land.

BARNARDO I think it be no other but e'en so;

Well may it sort that this portentous figure

Comes armed through our watch so like the king

That was and is the question of these wars.

HORATIO A moth it is to trouble the mind's eye.

In the most high and palmy state of Rome,

A little ere the mightiest Julius fell,

The graves stood tenantless, and the sheeted dead

Did squeak and gibber in the Roman streets,

As stars with trains of fire and dews of blood,

Disasters in the sun; and the moist star,

Upon whose influence Neptune's empire stands,

Was sick almost to doomsday with eclipse.

And even the like precurse of fierce events,

As harbingers preceding still the fates

他失败了，哈姆莱特可以把他的土地没收一样。现在要说起那位福丁布拉斯的儿子，他生得一副未经锻炼的烈火也似的性格，在挪威四境召集了一群无赖之徒，供给他们衣食，驱策他们去干冒险的勾当，好叫他们显一显身手。他的唯一的目的，我们的当局看得很清楚，无非是要用武力和强迫性的条件，夺回他父亲所丧失的土地。照我所知道的，这就是我们种种准备的主要动机，我们这样戒备的唯一原因，也是全国所以这样慌忙骚乱的缘故。

勃 那 多 我想正是为了这个缘故。我们那位王上在过去和目前的战乱中间，都是一个主要的角色，所以无怪他的武装的形象要向我们出现示警了。

霍 拉 旭 那是扰乱我们心灵之眼的一点微尘。从前在富强繁盛的罗马，在那雄才大略的裘力斯·恺撒遇害前不久，披着殓衾的死人都从坟墓里出来，在街道上啾啾鬼语，星辰拖着火尾，露水带血，太阳变色，支配潮汐的月亮被吞蚀得像

And prologue to the omen coming on,

Have heaven and earth together demonstrated

Unto our climatures and countrymen,

   [*Re-enter Ghost.*]

But soft, behold, lo where it comes again!

I'll cross it though it blast me. Stay, illusion!

If thou hast any sound or use of voice,

Speak to me.

If there be any good thing to be done

That may to thee do ease, and grace to me,

Speak to me.

If thou art privy to thy country's fate

Which happily foreknowing may avoid,

O, speak!

Or if thou hast uphoarded in thy life

Extorted treasure in the womb of earth,

For which they say you spirits oft walk in death, [*A cock crows*]

Speak of it. Stay and speak. Stop it, Marcellus!

MARCELLUS	Shall I strike at it with my partisan?
HORATIO	Do if it will not stand.
BARNARDO	'Tis here!
HORATIO	'Tis here! [*Exit Ghost.*]
MARCELLUS	'Tis gone!

We do it wrong being so majestical

To offer it the show of violence,

For it is as the air, invulnerable,

And our vain blows malicious mockery.

BARNARDO   It was about to speak when the cock crew.

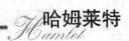

哈姆莱特

一个没有气色的病人；这一类预报重大变故的征兆，在我们国内的天上地下也已经屡次出现了。可是不要响！瞧！瞧！它又来了！

（鬼魂重上。）

我要挡住它的去路，即使它会害我。不要走，鬼魂！要是你能出声，会开口，对我说话吧；要是我有可以为你效劳之处，使你的灵魂得到安息，那么对我说话吧；要是你预知祖国的命运，靠着你的指示，也许可以及时避免未来的灾祸，那么对我说话吧；或者你在生前曾经把你搜括得来的财宝埋藏在地下，我听见人家说，鬼魂往往在他们藏金的地方徘徊不散，（鸡啼）要是有这样的事，你也对我说吧；不要走，说呀！拦住它，马西勒斯。

马西勒斯　要不要我用我的戟刺它？

霍拉旭　好的，要是它不肯站定。

勃那多　它在这儿！

霍拉旭　它在这儿！（鬼魂下。）

马西勒斯　它走了！我们不该用暴力对待这样一个尊严的亡魂；因为它是像空气一样不可侵害的，我们无益的打击不过是恶意的徒劳。

勃那多　它正要说话的时候，鸡就啼了。

莎士比亚经典戏剧

HORATIO	And then it started like a guilty thing,
	Upon a fearful summons; I have heard
	The cock that is the trumpet to the morn
	Doth with his lofty and shrill-sounding throat
	Awake the god of day, and at his warning
	Whether in sea or fire, in earth or air,
	Th'extravagant and erring spirit hies
	To his confine, and of the truth herein
	This present object made probation.
MARCELLUS	It faded on the crowing of the cock.
	Some say that ever ' gainst that season comes
	Wherein our Saviour's birth is celebrated
	This bird of dawning singeth all night long,
	And then they say no spirit dare stir abroad,
	The nights are wholesome, then no planets strike,
	No fairy takes, nor witch hath power to charm,
	So hallowed, and so gracious is that time.
HORATIO	So have I heard and do in part believe it.
	But look, the morn in russet mantle clad
	Walks o' er the dew of yon high eastward hill.
	Break we our watch up and by my advice
	Let us impart what we have seen tonight
	Unto young Hamlet, for upon my life
	This spirit, dumb to us, will speak to him.
	Do you consent we shall acquaint him with it,
	As needful in our loves, Fitting our duty?
MARCELLUS	Let' s do' t, I pray, and I this morning know
	Where we shall find him most convenient. [*Exeunt.*]

Shakespeare Classics

霍 拉 旭	于是它就像一个罪犯听到了可怕的召唤似的惊跳起来。我听人家说，报晓的雄鸡用它高锐的啼声，唤醒了白昼之神，一听到它的警告，那些在海里、火里、地下、空中到处浪游的有罪的灵魂，就一个个钻回自己的巢穴里去；这句话现在已经证实了。
马西勒斯	那鬼魂正是在鸡鸣的时候隐去的。有人说，在我们每次欢庆圣诞之前不久，这报晓的鸟儿总会彻夜长鸣；那时候，他们说，没有一个鬼魂可以出外行走，夜间的空气非常清净，没有一颗星用毒光射人，没有一个神仙用法术迷人，妖巫的符咒也失去了力量，一切都是圣洁而美好的。
霍 拉 旭	我也听人家这样说过，倒有几分相信。可是瞧，清晨披着赤褐色的外衣，已经踏着那边东方高山上的露水走过来了。我们也可以下班了。照我的意思，我们应该把我们今夜看见的事情告诉年轻的哈姆莱特；因为凭着我的生命起誓，这一个鬼魂虽然对我们不发一言，见了他一定有话要说。你们以为按着我们的交情和责任说起来，是不是应当让他知道这件事情？
马西勒斯	很好，我们决定去告诉他吧；我知道今天早上在什么地方最容易找到他。（同下。）

SCENE 2

A room of state in the castle

[*Enter King Claudius, Queen Gertrude, Hamlet, Polonius, Laertes, Voltimand, Cornelius, Lords, and Attendants.*]

KING   Though yet of Hamlet our dear brother's death

The memory be green, and that it us befitted

To bear our hearts in grief, and our whole kingdom

To be contracted in one brow of woe,

Yet so far hath discretion fought with nature,

That we with wisest sorrow think on him

Together with remembrance of ourselves;

Therefore our sometime sister, now our queen,

Th'imperial jointress to this warlike state,

Have we as 'twere with a defeated joy,

With an auspicious, and a dropping eye,

With mirth in funeral, and with dirge in marriage,

In equal scale weighing delight and dole,

Taken to wife: nor have we herein barred

Your better wisdoms, which have freely gone

With this affair along, for all, our thanks.

Now follows that you know, young Fortinbras,

Holding a weak supposal of our worth,

Or thinking by our late dear brother's death

Our state to be disjoint and out of frame,

第二场　城堡中的大厅

（国王、王后、哈姆莱特、波洛涅斯、雷欧提斯、伏提曼德、考尼律斯、群臣、侍从等上。）

国　　王　虽然我们亲爱的王兄哈姆莱特新丧未久，我们的心里应当充满了悲痛，我们全国都应当表示一致的哀悼，可是我们凛于后死者责任的重大，不能不违情逆性，一方面固然要用适度的悲哀纪念他，一方面也要为自身的利害着想；所以，在一种悲喜交集的情绪之下，让幸福和忧郁分据了我的两眼，殡葬的挽歌和结婚的笙乐同时并奏，用盛大的喜乐抵消沉重的不幸，我已经和我旧日的长嫂，当今的王后，这一个多事之国的共同的统治者，结为夫妇；这一次婚姻事先曾经征求各位的意见，多承你们诚意的赞助，这是我必须向大家致谢的。现在我要告诉你们知道，年轻的福丁布拉斯看轻了我们的实力，也许他以为自从我们亲爱的王兄驾崩以后，我们的国家已经瓦解，所以挟着他的从中取利的梦想，不断向

Colleagued with this dream of his advantage,

He hath not failed to pester us with message

Importing the surrender of those lands

Lost by his father, with all bands of law,

To our most valiant brother, so much for him,

Now for ourself, and for this time of meeting.

Thus much the business is: We have here writ

To Norway, uncle of young Fortinbras,

Who impotent and bed-rid scarcely hears

Of this his nephew's purpose, to suppress

His further gait herein, in that the levies,

The lists, and full proportions, are all made

Out of his subject. And we here dispatch

You good Cornelius, and you Valtemand,

For bearers of this greeting to old Norway,

Giving to you no further personal power

To business with the king, more than the scope

Of these delated articles allow.

Farewell, and let your haste commend your duty.

CORNELIUS VALTEM'D

In that, and all things, will we show our duty.

KING

We doubt it nothing, heartily farewell.

[*Exeunt Valtemand and Cornelius.*]

And now, laertes, what's the news with you?

You told us of some suit, what is' t, Laertes?

You cannot speak of reason to the Dane,

And lose your voice; What wouldst thou beg, Laertes,

That shall not be my offer, not thy asking?

我们书面要求把他的父亲依法割让给我们英勇的王兄的土地归还。这是他一方面的话。现在要讲到我们的态度和今天召集各位来此的目的。我们的对策是这样的：我这儿已经写好了一封信给挪威国王，年轻的福丁布拉斯的叔父——他因为卧病在床，不曾与闻他侄子的企图——在信里我请他注意他的侄子擅自在国内征募壮丁，训练士卒，积极进行各种准备的事实，要求他从速制止他的进一步的行动；现在我就派遣你，考尼律斯，还有你，伏提曼德，替我把这封信送给挪威老王，除了训令上所规定的条件以外，你们不得僭用你们的权力，和挪威成立逾越范围的妥协。你们赶紧去吧，再会！

考尼律斯
伏提曼德　我们敢不尽力执行陛下的旨意。

国　　王　我相信你们的忠心；再会！（伏提曼德、考尼律斯同下。）现在，雷欧提斯，你有什么话说？你对我说你有一个请求；是什么请求，雷欧提斯？只要是合理的事情，你向丹麦王说了，他总不会不答应你。你有什么要求，雷欧提斯，不是你未开口我就自动许给了你？丹麦王室和你父亲

The head is not more native to the heart,

The hand more instrumental to the mouth,

Than is the throne of Denmark to thy father.

What wouldst thou have, Laertes?

LAERTES　My dread lord,

Your leave and favour to return to France,

From whence though willingly I came to Denmark,

To show my duty in your coronation;

Yet now I must confess, that duty done,

My thoughts and wishes bend again toward France,

And bow them to your gracious leave and pardon.

KING　Have you your father's leave? What says Polonius?

POLONIUS　He hath my lord, wrung from me my slow leave

By laboursome petition, and at last

Upon his will I sealed my hard consent.

I do beseech you give him leave to go.

KING　Take thy fair hour, Laertes, time be thine,

And thy best graces spend it at thy will.

But now my cousin Hamlet, and my son —

HAMLET　[*Aside*] A little more than kin, and less than kind.

KING　How is it that the clouds still hang on you?

HAMLET　Not so, my lord, I am too much in the sun.

QUEEN　Good Hamlet, cast thy nighted colour off,

And let thine eye look like a friend on Denmark;

Do not for eve with thy vailed lids

Seek for thy noble father in the dust;

Thou know' st ' tis common, all that lives must die,

Passing through nature to eternity.

的关系，正像头脑之于心灵一样密切；丹麦国王乐意为你父亲效劳，正像双手乐于为嘴服役一样。你要些什么，雷欧提斯？

雷欧提斯 陛下，我要请求您允许我回到法国去。这一次我回国参加陛下加冕的盛典，略尽臣子的微忱，实在是莫大的荣幸；可是现在我的任务已尽，我的心愿又向法国飞驰，但求陛下开恩允准。

国　　王 你父亲已经答应你了吗？波洛涅斯怎么说？

波洛涅斯 陛下，我却不过他几次三番的恳求，已经勉强答应他了；请陛下放他去吧。

国　　王 好好利用你的时间，雷欧提斯，尽情发挥你的才能吧！可是来，我的侄儿哈姆莱特，我的孩子——

哈姆莱特 （旁白）超乎寻常的亲族，漠不相干的路人。

国　　王 为什么愁闷依旧笼罩在你的身上？

哈姆莱特 不，陛下；我已经在太阳里晒得太久了。

王　　后 好哈姆莱特，抛开你阴郁的神气吧，对丹麦王应该和颜悦色一点；不要老是垂下了眼皮，在泥土之中找寻你的高贵的父亲。你知道这是一件很普通的事情，活着的人谁都要死去，从生活踏进永久的宁静。

HAMLET	Ay, madam, it is common.
QUEEN	If it be, why seems it so particular with thee?
HAMLET	Seems, madam! Nay it is, I know not 'seems'.

'Tis not alone my inky cloak, good mother,

Nor customary suits of solemn black,

Nor windy suspiration of forced breath,

No, nor the fruitful river in the eye,

Nor the dejected haviour of the visage,

Together with all forms, motes, shapes of grief,

That can denote me truly. These 'indeed seem,

For they are actions that a man might play,

But I have that within which passes show,

These but the trappings and the suits of woe.

KING   'Tis sweet and commendable in your nature, Hamlet,

To give these mourning duties to your father,

But you must know your father lost a father,

That father lost, lost his, and the survivor bound

In filial obligation for some term

To do obsequious sorrow. But to persever

In obstinate condolement is a course

Of impious stubbornness, 'tis unmanly grief,

It shows a will most incorrect to heaven,

A heart unfortified, a mind impatient,

An understanding simple and unschooled.

For what we know must be and is as common

As any the most vulgar thing to sense,

Why should we in our peevish opposition

Take it to heart? Fie, 'tis a fault to heaven,

哈姆莱特

哈 姆 莱 特　嗯，母亲，这是一件很普通的事情。

王　　后　既然是很普通的，那么你为什么瞧上去好像老是这样郁郁于心呢？

哈 姆 莱 特　好像，母亲！不，是这样就是这样，我不知道什么"好像"不"好像"。好妈妈，我的墨黑的外套、礼俗上规定的丧服、难以吐出来的叹气、像滚滚江流一样的眼泪、悲苦沮丧的脸色，以及一切仪式、外表和忧伤的流露，都不能表示出我的真实的情绪。这些才真是给人瞧的，因为谁都可以做作成这种样子。它们不过是悲哀的装饰和衣服；可是我的郁结的心事却是无法表现出来的。

国　　王　哈姆莱特，你这样孝思不匮，原是你天性中纯笃过人之处；可是你要知道，你的父亲也曾失去过一个父亲，那失去的父亲自己也失去过父亲；那后死的儿子为了尽他的孝道，必须有一个时期服丧守节，然而固执不变的哀伤，却是一种逆天悖理的愚行，不是堂堂男子所应有的举动；它表现出一个不肯安于天命的意志，一个经不起艰难痛苦的心，一个缺少忍耐的头脑和一个简单愚昧的理性。既然我们知道那是无可避免的事，无论谁都要遭遇到同样的经验，那么我们为什么要这样固执地把它介介于怀呢？嘿！那是对上天的罪戾，对死者的罪戾，也是违反人情的罪戾；在理智上它是完全荒谬的，因为从第

A fault against the dead, a fault to nature,

To reason most absurd, whose common theme

Is death of fathers, and who still hath cried,

From the first corse till he that died today,

'This must be so'. We pray you throw to earth

This unprevailing woe, and think of us

As of a father, for let the world take note

You are the most immediate to our throne,

And with no less nobility of love

Than that which dearest father bears his son,

Do I impart toward you. For your intent

In going back to school in Wittenberg,

It is most retrograde to our desire,

And we beseech you, bend you to remain

Here in the cheer and comfort of our eye,

Our chiefest courtier, cousin, and our son.

QUEEN Let not thy mother lose her prayers, Hamlet;

I pray thee stay with us, go not to Wittenberg.

HAMLET I shall in all my best obey you, madam.

KING Why, 'tis a loving and a fair reply,

Be as ourself in Denmark. Madam, come.

This gentle and unforced accord of Hamlet,

Sits smiling to my heart, in grace whereof,

No jocund health that Denmark drinks today,

But the great cannon to the clouds shall tell,

And the king's rouse the heaven shall bruit again,

Re-speaking earthly thunder; come away.

[*Exeunt all but Hamlet.*]

一个死了的父亲起，直到今天死去的最后一个父亲为止，理智永远在呼喊，"这是无可避免的。"我请你抛弃了这种无意的悲伤，把我当作你的父亲；因为我要让全世界知道，你是王位的直接的继承者，我要给你的尊荣和恩宠，不亚于一个最慈爱的父亲之于他的儿子。至于你要回到威登堡去继续求学的意思，那是完全违反我们的愿望的；请你听从我的劝告，不要离开这里，在朝廷上领袖群臣，做我们最亲近的国亲和王子，使我们因为每天能看见你而感到欢欣。

王　　后　不要让你母亲的祈求全归无用，哈姆莱特；请你不要离开我们，不要到威登堡去。

哈姆莱特　我将要勉力服从您的意志，母亲。

国　　王　啊，那才是一句有孝心的答复；你将在丹麦享有和我同等的尊荣。御妻，来。哈姆莱特这一种自动的顺从使我非常高兴；为了表示庆祝，今天丹麦王每一次举杯祝饮的时候，都要放一响高入云霄的祝炮，让上天应和着地上的雷鸣，发出欢乐的回声。来。（除哈姆莱特外均下。）

HAMLET   O, that this too too solid flesh would melt,

Thaw and resolve itself into a dew,

Or that the Everlasting had not fixed

His canon ' gainst self-slaughter. O God, God,

How weary, stale, flat, and unprofitable

Seem to me all the uses of this world!

Fie on' t, ah fie, ' tis an unweeded garden

That grows to seed, things rank and gross in nature

Possess it merely. That it should come to this,

But two months dead, nay not so much, not two,

So excellent a king, that was to this

Hyperion to a satyr, so loving to my mother,

That he might not beteem the winds of heaven

Visit her face too roughly-heaven and earth,

Must I remember? Why, she would hang on him

As if increase of appetite had grown

By what it fed on, and yet within a month,

Let me not think on' t. Frailty, thy name is woman!

A little month or ere those shoes were old

With which she followed my poor father's body,

Like Niobe all tears, why she, even she——

O God, a beast that wants discourse of reason

Would have mourned longer——married with my uncle

My father's brother, but no more like my father

Than I to Hercules, Within a month,

Ere yet the salt of most unrighteous teats

Had left the flushing in her galled eyes

She married. O most wicked speed, to post

哈姆莱特

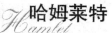

哈姆莱特	啊，但愿这一个太坚实的肉体会融解、消散，化成一堆露水！或者那永生的真神未曾制定禁止自杀的律法！上帝啊！上帝啊！人世间的一切在我看来是多么可厌、陈腐、乏味而无聊！哼！哼！那是一个荒芜不治的花园，长满了恶毒的莠草。想不到居然会有这种事情！刚死了两个月！不，两个月还不满！这样好的一个国王，比起当前这个来，简直是天神和丑怪；这样爱我的母亲，甚至于不愿让天风吹痛了她的脸。天地呀！我必须记着吗？嘿，她会偎依在他的身旁，好像吃了美味的食物，格外促进了食欲一般；可是，只有一个月的时间，我不能再想下去了！脆弱啊，你的名字就是女人！短短的一个月以前，她哭得像个泪人儿似的，送我那可怜的父亲下葬；她在送葬的时候所穿的那双鞋子还没有破旧，她就，她就——上帝啊！一头没有理性的畜生也要悲伤得长久一些——她就嫁给我的叔父，我的父亲的弟弟，可是他一点不像我的父亲，正像我一点不像赫剌克勒斯一样。只有一个月的时间，她那流着虚伪之泪的眼睛还没有消去红肿，她就嫁了人了。啊，罪恶的匆促，这样迫不及待地钻进了乱伦的衾被！那不是好

With such dexterity to incestuous sheets！

It is not, nor it cannot come to good,

But break my heart, for I must hold my tongue.

[*Enter Horatio, Marcellus and Barnardo.*]

HORATIO	Hail to your lordship！
HAMLET	I am glad to see you well；
	Horatio, or I do forget myself！
HORATIO	The same, my lord, and your poor servant ever.
HAMLET	Sir, my good friend, I'll change that name with you. And
	what make you from Wittenberg, Horatio？
	Marcellus.
MARCELLUS	My good lord！
HAMLET	I am very glad to see you：good even, sir.

[*He bows to Barnardo*]

But what in faith make you from Wittenberg？

HORATIO	A truant disposition, good my lord.
HAMLET	I would not hear your enemy say so,
	Nor shall you do mine ear that violence
	To make it truster of your own report
	Against yourself. I know you are no truant,
	But what is your affair in Elsinore？
	We'll teach you to drink deep ere you depart.
HORATIO	My lord, I came to see your father's funeral.
HAMLET	I prithee do not mock me, fellow-student,
	I think it was to see my mother's wedding.
HORATIO	Indeed, my lord, it followed hart upon.
HAMLET	Thrift, thrift, Horatio, the funeral baked meats
	Did coldly furnish forth the marriage tables.

事，也不会有好结果；可是碎了吧，我的心，因为我必须噤住我的嘴！

（霍拉旭、马西勒斯、勃那多同上。）

霍　拉　旭　祝福，殿下！

哈　姆　莱　特　我很高兴看见你身体健康。你不是霍拉旭吗？绝对没有错。

霍　拉　旭　正是，殿下；我永远是您的卑微的仆人。

哈　姆　莱　特　不，你是我的好朋友；我愿意和你朋友相称。你怎么不在威登堡，霍拉旭？马西勒斯！

马　西　勒　斯　殿下——

哈　姆　莱　特　我很高兴看见你。（向勃那多）你好，朋友。——可是你究竟为什么离开威登堡？

霍　拉　旭　无非是偷闲躲懒罢了，殿下。

哈　姆　莱　特　我不愿听见你的仇敌说这样的话，你也不能用这样的话刺痛我的耳朵，使它相信你对你自己所作的诽谤；我知道你不是一个偷闲躲懒的人。可是你到艾尔西诺来有什么事？趁你未去之前，我们要陪你痛饮几杯哩。

霍　拉　旭　殿下，我是来参加您的父王的葬礼的。

哈　姆　莱　特　请你不要取笑，我的同学；我想你是来参加我的母后的婚礼的。

霍　拉　旭　真的，殿下，这两件事情相去得太近了。

哈　姆　莱　特　这是一举两便的办法，霍拉旭！葬礼中剩下来的残羹冷炙，正好宴请婚筵上的宾客。霍拉旭，我宁愿在天上遇见

Would I had met my dearest foe in heaven

Or ever I had seen that day, Horatio.

My father, methinks I see my father.

HORATIO   Where, my lord?

HAMLET   In my mind's eye, Horatio.

HORATIO   I saw him once, he was a goodly king.

HAMLET   He was a man, take him for all in all,

I shall not look upon his like again.

HORATIO   My lord, I think I saw him yesternight.

HAMLET   Saw, who?

HORATIO   My lord, the king your father.

HAMLET   The king my father!

HORATIO   Season your admiration for a while

With an attent ear till I may deliver

Upon the witness of these gentlemen

This marvel to you.

HAMLET   For God's love let me hear!

HORATIO   Two nights together had these gentlemen,

Marcellus and Barnardo, on their watch

In the dead waste and middle of the night,

Been thus encountered. A figure like your father,

Armed at point exactly, cap-a-pe,

Appears before them, and with solemn march,

Goes slow and stately by them; thrice he walked

By their oppressed and fear-surprised eyes

Within his truncheon's length, whilst they distilled

Almost to jelly with the act of fear,

Stand dumb and speak not to him; this to me

　　　　　　我的最痛恨的仇人，也不愿看到那样的一天！我的父亲，
　　　　　　我仿佛看见我的父亲。

霍　拉　旭　啊，在什么地方，殿下？

哈姆莱特　在我的心灵的眼睛里，霍拉旭。

霍　拉　旭　我曾经见过他一次；他是一位很好的君王。

哈姆莱特　他是一个堂堂男子；整个说起来，我再也见不到像他那样
　　　　　　的人了。

霍　拉　旭　殿下，我想我昨天晚上看见他。

哈姆莱特　看见谁？

霍　拉　旭　殿下，我看见您的父王。

哈姆莱特　我的父王！

霍　拉　旭　不要吃惊，请您静静地听我把这件奇事告诉您，这两位可
　　　　　　以替我做见证。

哈姆莱特　看在上帝的份上，讲给我听。

霍　拉　旭　这两位朋友，马西勒斯和勃那多，在万籁俱寂的午夜守望
　　　　　　的时候，曾经连续两夜看见一个自顶至踵全身甲胄、像您
　　　　　　父亲一样的人形，在他们的面前出现，用庄严而缓慢的步
　　　　　　伐走过他们的身边。在他们惊奇骇愕的眼前，它三次走过
　　　　　　去，它手里所握的鞭杖可以碰到他们的身上；他们吓得几
　　　　　　乎浑身都瘫痪了，只是呆立着不动，一句话也没有对它
　　　　　　说。怀着惴惧的心情，他们把这件事悄悄地告诉了我，我

In dreadful secrecy impart they did,

And I with them the third night kept the watch,

Where, as they had delivered, both in time,

Form of the thing, each word made true and good,

The apparition comes. I knew your father,

These hands are not more like.

HAMLET   But where was this?

MARCELLUS   My lord, upon the platform where we watch.

HAMLET   Did you not speak to it?

HORATIO   My lord, I did,

But answer made it none, yet once methought

It lifted up it head, and did address

Itself to motion like as it would speak,

But even then the morning cock crew loud,

And at the sound it shrunk in haste away

And vanished from our sight.

HAMLET   'Tis very strange.

HORATIO   As I do live, my honoured lord, 'tis true,

And we did think it writ down in our duty

To let you know of it.

HAMLET   Indeed, indeed, sirs, but this troubles me.

Hold you the watch tonight?

MARCELLUS
BARNARDO   We do, my lord.

HAMLET   Armed, say you?

MARCELLUS
BARNARDO   Armed, my lord.

就在第三夜陪着他们一起守望；正像他们所说的一样，那鬼魂又出现了，出现的时间和它的形状，证实了他们的每一个字都是正确的。我认识您的父亲；那鬼魂是那样酷肖它的生前，我这两手也不及他们彼此的相似。

哈 姆 莱 特 可是这是在什么地方？

马 西 勒 斯 殿下，就在我们守望的露台上。

哈 姆 莱 特 你们有没有和它说话？

霍 拉 旭 殿下，我说了，可是它没有回答我；不过有一次我觉得它好像抬起头来，像要开口说话似的，可是就在那时候，晨鸡高声啼了起来，它一听见鸡声，就很快地隐去不见了。

哈 姆 莱 特 这很奇怪。

霍 拉 旭 凭着我的生命起誓，殿下，这是真的；我们认为按着我们的责任，应该让您知道这件事。

哈 姆 莱 特 不错，不错，朋友们；可是这件事情很使我迷惑。你们今晚仍旧要去守望吗？

马 西 勒 斯
勃 那 多 是，殿下。

HAMLET	From top to toe?
MARCELLUS	
BARNARDO	My lord, from head to foot.
HAMLET	Then saw you not his face.
HORATIO	O yes, my lord, he wore his beaver up.
HAMLET	What, looked he frowningly?
HORATIO	A countenance more in sorrow than in anger.
HAMLET	Pale, or red?
HORATIO	Nay, very pale.
HAMLET	And fixed his eyes upon you?
HORATIO	Most constantly.
HAMLET	I would I had been there.
HORATIO	It would have much amazed you.
HAMLET	Very like, very like. Stayed it long?
HORATIO	While one with moderate haste might tell a hundred.
MARCELLUS	
BARNARDO	Longer, longer
HORATIO	Not when I saw' t.
HAMLET	His beard was grizzled, no?
HORATIO	It was as I have seen it in his life,
	A sable silvered.
HAMLET	I will watch tonight,
	Perchance ' twill walk again.
HORATIO	I war' nt it win.
HAMLET	If it assume my noble father's person,
	I'll speak to it though hell itself should gape
	And bid me hold my peace; I pray you all

哈 姆 莱 特	你们说它穿着甲胄吗？
马 西 勒 斯 勃 那 多	是，殿下。
哈 姆 莱 特	从头到脚？
马 西 勒 斯 勃 那 多	从头到脚，殿下。
哈 姆 莱 特	那么你们没有看见它的脸吗？
霍 拉 旭	啊，看见的，殿下；它的脸甲是掀起的。
哈 姆 莱 特	怎么，它瞧上去像在发怒吗？
霍 拉 旭	它的脸上悲哀多于愤怒。
哈 姆 莱 特	它的脸色是惨白的还是红红的？
霍 拉 旭	非常惨白。
哈 姆 莱 特	它把眼睛注视着你吗？
霍 拉 旭	它直盯着我瞧。
哈 姆 莱 特	我真希望当时我也在场。
霍 拉 旭	那一定会使您吃惊万分。
哈 姆 莱 特	多半会的，多半会的。它停留得长久吗？
霍 拉 旭	大概有一个人用不快不慢的速度从一数到一百的那段时间。
马 西 勒 斯 勃 那 多	还要长久一些，还要长久一些。
霍 拉 旭	我看见它的时候，不过这么久。
哈 姆 莱 特	它的胡须是斑白的吗？
霍 拉 旭	是的，正像我在它生前看见的那样，乌黑的胡须里略有几根变成白色。
哈 姆 莱 特	我今晚也要守夜去；也许它还会出来。
霍 拉 旭	我可以担保它一定会出来。
哈 姆 莱 特	要是它借着我的父王的形貌出现，即使地狱张开嘴来，叫我不要作声，我也一定要对它说话。要是你们到现在还没

If you have hitherto concealed this sight,

Let it be tenable in your silence still,

And whatsomever else shall hap tonight,

Give it an understanding but no tongue.

I will requite your loves, so fare you well;

Upon the platform ' twixt eleven and twelve

I'll visit you.

ALL   Our duty to your honour.

HAMLET   Your loves as mine to you. Farewell. [*Exeunt all but Hamlet.*]

My father's spirit in arms! all is not well,

I doubt some foul play. Would the night were come;

Till then sit still my soul, foul deeds will rise,

Though all the earth o' erwhelm them, to men' s eyes. [*Exit.*]

SCENE 3

A room in the house of Polonius

[*Enter Laertes and Ophelia.*]

LAERTES   My necessaries are embarked, farewell,

And sister, as the winds give benefit

And convoy is assistant, do not sleep,

But let me hear from you.

OPHELIA   Do you doubt that?

LAERTES   For Hamlet, and the trifling of his favour,

Hold it a fashion, and a toy in blood,

A violet in the youth of primy nature,

Forward, not permanent, sweet, not lasting,

The perfume and suppliance of a minute,

有把你们所看见的告诉别人，那么就要请求你们大家继续保持沉默；无论今夜发生什么事情，都请放在心里，不要在口舌之间泄漏出去。我一定会报答你们的忠诚。好，再会；今晚十一点钟到十二点钟之间，我要到露台上来看你们。

众 人 我们愿意为殿下尽忠。

哈 姆 莱 特 让我们彼此保持着不渝的交情；再会！（霍拉旭、马西勒斯、勃那多同下。）我父亲的灵魂披着甲胄！事情有些不妙；我想这里面一定有奸人的恶计。但愿黑夜早点到来！静静地等着吧，我的灵魂；罪恶的行为总有一天会发现，虽然地上所有的泥土把它们遮掩。（下。）

第三场　波洛涅斯家中一室

（雷欧提斯及奥菲利娅上。）

雷 欧 提 斯 我需要的物件已经装在船上，再会了；妹妹，在好风给人方便、船只来往无阻的时候，不要贪睡，让我听见你的消息。

奥 菲 利 娅 你还不相信我吗？

雷 欧 提 斯 对于哈姆莱特和他的调情献媚，你必须把它认作年轻人一时的感情冲动，一朵初春的紫罗兰早熟而易凋，馥郁而不能持久，一分钟的芬芳和喜悦，如此而已。

No more.

OPHELIA No more but so?

LAERTES Think it no more.

For nature crescent does not grow alone

In thews and bulk, but as this temple waxes

The inward service of the mind and soul

Grows wide withal. Perhaps he loves you now,

And now no soil nor cautel doth besmirch

The virtue of his will. But you must fear,

His greatness weighed, his will is not his own,

For he himself is subject to his birth.

He may not, as unvalued persons do,

Carve for himself, for on his choice depends

The sanity and health of this whole state,

And therefore must his choice be circumscribed

Unto the voice and yielding of that body

Whereof he is the head. Then if he says he loves you,

It fits your wisdom so far to believe it

As he in his particular act and place

Msy give his saying deed, which is no further

Than the main voice of Denmark goes withal.

Then weigh what loss your honour may sustain

If with too credent ear you list his songs,

Or lose your heart, or your chaste treasure open

To his unmast' red importunity.

Fear it Ophelia, fear it my dear sister,

And keep you in the rear of your affection,

Out of the shot and danger of desire.

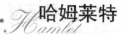

哈姆莱特

奥 菲 利 娅	不过如此吗？
雷 欧 提 斯	不过如此；因为一个人成长的过程，不仅是肌肉和体格的增强，而且随着身体的发展，精神和心灵也同时扩大。也许他现在爱你，他的真诚的意志是纯洁而不带欺诈的；可是你必须留心，他有这样高的地位，他的意志并不属于他自己，因为他自己也要被他的血统所支配；他不能像一般庶民一样为自己选择，因为他的决定足以影响到整个国家的安危，他是全身的首脑，他的选择必须得到各部分肢体的同意；所以要是他说，他爱你，你不可贸然相信，应该明白：照他的身份地位说来，他要想把自己的话付诸实现，决不能越出丹麦国内普遍舆论所同意的范围。你再想一想，要是你用过于轻信的耳朵倾听他的歌曲，让他攫走了你的心，在他的狂妄的渎求之下，打开了你的宝贵的童贞，那时候你的名誉将要蒙受多大的损失。留心，奥菲利娅，留心，我的亲爱的妹妹，不要放纵你的爱情，不要让欲望的利箭把你射中。一个自爱的女郎，若是向月亮显露

The chariest maid is prodigal enough

If she unmask her beauty to the moon.

Virtue itseff 'scapes not calumnious strokes.

The canker galls the infants of the spring

Too oft before their buttons be disclosed,

And in the morn and liquid dew of youth

Contagious blastments are most imminent.

Be wary then, best safety lies in fear,

Youth to itself rebels, though none else near.

OPHELIA　I shall the effect of this good lesson keep

As watchman to my heart. But good my brother,

Do not, as some ungracious pastors do,

Show me the steep and thorny way to heaven,

Whiles like a puffed and reckless libertine

Himself the primrose path of dalliance treads,

And recks not his own rede.

[*Enter Polonius.*]

LAERTES　O fear me not;

I stay too long; but here my father comes.

A double blessing is a double grace,

Occasion smiles upon a second leave.

POLONIUS　Yet here, Laertes? Aboard, aboard for shame!

The wind sits in the shoulder of your sail,

And you are stayed for. There, my blessing with thee, And

these few precepts in thy memory

Look thou character. Give thy thoughts no tongue,

Nor any unproportioned thought his act.

Be thou familiar, but by no means vulgar;

　　她的美貌就算是极端放荡了；圣贤也不能逃避谗口的中伤；春天的草木往往还没有吐放它们的蓓蕾，就被蛀虫蠹蚀；朝露一样晶莹的青春，常常会受到罡风的吹打。所以留心吧，戒惧是最安全的方策；即使没有旁人的诱惑，少年的血气也要向他自己叛变。

奥菲利娅 我将要记住你这个很好的教训，让它看守着我的心。可是，我的好哥哥，你不要像有些坏牧师一样，指点我上天去的险峻的荆棘之途，自己却在花街柳巷流连忘返，忘记了自己的箴言。

雷欧提斯 啊！不要为我担心。我耽搁得太久了；可是父亲来了。

　　　　　　（波洛涅斯上。）

雷欧提斯 两度的祝福是双倍的福分；第二次的告别是格外可喜的。

波洛涅斯 还在这儿，雷欧提斯！上船去，上船去，真好意思！风息在帆顶上，人家都在等着你哩。好，我为你祝福！还有几句教训，希望你铭刻在记忆之中：不要想到什么就说什么，凡事必须三思而行。对人要和气，可是不要过分狎昵。

Those friends thou hast, and their adoption tried,

Grapple them unto thy soul with hoops of steel,

But do not dull thy palm with entertainment

Of each new-hatched unfledged courage. Beware

Of entrance to a quarrel, but being in,

Bear' t that th'opposed may beware of thee.

Give every man thy ear, but few thy voice;

Take each man's censure, but reserve thy judgment.

Costly thy habit as thy purse can buy,

But not expressed in fancy; rich not gaudy.

For the apparel oft proclaims the man,

And they in France of the best rank and station,

Or of a most select and generous, chief in that.

Neither a borrower nor a lender be,

For loan oft loses both itself and friend,

And borrowing dulls the edge of husbandry;

This above all, to thine own self be trne

And it must follow as the night the day

Thou canst not then be false to any man.

Farewell; my blessing season this in thee.

LAERTES	Most humbly do I take my leave, my lord.
POLONIUS	The time invites you, go, your servants tend.
LAERTES	Farewell, Ophelia, and remember well
	What I have said to you.
OPHELIE	'Tis in my memory locked,
	And you yourself shall keep the key of it.
LAERTES	Farewell. [*Exit*]
POLONIUS	What is' t, Ophelia, he hath said to you?

相知有素的朋友，应该用钢圈箍在你的灵魂上，可是不要对每一个泛泛的新知滥施你的交情。留心避免和人家争吵；可是万一争端已起，就应该让对方知道你不是可以轻侮的。倾听每一个人的意见，可是只对极少数人发表你的意见；接受每一个人的批评，可是保留你自己的判断。尽你的财力购制贵重的衣服，可是不要炫新立异，必须富丽而不浮艳，因为服装往往可以表现人格；法国的名流要人，就是在这点上显得最高尚，与众不同。不要向人告贷，也不要借钱给人；因为债款放了出去，往往不但丢了本钱，而且还失去了朋友；向人告贷的结果，容易养成因循懒惰的习惯。尤其要紧的，你必须对你自己忠实；正像有了白昼才有黑夜一样，对自己忠实，才不会对别人欺诈。再会；愿我的祝福使这一番话在你的行事中奏效！

雷欧提斯　父亲，我告别了。

波洛涅斯　时候不早了；去吧，你的仆人都在等着。

雷欧提斯　再会，奥菲利娅，记住我对你说的话。

奥菲利娅　你的话已经锁在我的记忆里，那钥匙你替我保管着吧。

雷欧提斯　再会！（下。）

波洛涅斯　奥菲利娅，他对你说些什么话？

OPHELIA	So please you, something touching the Lord Hamlet.
POLONIUS	Marry, well bethought.
	'Tis told me he hath very oft of late
	Given private time to you, and you yourself
	Have of your audience been most free and bounteous.
	If it be so, as so 'tis put on me,
	And that in way of caution——I must tell you,
	You do not understand yourself so clearly
	As it behoves my daughter and your honour.
	What is between you? Give me up the truth.
OPHELIA	He hath, my lord, of late made many tenders
	Of his affection to me.
POLONIUS	Affection, pooh! You speak like a green girl
	Unsifted in such perilous circumstance.
	Do you believe his tenders, as you call them?
OPHELIA	I do not know, my lord, what I should think.
POLONIUS	Marry, I will teach you; think yourself a baby
	That you have ta'en these tenders for true pay
	Which are not sterling. Tender yourself more dearly,
	Or—not to crack the wind of the poor phrase,
	Running it thus — you'll tender me a fool.
OPHELIA	My lord, he hath importuned me with love
	In honourable fashion.
POLONIUS	Ay, fashion you may call it, go to, go to.
OPHELIA	And hath given countenance to his speech, my lord,
	With almost all the holy vows of heaven.
POLONIUS	Ay, springes to catch woodcocks. I do know
	When the blood burns, how prodigal the soul

奥菲利娅	回父亲的话，我们刚才谈起哈姆莱特殿下的事情。
波洛涅斯	嗯，这是应该考虑一下的。听说他近来常常跟你在一起，你也从来不拒绝他的求见；要是果然有这种事——人家这样告诉我，也无非是叫我注意的意思——那么我必须对你说，你还没有懂得你做了我的女儿，按照你的身份，应该怎样留心你自己的行动。究竟在你们两人之间有些什么关系？老实告诉我。
奥菲利娅	父亲，他最近曾经屡次向我表示他的爱情。
波洛涅斯	爱情！呸！你讲的话完全像是一个不曾经历过这种危险的不懂事的女孩子。你相信你所说的他的那种表示吗？
奥菲利娅	父亲，我不知道我应该怎样想才好。
波洛涅斯	好，让我来教你；你应该这样想，你是一个毛孩子，竟然把这些假意的表示当作了真心的奉献。你应该"表示"出一番更大的架子，要不然——就此打住吧，这个可怜的字眼被我使唤得都快断气了——你就"表示"你是个十足的傻瓜。
奥菲利娅	父亲，他向我求爱的态度是很光明正大的。
波洛涅斯	不错，那只是态度；算了，算了。
奥菲利娅	而且，父亲，他差不多用尽一切指天誓日的神圣的盟约，证实他的言语。
波洛涅斯	嗯，这些都是捕捉愚蠢的山鹬的圈套。我知道在热情燃烧的时候，一个人无论什么盟誓都会说出口来；这些火焰，

Lencts the tongue vows. These blazes, daughter,

Giving more light than heat, extinct in both,

Even in their promise, as it is a-making,

You must not take for fire. From this time

Be something scanter of your maiden presence,

Set your entreatments at a higher rate

Than a command to parle; for Lord Hamlet,

Believe so much in him that he is young,

And with a larger tether may he walk

Than may be given you. in few, Ophelia,

Do not believe his vows, for they are brokers

Not of that dye which their investments show,

But mere implorators of unholy suits,

Breathing like sanctified and pious bonds

The better to beguile. This is for all,

I would not in plain terms from this time forth

Have you so slander any moment leisure

As to give words or talk with the Lord Hamlet.

Look to' t, I charge you, come your ways.

OPHELIA   I shall obey, my lord.   [*Exeunt.*]

SCENE 4

The platform

[*Enter Hamlet, Horatio and Marcellus.*]

HAMLET   The air bites shrewdly, it is very cold.

HORATIO   It is a nipping and an eager air.

HAMLET   What hour now?

女儿，是光多于热的，刚刚说出口就会光销焰灭，你不能把它们当作真火看待。从现在起，你还是少露一些你的女儿家的脸；你应该抬高身价，不要让人家以为你是可以随意呼召的。对于哈姆莱特殿下，你应该这样想，他是个年轻的王子，他比你在行动上有更大的自由。总而言之，奥菲利娅，不要相信他的盟誓，它们不过是淫媒，内心的颜色和服装完全不一样，只晓得诱人干一些龌龊的勾当，正像道貌岸然大放厥词的鸨母，只求达到骗人的目的。我的言尽于此，简单一句话，从现在起，我不许你一有空闲就跟哈姆莱特殿下聊天。你留点儿神吧；进去。

奥菲利娅　我一定听从您的话，父亲。（同下。）

第四场　露　台

（哈姆莱特、霍拉旭及马西勒斯上。）

哈姆莱特　风吹得人怪痛的，这天气真冷。
霍拉旭　是很凛冽的寒风。
哈姆莱特　现在什么时候了？

HORATIO	I think it lacks of twelve.
MARCELLUS	No, it is struck.
HORATIO	Indeed? I heard it not, it then draws near the season,
	Wherein the spirit held his wont to walk.

[*A flourish of trumpets, and ordnance shot off*]

	What does this mean, my lord?
HAMLET	The King doth wake tonight and takes his rouse,
	Keeps wassail and the swagg' ring upspring reels:
	And as he drains his draughts of Rhenish down,
	The kettle-drmn and trumpet thus bray out
	The triumph of his pledge.
HORATIO	Is it a custom?
HAMLET	Ay marry is' t,
	But to my mind, though I am native here
	And to the manner born, it is a custom
	More honoured in the breach than the observance.
	This heavy-headed revel east and west
	Makes us traduced and taxed of other nations.
	They clepe us drunkards and with swinish phrase
	Soil our addition, and indeed it takes
	From our achievements, though performed at height,
	The pith and marrow of our attribute.
	So, oft it chances in particular men,
	That for some vicious mole of nature in them:
	As in their birth, wherein they are not guilty——
	Since nature cannot choose his origin,
	By the o'ergrowth of some complexion;
	Oft breaking down the pales and forts of reason,

哈姆莱特
Hamlet

霍 拉 旭	我想还不到十二点。
马 西 勒 斯	不，已经打过了。
霍 拉 旭	真的？我没有听见；那么鬼魂出现的时候快要到了。（内喇叭奏花腔及鸣炮声）这是什么意思，殿下？
哈 姆 莱 特	王上今晚大宴群臣，作通宵的醉舞；每次他喝下了一杯葡萄美酒，铜鼓和喇叭便吹打起来，欢祝万寿。
霍 拉 旭	这是向来的风俗吗？
哈 姆 莱 特	嗯，是的。可是我虽然从小就熟习这种风俗，我却以为把它破坏了倒比遵守它还体面些。这一种酗酒纵乐的风俗，使我们在东西各国受到许多非议；他们称我们为财徒醉汉，将下流的污名加在我们头上，使我们各项伟大的成就都因此而大为减色。在个人方面也常常是这样，由于品性上有某些丑恶的瘢痣：或者是天生的——这就不能怪本人，因为天性不能由自己选择；或者是某种脾气发展到反常地步，冲破了理智的约束和防卫；或者是某种习惯玷污

Or by some habit, that too much o' er-leavens

The form of plausive manners, that these men,

Carrying I say the stamp of one defect——

Being nature' s livery, or fortune' s star——

His virtues else be they as pure as grace,

As infinite as man may undergo,

Shall in the general censure take corruption

From that particular fault; the dram of evil

Doth all the noble substance of a doubt,

To his own scandal.

    [*Enter the Ghost.*]

HORATIO   Look, my lord, it comes !

HAMLET   Angels and ministers of grace defend us!

Be thou a spirit of health, or goblin damned,

Bring with thee airs from heaven, or blasts from hell,

Be thy intents wicked, or charitable,

Thou com' st in such a questionable shape,

That I will speak to thee. I'll call thee Hamlet,

King, father, royal Dane. O, answer me!

Let me not burst in ignorance, but tell

Why thy canonized bones hearsed in death

Have burst their cerements? why the sepulchre,

Wherein we saw thee quietly inurned,

Hath oped his ponderous and marble jaws

To cast thee up again? what may this mean

That thou, dead corse, again in complete steel

Revisits thus the glimpses of the moon,

Making night hideous, and we fools of nature

了原来令人喜爱的举止；这些人只要带着上述一种缺点的烙印——天生的标记或者偶然的机缘——不管在其余方面他们是如何圣洁，如何具备一个人所能有的无限美德，由于那点特殊的毛病，在世人的非议中也会感染溃烂；少量的邪恶足以勾销全部高贵的品质，害得人声名狼藉。

（鬼魂上。）

霍 拉 旭	瞧，殿下，它来了！
哈 姆 莱 特	天使保佑我们！不管你是一个善良的灵魂或是万恶的妖魔，不管你带来了天上的和风或是地狱中的罡风，不管你的来意好坏，因为你的形状是这样引起我的怀疑，我要对你说话；我要叫你哈姆莱特，君王，父亲！尊严的丹麦先王，啊，回答我！不要让我在无知的蒙昧里抱恨终天；告诉我为什么你的长眠的骸骨不安窀穸，为什么安葬着你的遗体的坟墓张开它的沉重的大理石的两颚，把你重新吐放出来。你这已死的尸体这样全身甲胄，出现在月光之下，使黑夜变得这样阴森，使我们这些为造化所玩弄的愚人由

So horridly to shake our disposition

With thoughts beyond the reaches of our souls?

Say why is this? Wherefore? What should we do?

   [*Ghost beckons Hamlet.*]

HORATIO   It beckons you to go away with it,

As if it some impartment did desire

To you alone.

MARCELLUS   Look with what courteous action

It wares you to a more removed ground,

But do not go with it.

HORATIO   No, by no means.

HAMLET   It will not speak, then I will follow it.

HORATIO   Do not my lord.

HAMLET   Why, what should be the fear?

I do not set my life at a pin's fee,

And for my soul, what can it do to that

Being a thing immortal as itself;

It waves me forth again, I'll follow it.

HORATIO   What if it tempt you toward the flood, my lord,

Or to the dreadful summit of the cliff

That beetles o' er his base into the sea,

And there assume some other borrible form,

Which might deprive your sovereignty of reason,

And draw you into madness? Think of it,

The very place puts toys of desperation,

Without more motive, into every brain

That looks so many fathoms to the sea

And hears it roar beneath.

于不可思议的恐怖而心惊胆战，究竟是什么意思呢？说，这是为了什么？你要我们怎样？（鬼魂向哈姆莱特招手。）

霍　拉　旭　它招手叫您跟着它去，好像它有什么话要对您一个人说似的。

马西勒斯　瞧，它用很有礼貌的举动，招呼您到一个偏远的所在去；可是别跟它去。

霍　拉　旭　千万不要跟它去。

哈姆莱特　它不肯说话；我还是跟它去。

霍　拉　旭　不要去，殿下。

哈姆莱特　嗨，怕什么呢？我把我的生命看得不值一枚针；至于我的灵魂，那是跟它自己同样永生不灭的，它能够加害它吗？它又在招手叫我前去了；我要跟它去。

霍　拉　旭　殿下，要是它把您诱到潮水里去，或者把您领到下临大海的峻峭的悬崖之巅，在那边它现出了狰狞的面貌，吓得您丧失理智，变成疯狂，那可怎么好呢？您想，无论什么人一到了那样的地方，望着下面千仞的峭壁，听见海水奔腾的怒吼，即使没有别的原因，也会起穷凶极恶的怪念的。

HAMLET	It waves me still.
	Go on, I'll follow thee.
MARCELLUS	You shall not go, my lord.
HAMLET	Hold off your hands.
HORATIO	Be ruled, you shall not go.
HAMLET	My fate cries out, and makes each petty artere in this body
	As hardy as the Nemean lion's nerve. [*The Ghost beckons*]
	Still am I called, unhand me gentlemen,
	[*He breaks from them*]
	By heaven, I'll make a ghost of him that lets me!
	I say, away! Go on, I'll follow thee.
	[*Exeunt the Ghost and Hamlet.*]
HORATIO	He waxes desperate with imagination.
MARCELLUS	Lets follow, 'tis not fit thus to obey him.
HORATIO	Have after, to what issue will this come?
MARCELLUS	Something is rotten in the state of Denmark.
HORATIO	Heaven will direct it.
MARCELLUS	Nay, let's follow him. [*Exeunt.*]

SCENE 5

Another part of the platform

[*Enter Ghost and Hamlet.*]

HAMLET	Whither wilt thou lead me? speak, I'll go no further.
GHOST	Mark me.
HAMLET	I will.
GHOST	My hour is almost come,
	When I to sulph' rous and tormenting flames

哈姆莱特

Hamlet

哈 姆 莱 特　它还在向我招手。去吧，我跟着你。

马 西 勒 斯　您不能去，殿下。

哈 姆 莱 特　放开你们的手！

霍 拉 旭　听我们的劝告，不要去。

哈 姆 莱 特　我的命运在高声呼喊，使我全身每一根微细的血管都变得像怒狮的筋骨一样坚硬。（鬼魂招手）它仍旧在招我去。放开我，朋友们；（挣脱二人之手）凭着上天起誓，谁要是拉住我，我要叫他变成一个鬼！走开！去吧，我跟着你。（鬼魂及哈姆莱特同下。）

霍 拉 旭　幻想占据了他的头脑，使他不顾一切。

马 西 勒 斯　让我们跟上去；我们不应该服从他的话。

霍 拉 旭　那么跟上去吧。这种事情会引出些什么结果来呢？

马 西 勒 斯　丹麦国里恐怕有些不可告人的坏事。

霍 拉 旭　上帝的旨意支配一切。

马 西 勒 斯　得了，我们还是跟上去吧。（同下。）

第五场　露台的另一部分

（鬼魂及哈姆莱特上。）

哈 姆 莱 特　你要领我到什么地方去？说；我不愿再前进了。

鬼 　 魂　听我说。

哈 姆 莱 特　我在听着。

鬼 　 魂　我的时间快到了，我必须再回到硫黄的烈火里去受煎熬的

	Must render up myself.
HAMLET	Alas, poor ghost!
GHOST	Pity me not, but lend thy serious hearing
	To what I shall unfold.
HAMLET	Speak, I am bound to hear.
GHOST	So art thou to revenge, when thou shalt hear.
HAMLET	What?
GHOST	I am thy father's spirit,
	Doomed for a certain term to walk the night,
	And for the day confined to fast in fires,
	Till the foul crimes done in my days of nature
	Are burnt and purged away. but that I am forbid
	To tell the secrets of my prison-house,
	I could a tale unfold whose lightest word
	Would harrow up thy soul, freeze thy young blood,
	Make thy two eyes like stars start from their spheres,
	Thy knotted and combined locks to part,
	And each particular hair to stand an end,
	Like quills upon the fretful porpentine.
	But this eternal blazon must not be
	To ears of flesh and blood. List, list, O list!
	If thou didst ever thy dear father love.
HAMLET	O God!
GHOST	Revenge his foul and most unnatural murder.
HAMLET	Murder!
GHOST	Murder most foul, as in the best it is,
	But this most foul, strange and unnatural.
HAMLET	Haste me to know't, that I with wings as swift

痛苦。

哈 姆 莱 特　唉，可怜的亡魂！

鬼　　　魂　不要可怜我，你只要留心听着我要告诉你的话。

哈 姆 莱 特　说吧；我自然要听。

鬼　　　魂　你听了以后，也自然要替我报仇。

哈 姆 莱 特　什么？

鬼　　　魂　我是你父亲的灵魂，因为生前孽障未尽，被判在晚间游行地上，白昼忍受火焰的烧灼，必须经过相当的时期，等生前的过失被火焰净化以后，方才可以脱罪。若不是因为我不能违犯禁令，泄漏我的狱中的秘密，我可以告诉你一桩事，最轻微的几句话，都可以使你魂飞魄散，使你年轻的血液凝冻成冰，使你的双眼像脱了轨道的星球一样向前突出，使你的纠结的鬈发根根分开，像愤怒的豪猪身上的刺毛一样森然耸立；可是这一种永恒的神秘，是不能向血肉的凡耳宣示的。听着，听着，啊，听着！要是你曾经爱过你的亲爱的父亲——

哈 姆 莱 特　上帝啊！

鬼　　　魂　你必须替他报复那逆伦惨恶的杀身的仇恨。

哈 姆 莱 特　杀身的仇恨！

鬼　　　魂　杀人是重大的罪恶；可是这一件谋杀的惨案，更是骇人听闻而伤天害理的罪行。

哈 姆 莱 特　赶快告诉我，让我驾着像思想和爱情一样迅速的翅膀，飞

As meditation or the thoughts of love,

May sweep to my revenge.

GHOST   I find thee apt,

And duller shouldst thou be than the fat weed

That rots itself in ease on Lethe wharf,

Wouldst thou not stir in this; now Hamlet hear,

'Tis given out, that sleeping in my orchard,

A serpent stung me, so the whole ear of Denmark

Is by a forged process of my death

Rankly abused; but know, thou noble youth,

The serpent that did sting thy father's life

Now wears his crown.

HAMLET   O, my prophetic soul!

My uncle?

GHOST   Ay, that incestuous, that adulterate beast,

With witchcraft of his wit, with traitorous gifts,

O wicked wit and gifts, that have the power

So to seduce; won to his shameful lust

The will of my most seeming-virtuous queen;

O Hamlet, what a falling-off was there!

From me whose love was of that dignity,

That it went hand in hand even with the vow

I made to her in marriage, and to decline

Upon a wretch whose natural gifts were poor

To those of mine; but virtue, as it never will be moved,

Though lewdness court it in a shape of heaven,

So lust, though to a radiant angel linked,

Will sate itself in a celestial bed and prey on garbage.

去把仇人杀死。

鬼　　魂　我的话果然激动了你；要是你听见了这种事情而漠然无动于衷，那你除非比舒散在忘河之滨的蔓草还要冥顽不灵。现在，哈姆莱特，听我说；一般人都以为我在花园里睡觉的时候，一条蛇来把我螫死，这一个虚构的死状，把丹麦全国的人都骗过了；可是你要知道，好孩子，那毒害你父亲的蛇，头上戴着王冠呢。

哈 姆 莱 特　啊，我的预感果然是真的！我的叔父！

鬼　　魂　嗯，那个乱伦的、奸淫的畜生，他有的是过人的诡诈，天赋的奸恶，凭着他的阴险的手段，诱惑了我的外表上似乎非常贞淑的王后，满足他的无耻的兽欲。啊，哈姆莱特，那是一个多么卑鄙无耻的背叛！我的爱情是那样纯洁真诚，始终信守着我在结婚的时候对她所作的盟誓；她却会对一个天赋的才德远不如我的恶人降心相从！可是正像一个贞洁的女子，虽然淫欲罩上神圣的外表，也不能把她煽动一样，一个淫妇虽然和光明的天使为偶，也会有一天厌倦于天上的唱随之乐，而宁愿搂抱人间的朽骨。可是且慢！我仿佛嗅到了清晨的空气；让我把话说得

But soft, methinks I scent the morning air,

Brief let me be; sleeping within my orchard,

My custom always of the afternoon,

Upon my secure hour thy uncle stole

With juice of cursed hebona in a vial,

And in the porches of my ears did pour

The leperous distilment, whose effect

Holds such an enmity with blood of man,

That swift as quicksilver it courses through

The natural gates and alleys of the body,

And with a sudden vigour it doth posset

And curd, like eager droppings into milk,

The thin and wholesome blood; so did it mine,

And a most instant tetter barked about

Most lazar-like with vile and loathsome crust

All my smooth body. Thus was I sleeping by a brother's

hand,

Of life, of crown, of queen at once dispatched,

Cut off even in the blossoms of my sin,

Unhouseled, disappointed, unaneled,

No reck' ning made, but sent to my account

With all my imperfections on my head.

O, horrible! O, horrible! Most horrible!

If thou hast nature in thee bear it not,

Let not the royal bed of Denmark be

A couch for luxury and damned incest.

But howsomever thou pursues this act,

Taint not thy mind, nor let thy soul contrive

简短一些。当我按照每天午后的惯例，在花园里睡觉的时候，你的叔父乘我不备，悄悄溜了进来，拿着一个盛着毒草汁的小瓶，把一种使人麻痹的药水注入我的耳腔之内，那药性发作起来，会像水银一样很快地流过全身的大小血管，像酸液滴进牛乳一般把淡薄而健全的血液凝结起来；它一进入我的身体，我全身光滑的皮肤上便立刻发生无数疱疹，像害着癞病似的满布着可憎的鳞片。这样，我在睡梦之中，被一个兄弟同时夺去了我的生命、我的王冠和我的王后；甚至于不给我一个忏罪的机会，使我在没有领到圣餐也没有受过临终涂膏礼以前，就一无准备地负着我的全部罪恶去对簿阴曹。可怕啊，可怕！要是你有天性之情，不要默尔而息，不要让丹麦的御寝变成了藏奸养逆的卧榻；可是无论你怎样进行复仇，不要胡乱猜疑，更不可对你的母亲有什么不利的图谋，她自

Against thy mother aught, leave her to heaven,

And to those thorns that in her bosom lodge

To prick and sting her. Fare thee well at once,

The glow-worm shows the matin to be near,

And 'gins to pale his uneffectual fire.

Adieu, adieu, adieu, remember me.　　　　[*Exit.*]

HAMLET　　O all you host of heaven! O earth! What else?

And shall I couple hell? O fie! Hold, hold, my heart,

And you, my sinews, grow not instant old,

But bear me stiffly up. Remember thee?

Ay thou poor ghost, whiles memory holds a seat

In this distracted globe. Remember thee?

Yea, from the table of my memory

I'll wipe away all trivial fond records,

All saws of books, all forms, all pressures past

That youth and observation copied there,

And thy commandment all alone shall live

Within the book and volume of my brain,

Unmixed with baser matter, yes by heaven!

O most pernicious woman!

O villain, villain, smiling damned villain!

My tables, meet it is I set it down　　　　[*He writes*]

That one may smile, and smile, and be a villain,

At least I am sure it may be so in Denmark.

So, uncle, there you are. Now, to my word,

It is ' Adieu, adieu, remember me. '

I have sworn' t

HORATIO　　[*Within*] My lord, my lord!

会受到上天的裁判，和她自己内心中的荆棘的刺戳。现在我必须去了！萤火的微光已经开始暗淡下去，清晨快要到来了；再会，再会！哈姆莱特，记着我。（下。）

哈姆莱特 天上的神明啊！地啊！再有什么呢？我还要向地狱呼喊吗？啊，呸！忍着吧，忍着吧，我的心！我的全身的筋骨，不要一下子就变成衰老，支持着我的身体呀！记着你！是的，我可怜的亡魂，当记忆不曾从我这混乱的头脑里消失的时候，我会记着你的。记着你！是的，我要从我的记忆的碑版上，拭去一切琐碎愚蠢的记录、一切书本上的格言、一切陈言套语、一切过去的印象、我的少年的阅历所留下的痕迹，只让你的命令留在我的脑筋的书卷里，不掺杂一些下贱的废料；是的，上天为我作证！啊，最恶毒的妇人！啊，奸贼，奸贼，脸上堆着笑的万恶的奸贼！我的记事簿呢？我必须把它记下来：一个人可以尽管满面都是笑，骨子里却是杀人的奸贼；至少我相信在丹麦是这样的。（写字）好，叔父，我把你写下来了。现在我要记下我的座右铭那是，"再会，再会！记着我。"我已经发过誓了。

霍拉旭 （在内）殿下！殿下！

莎士比亚经典戏剧

MARCELLUS	[*Within*] Lord Hamlet !
HORATIO	[*Within*] Heaven secure him!
HAMLET	[*Within*] So be it!
HORATIO	[*Within*]Illo, ho, ho, my lord!
HAMLET	Hillo, ho, ho, boy! Come, bird, come.

[*Enter Horatio and Marcellus.*]

MARCELLUS	How is' t, my noble lord?
HORATIO	What news, my lord?
HAMLET	O, wonderful!
HORATIO	Good my lord, tell it.
HAMLET	No, you will reveal it.
HORATIO	Not I, my lord, by heaven.
MARCELLUS	Nor I, my lord.
HAMLET	How say you then, would heart of man once think it?
	But you'll be secret?
HORATIO **MARCELLUS**	Ay, by heaven, my lord.
HAMLET	There's ne' er a villain dwelling in all Denmark
	But he's an arrant knave.
HORATIO	There needs no ghost, my lord, come from the grave,
	To tell us this.
HAMLET	Why right, you are in the right,
	And so without more circumstance at all
	I hold it fit that we shake hands and part,
	You, as your business and desire shall point you,
	For every man hath business and desire
	Such as it is, and for my own poor part,
	Look you, I will go pray.

哈姆莱特

马西勒斯 （在内）哈姆莱特殿下！

霍 拉 旭 （在内）上天保佑他！

哈姆莱特 （在内）但愿如此！

霍 拉 旭 （在内）喂，呵，呵，殿下！

哈姆莱特 喂，呵，呵，孩儿！来，鸟儿，来。

（霍拉旭及马西勒斯上。）

马西勒斯 怎样，殿下！

霍 拉 旭 有什么事，殿下？

哈姆莱特 啊！奇怪！

霍 拉 旭 好殿下，告诉我们。

哈姆莱特 不，你们会泄漏出去的。

霍 拉 旭 不，殿下，凭着上天起誓，我一定不泄漏。

马西勒斯 我也一定不泄漏，殿下。

哈姆莱特 那么你们说，哪一个人会想得到有这种事？可是你们能够
保守秘密吗？

霍 拉 旭
马西勒斯 是，上天为我们作证，殿下。

哈姆莱特 全丹麦从来不曾有哪一个奸贼不是一个十足的坏人。

霍 拉 旭 殿下，这样一句话是用不着什么鬼魂从坟墓里出来告诉我
们的。

哈姆莱特 啊，对了，你说得有理；所以，我们还是不必多说废话，
大家握握手分开了吧。你们可以去照你们自己的意思干你
们自己的事——因为各人都有各人的意思和各人的事，这
是实际情况——至于我自己，那么我对你们说，我是要祈
祷去的。

HORATIO	These are but wild and whirling words, my lord.
HAMLET	I am sorry they offend you, heartily, yes, faith, heartily.
HORATIO	There's no offence, my lord.
HAMLET	Yes, by Saint Patrick, but there is. Horatio,
	And much offence too, touching this vision here.
	It is an honest ghost, that let me tell you,
	For your desire to know what is between us.
	O' ermaster't as you may. And now, good friends,
	As you are friends, scholars, and soldiers,
	Give me one poor request.
HORATIO	What is't, my lord. ? we will.
HAMLET	Never make known what you have seen tonight.
BOTH	My lord, we will not.
HAMLET	Nay, but swear' t.
HORATIO	In faith, my lord, not I.
MARCELLUS	Nor I, my lord, in faith.
HAMLET	Upon my sword.
MARCELLUS	We have sworn, my lord, already.
HAMLET	Indeed, upon my sword, indeed.
GHOST	[*Beneath*] Swear.
HAMLET	Ha, ha, boy! Say'st thou so? Art thou there, truepenny?
	Come on, you hear this fellow in the cellarage,
	Consent to swear.
HORATIO	Propose the oath, my lord.
HAMLET	Never to speak of this that you have seen,
	Swear by my sword.
GHOST	[*Beneath*] Swear.
HAMLET	Hic et ubique? Then we'll shift our ground.

哈姆莱特

Hamlet

霍 拉 旭	殿下，您这些话好像有些疯疯癫癫似的。
哈姆莱特	我的话得罪了你，真是非常抱歉；是的，我从心底里抱歉。
霍 拉 旭	谈不上得罪，殿下。
哈姆莱特	不，凭着圣伯特力克的名义，霍拉旭，谈得上，而且罪还不小呢。讲到这一个幽灵，那么让我告诉你们，它是一个老实的亡魂；你们要是想知道它对我说了些什么话，我只好请你们暂时不必动问。现在，好朋友们，你们都是我的朋友，都是学者和军人，请你们允许我一个卑微的要求。
霍 拉 旭	是什么要求，殿下？我们一定允许您。
哈姆莱特	永远不要把你们今晚所见的事情告诉别人。
霍 拉 旭 马 西 勒 斯	殿下，我们一定不告诉别人。
哈姆莱特	不，你们必须宣誓。
霍 拉 旭	凭着良心起誓，殿下，我决不告诉别人。
马 西 勒 斯	凭着良心起誓，殿下，我也决不告诉别人。
哈姆莱特	把手按在我的剑上宣誓。
马 西 勒 斯	殿下，我们已经宣誓过了。
哈姆莱特	那不算，把手按在我的剑上。
鬼 魂	（在下）宣誓！
哈姆莱特	啊哈！孩儿！你也这样说吗？你在那儿吗，好家伙？来；你们不听见这个地下的人怎么说吗？宣誓吧。
霍 拉 旭	请您教我们怎样宣誓，殿下。
哈姆莱特	永不向人提起你们所看见的这一切。把手按在我的剑上宣誓。
鬼 魂	（在下）宣誓！
哈姆莱特	"说哪里，到哪里"吗？那么我们换一个地方。过来，朋

71

Come hither gentlemen, and lay your hands again upon my
sword.

Swear by my sword, never to speak of this that you have
heard.

GHOST	[*Beneath*] Swear by his sword.
HAMLET	Well said, old mole! Canst work i' th'earth so fast?
	A worthy pioneer! Once, more remove, good friends.
HORATIO	O day and night, but this is wondrous strange!
HAMLET	And therefore as a stranger give it welcome. There are
	more things in heaven and earth, Horatio,
	Than are dreamt of in your philosophy.
	But come, here as before, never, so help you mercy,
	How strange or odd some'er I bear myself;
	As I perchance hereafter shall think meet,
	To put an antic disposition on,
	That you at such times seeing me, never shall
	With arms encumbered thus, or this head-shake,
	Or by pronouncing of some doubtful phrase,
	As 'Well, well, we know', or 'We could an if we would',
	Or 'If we list to speak', or 'There be an if they might',
	Or such ambiguous giving out, to note
	That you know aught of me; this not to do,
	So grace and mercy at your most need help you! Swear
GHOST	[*Beneath*] Swear.
HAMLET	Rest, rest, perturbed spirit!
	So, gentlemen,
	With all my love I do commend me to you,

友们。把你们的手按在我的剑上，宣誓永不向人提起你们所听见的这件事。

鬼　　魂　（在下）宣誓！

哈姆莱特　说得好，老鼹鼠！你能够在地底钻得这么快吗？好一个开路的先锋！好朋友们，我们再来换一个地方。

霍　拉　旭　哎哟，真是不可思议的怪事！

哈姆莱特　那么你还是用见怪不怪的态度对待它吧。霍拉旭，天地之间有许多事情，是你们的哲学里所没有梦想到的呢。可是，来，上帝的慈悲保佑你们，你们必须再作一次宣誓。我今后也许有时候要故意装出一副疯疯癫癫的样子，你们要是在那时候看见了我的古怪的举动，切不可像这样交叉着手臂，或者这样摇头摆脑的，或者嘴里说一些吞吞吐吐的言词，例如"呃，呃，我们知道"，或者"只要我们高兴，我们就可以"，或是"要是我们愿意说出来的话"，或是"有人要是怎么怎么"，诸如此类的含糊其辞的话语，表示你们知道我有些什么秘密；你们必须答应我避开这一类言词，上帝的恩惠和慈悲保佑着你们，宣誓吧。

鬼　　魂　（在下）宣誓！（二人宣誓。）

哈姆莱特　安息吧，安息吧，受难的灵魂！好，朋友们，我以满怀的热情，信赖着你们两位；要是在哈姆莱特的微弱的能力以

And what so poor a man as Hamlet is

May do t' express his love and friending to you

God willing shall not lack. Let us go in together,

And still your fingers on your lips I pray.

The time is out of joint, O cursed spite,

That ever I was bom to set it right!

Nay come, let's go together.   [Exeunt.]

内，能够有可以向你们表示他的友情之处，上帝在上，我一定不会有负你们。让我们一同进去；请你们记着无论在什么时候都要守口如瓶。这是一个颠倒混乱的时代，唉，倒霉的我却要负起重整乾坤的责任！来，我们一块儿去吧。（同下。）

ACT 2   SCENE 1

A room in the house of Polonius

[*Enter Polonius and Reynaldo.*]

POLONIUS	Give him this money, and these notes, Reynaldo,
REYNALDO	I will, my lord.
POLONIUS	You shall do marvellous wisely, good Reynaldo,
	Before you visit him, to make inquire
	Of his behaviour.
REYNALDO	My lord, I did intend it.
POLONIUS	Marry, well said, very well said; look you sir,
	Inquire me first what Danskers are in Paris,
	And how, and who, what means, and where they keep,
	What company, at what expense, and finding
	By this encompassment and drift of question
	That they do know my son, come you more nearer
	Than your particular demands will touch it,
	Take you as ' twere some distant knowledge of him,
	As thus, I' know his father, and his friends,
	And in part him'. Do you mark this, Reynaldo?
REYNALDO	Ay, very well, my lord.
POLONIUS	'And in part him, but,' you may say, 'not well,
	But if' t he he I mean, he's very wild,
	Addicted so and so.' And there put on him
	What forgeries you please, marry none so rank
	As may dishonour him, take heed of that,

第 二 幕

第一场　波洛涅斯家中一室

（波洛涅斯及雷奈尔多上。）

波洛涅斯　把这些钱和这封信交给他，雷奈尔多。

雷奈尔多　是，老爷。

波洛涅斯　好雷奈尔多，你在没有去看他以前，最好先探听探听他的行为。

雷奈尔多　老爷，我本来就是这个意思。

波洛涅斯　很好，很好，好得很。你先给我调查调查有些什么丹麦人在巴黎，他们是干什么的，叫什么名字，有没有钱，住在什么地方，跟哪些人做伴，用度大不大；用这种转弯抹角的方法，要是你打听到他们也认识我的儿子，你就可以更进一步，表示你对他也有相当的认识；你可以这样说："我知道他的父亲和他的朋友，对他也略为有点认识。"你听见没有，雷奈尔多？

雷奈尔多　是，我在留心听着，老爷。

波洛涅斯　"对他也略为有点认识，可是，"你可以说，"不怎么熟悉；不过假如果然是他的话，那么他是个很放浪的人，有些怎样怎样的坏习惯。"说到这里，你就可以随便捏造一些关于他的坏话；当然罗，你不能把他说得太不成样子，

But sir such wanton, wild, and usual slips

As are companions noted and most known

To youth and liberty.

REYNALDO   As gaming, my lord

POLONIUS   Ay, or drinking, fencing, swearing, quarrelling,

Drabbing. You may go so far.

REYNALDO   My lord, that would dishonour him.

POLONIUS   Faith no, as you may season it in the charge.

You must not put another scandal on him,

That he is open to incontinency,

That's not my meaning, but breathe his faults so quaintly

That they may seem the taints of liberty,

The flash and outbreak of a fiery mind,

A savageness in unreclaimed blood,

Of general assault.

REYNALDO   But, my good lord—

POLONIUS   Wherefore should you do this?

REYNALDO   Ay my lord,

I would know that.

POLONIUS   Marry sir, here's my drift,

And l believe it is a fetch of warrant,

You laying these slight sullies on my son,

As ' twere a thing a little soiled i' th' working,

Mark you, your party in converse, him you would sound,

Having ever seen in the prenominate crimes

The youth you breathe Of guilty, be assured

He closes with you in this consequence,

'Good sir——', or so, or 'friend', or 'gentleman',

那是会损害他的名誉的，这一点你必须注意；可是你不妨举出一些纨袴子弟们所犯的最普通的浪荡的行为。

雷奈尔多　譬如赌钱，老爷。

波洛涅斯　对了，或是喝酒、斗剑、赌咒、吵嘴、嫖妓之类，你都可以说。

雷奈尔多　老爷，那是会损害他的名誉的。

波洛涅斯　不，不，你可以在言语之间说得轻淡一些。你不能说他公然纵欲，那可不是我的意思；可是你要把他的过失讲得那么巧妙，让人家听着好像那不过是行为上的小小的不检，一个躁急的性格不免会有的发作，一个血气方刚的少年的一时胡闹，算不了什么。

雷奈尔多　可是老爷——

波洛涅斯　为什么叫你做这种事？

雷奈尔多　是的，老爷，请您告诉我。

波洛涅斯　呃，我的用意是这样的，我相信这是一种说得过去的策略；你这样轻描淡写地说了我儿子的一些坏话，就像你提起一件略有污损的东西似的，听着，要是跟你谈话的那个人，也就是你向他探询的那个人，果然看见过你所说起的那个少年犯了你刚才所列举的那些罪恶，他一定会用这样的话向你表示同意："好先生——"也许他称你"朋友"，

According to the phrase, or the addition

Of man and country.

REYNALDO Very good, my lord.

POLONIUS And then sir, does he this, he does, what was I about to say?

By the mass I was about to say something.

Where did I leave?

REYNALDO At ' closes in the consequence';

At ' friend, or so, and gentleman'.

POLONIUS At ' closes in the consequence'. Ay marry,

He closes thus, 'I know the gentleman,

I saw him yesterday, or th' other day,

Or then, or then, with such or such, and as you say,

There was a' gaming, there o'ertook in's rouse,

There falling out at tennis; or perchance,

' I saw him enter such a house of sale;

Videlicet, a brothel, or so forth. See you now,

Your bait of falsehood takes this carp of truth,

And thus do we of wisdom, and of reach,

With windlasses, and with assays of bias,

By indirections find directions out,

So by my former lecture and advice

Shall you my son; you have me, have you not?

REYNALDO My lord, I have.

POLONIUS God bye ye, fare ye well.

REYNALDO Good, my lord.

POLONIUS Observe his inclination in yourself.

REYNALDO I shall, my lord.

POLONIUS And let him ply his music.

"仁兄"，按照着各人的身份和各国的习惯。

雷奈尔多 很好，老爷。

波洛涅斯 然后他就——他就——我刚才要说一句什么话？哎哟，我正要说一句什么话；我说到什么地方啦？

雷奈尔多 您刚才说到"用这样的话表示同意"；还有"朋友"或者"仁兄"。

波洛涅斯 说到"用这样的话表示同意"，嗯，对了；他会用这样的话对你表示同意："我认识这位绅士，昨天我还看见他，或许是前天，或许是什么什么时候，跟什么什么人在一起，正像您所说的，他在什么地方赌钱，在什么地方喝得酩酊大醉，在什么地方因为打网球而跟人家打起架来；"也许他还会说，"我看见他走进什么什么一家生意人家去，"那就是说窑子或是诸如此类的所在。你瞧，你用说谎的钓饵，就可以把事实的真相诱上你的钓钩；我们有智慧、有见识的人，往往用这种旁敲侧击的方法，间接达到我们的目的；你也可以照着我上面所说的那一番话，探听出我的儿子的行为。你懂得我的意思没有？

雷奈尔多 老爷，我懂得。

波洛涅斯 上帝和你同在；再会！

雷奈尔多 那么我去了，老爷。

波洛涅斯 你自己也得留心观察他的举止。

雷奈尔多 是，老爷。

波洛涅斯 叫他用心学习音乐。

REYNALDO	Well, my lord.
POLONIUS	Farewell. [*Exit Reynaldo.*]

[*Enter Ophelia.*]

POLONIUS	How now Ophelia, What's the matter?
OPHELIA	O my lord, my lord, I have been so affrighted!
POLONIUS	With what, i' th'name of God?
OPHELIA	My lord, as I was sewing in my closet,
	Lord Hamlet with his doublet all unbraced,
	No hat upon his head, his stockings fouled,
	Ungart' red, and down-gyved to his ankle,
	Pale as his shirt, his knees knocking each other,
	And with a look so piteous in purport
	As if he had been loosed out of hell
	To speak of horrors: he comes before me.
POLONIUS	Mad for thy love?
OPHELIA	My lord, I do not know,
	But truly I do fear it.
POLONIUS	What said he?
OPHELIA	He took me by the wrist, and held me hard,
	Then goes he to the length of all his arm,
	And with his other hand thus o'er his brow,
	He tails to such perusal of my face
	As he would draw it. Long stayed he so,
	At last, a little shaking of mine arm,
	And thrice his head thus waving up and down,
	He raised a sigh so piteous and profound
	As it did seem to shatter all his bulk,
	And end his being; that done, he lets me go,

雷奈尔多　是，老爷。

波洛涅斯　你去吧！（雷奈尔多下。）

（奥菲利娅上。）

波洛涅斯　啊，奥菲利娅！什么事？

奥菲利娅　哎哟，父亲，吓死我了！

波洛涅斯　凭着上帝的名义，怕什么？

奥菲利娅　父亲，我正在房间里缝纫的时候，哈姆莱特殿下跑了进来，走到我的面前；他的上身的衣服完全没有扣上纽子，头上也不戴帽子，他的袜子上沾着污泥，没有袜带，一直垂到脚踝上；他的脸色像他的衬衫一样白，他的膝盖互相碰撞，他的神气是那样凄惨，好像他刚从地狱里逃出来，要向人讲述地狱的恐怖一样。

波洛涅斯　他因为不能得到你的爱而发疯了吗？

奥菲利娅　父亲，我不知道，可是我想也许是的。

波洛涅斯　他怎么说？

奥菲利娅　他握住我的手腕紧紧不放，拉直了手臂向后退立，用他的另一只手这样遮在他的额角上，一眼不眨地瞧着我的脸，好像要把它临摹下来似的。这样经过了好久的时间，然后他轻轻地摇动一下我的手臂，他的头上上下下点了三次，于是他发出一声非常惨痛而深长的叹息，好像他的整个的胸部都要爆裂，他的生命就在这一声叹息中间完毕似的。

莎士比亚经典戏剧

And with his head over his shoulder turned

He seemed to find his way without his eyes,

For out adoors he went without their helps,

And to the last bended their light on me.

POLONIUS Come, go with me. I will go seek the king.

This is the very ecstasy of love.

Whose violent property fordoes itself,

And leads the will to desperate undertakings,

As oft as any passion under heaven

That does afflict our natures. I am sorry.

What, have you given him any hard words of late?

OPHELIA No, my good lord, but as you did command

I did repel his letters, and denied

His access to me.

POLONIUS That hath made him mad.

I am sorry that with better heed and judgment

I had not quoted him. I feared he did but trifle

And meant to wreck thee, but beshrew my jealousy

By heaven, it is as proper to our age

To cast beyond ourselves in our opinions,

As it is common for the younger sort

To lack discretion; come, go we to the king.

This must be known, which, being kept close, might move

More grief to hide, than hate to utter love.

Come. [*Exeunt.*]

然后他放松了我，转过他的身体，他的头还是向后回顾，好像他不用眼睛的帮助也能够找到他的路，因为直到他走出了门外，他的两眼还是注视在我的身上。

波洛涅斯 跟我来，我要见王上去。这正是恋爱不遂的疯狂。一个人受到这种剧烈的刺激，什么不顾一切的事情都会干得出来，其他一切能迷住我们本性的狂热，最厉害也不过如此。我真后悔。怎么，你最近对他说过什么使他难堪的话没有？

奥菲利娅 没有，父亲，可是我已经遵从您的命令，拒绝他的来信，并且不允许他来见我。

波洛涅斯 这就是使他疯狂的原因。我很后悔考虑得不够周到，看错了人。我以为他不过把你玩弄玩弄，恐怕贻误你的终身；可是我不该这样多疑！正像年轻人干起事来，往往不知道瞻前顾后一样，我们这种上了年纪的人，总是免不了鳃鳃过虑。来，我们见王上去。这种事情是不能蒙蔽起来的，要是隐讳不报，也许会闹出乱子来，比直言受责要严重得多。来。（同下。）

SCENE 2

A room in the castle

[*Enter the King and Queen followed by Rosencrantz,
Guildenstem , and Attendants.*]

KING   Welcome, dear Rosencrantz and Guildenstern!

Moreover that we much did long to see you,

The need we have to use you did provoke

Our hasty sending. Something have you heard

Of Hamlet's transformation: so I call it,

Sith nor th' exterior nor the inward man

Resembles that it was. What it should be,

More than his father's death, that thus hath put him

So much from th'understanding of himself,

I cannot dream of. I entreat you both,

That being of so young days brought up with him,

And sith so neighboured to his youth and haviour,

That you vouchsafe your rest here in our court

Some little time, so by your companies

To draw him on to pleasures, and to gather

So much as from occasion you may glean

Whether aught to us unknown afflicts him thus,

That opened lies within our remedy.

QUEEN   Good gentlemen, he hath much talked of you,

And sure I mn two men there are not living

To whom he more adheres. If it will please you

第二场　城堡中一室

（国王、王后、罗森格兰兹、吉尔登斯吞及侍从
等上。）

国　王　欢迎，亲爱的罗森格兰兹和吉尔登斯吞！这次匆匆召请你
们两位前来，一方面是因为我非常思念你们，一方面也是
因为我有需要你们帮忙的地方。你们大概已经听到哈姆莱
特的变化；我把它称为变化，因为无论在外表上或是精神
上，他已经和从前大不相同。除了他父亲的死以外，究竟
还有些什么原因，把他激成了这种疯疯癫癫的样子，我实
在无从猜测。你们从小便跟他在一起长大，素来知道他的
脾气，所以我特地请你们到我们宫廷里来盘桓几天，陪伴
陪伴他，替他解解愁闷，同时乘机窥探他究竟有些什么秘
密的心事，为我们所不知道的，也许一旦公开之后，我们
就可以替他对症下药。

王　后　他常常讲起你们两位，我相信世上没有哪两个人比你们更
为他所亲信了。你们要是不嫌怠慢，答应在我们这儿小作

To show us so much gentry and good will

As to expend your time with us awhile,

For the supply and profit of our hope,

Your visitation shall receive such thanks

As fits a king's remembrance.

ROSENC'Z   Both your majesties

Might by the sovereign power you have of us,

Put your dread pleasures more into command

Than to entreaty.

GUILD'RN   But we both obey,

And here give up ourselves in the full bent,

To lay our service freely at your feet

To be commanded.

KING   Thanks Rosencrantz, and gentle Guildenstern.

QUEEN   Thanks Guildenstern, and gentle Rosencrantz,

And I beseech you instantly to visit

My too much changed son. Go some of you

And bring these gentlemen where Hamlet is.

GUILD'RN   Heavens make our presence and our practices

Pleasant and helpful to him!

QUEEN   Ay, amen!

[*Exeunt Rosencrantz and Guildenstem.*]

[*Enter Polonius.*]

POLONIUS   The ambassadors from Norway, my good lord,

Are joyfully returned.

KING   Thou still hast been the father of good news.

POLONIUS   Have I, my lord? Assure you, my good liege,

I hold my duty as I hold my soul,

逗留，帮助我们实现我们的希望，那么你们的盛情雅意，一定会受到丹麦王室隆重的礼谢的。

罗森格兰兹 我们是两位陛下的臣子，两位陛下有什么旨意，尽管命令我们；像这样言重的话，倒使我们置身无地了。

吉尔登斯吞 我们愿意投身在两位陛下的足下，两位陛下无论有什么命令，我们都愿意尽力奉行。

国　　王 谢谢你们，罗森格兰兹和善良的吉尔登斯吞。

王　　后 谢谢你们，吉尔登斯吞和善良的罗森格兰兹。现在我就要请你们立刻去看看我的大大变了样子的儿子。来人，领这两位绅士到哈姆莱特的地方去。

吉尔登斯吞 但愿上天加佑，使我们能够得到他的欢心，帮助他恢复常态！

王　　后 阿门！（罗森格兰兹、吉尔登斯吞及若干侍从下。）
（波洛涅斯上。）

波洛涅斯 启禀陛下，我们派往挪威去的两位钦使已经喜气洋洋地回来了。

国　　王 你总是带着好消息来报告我们。

波洛涅斯 真的吗，陛下？不瞒陛下说，我把我对于我的上帝和我的

Both to my God and to my gracious king;

And I do think, or else this brain of mine

Hunts not the trail of policy so sure

As it hath used to do, that I have found

The very cause of Hamlet's lunacy.

KING   O speak of that, that do I long to hear.

POLONIUS   Give first admittance to th' ambassadors.

My news shall be the fruit to that great feast.

KING   Thyself do grace to them, and bring them in.

[*Exit Polonius.*]

He tells me, my dear Gertrude, he hath found

The head and source of all your son's distemper.

QUEEN   I doubt it is no other but the main,

His father's death and our o'erhasty marriage.

KING   Well, we shall sift him.

[*Re-enter Polonius with Valtemand and Cornelius.*]

Welcome, my good friends!

Say Valtemand, what from our brother Norway?

VALTEM'D   Most fair return of greetings and desires;

Upon our first, he sent out to suppress

His nephew's levies, which to him appeared

To be a preparation 'gainst the Polack,

But better looked into, he truly found

It was against your highness, whereat grieved

That so his sickness, age and impotence

Was falsely borne in hand, sends out arrests

On Fortinbras, which he in brief obeys,

Receives rebuke from Norway, and in fine,

宽仁厚德的王上的责任，看得跟我的灵魂一样重呢。此外，除非我的脑筋在观察问题上不如过去那样有把握了，不然我肯定相信我已经发现了哈姆莱特发疯的原因。

国　　王　啊！你说吧，我急着要听呢。

波洛涅斯　请陛下先接见了钦使；我的消息留着做盛筵以后的佳果美点吧。

国　　王　那么有劳你去迎接他们进来。（波洛涅斯下。）我的亲爱的乔特鲁德，他对我说他已经发现了你的儿子心神不定的原因。

王　　后　我想主要的原因还是他父亲的死和我们过于迅速的结婚。

国　　王　好，等我们仔细问问。

　　　　　（波洛涅斯率伏提曼德及考尼律斯重上。）

　　　　　欢迎，我的好朋友们！伏提曼德，我们的挪威王兄怎么说？

伏提曼德　他叫我们向陛下转达他的友好的问候。他听到了我们的要求，就立刻传谕他的侄儿停止征兵；本来他以为这种举动是准备对付波兰人的，可是一经调查，才知道它的对象原来是陛下；他知道此事以后，痛心自己因为年老多病，受人欺罔，震怒之下，传令把福丁布拉斯逮捕；福丁布拉斯并未反抗，受到了挪威王一番申斥，最后就在他的叔父面

Makes vow before his uncle never more

To give th' assay of arms against your majesty.

Whereon old Norway, overcome with joy,

Gives him threescore thousand crowns in annual fee,

And his commission to employ those soldiers,

So levied, as before, against the Polack,

With an entreaty, herein further shown,

That it might please you to give quiet pass

Through your dominions for this enterprise,

On such regards of safety and allowance

As therein are set down.

KING   It likes us well,

And at our more considered time, we'll read,

Answer, and think upon this business:

Meantime, we thank you for your well-took labour

Go to your rest, at night we'll feast together.

Most welcome home!

[*Exeunt Valtemand and Cornelius.*]

POLONIUS   This business is well ended.

My liege and madam, to expostulate

What majesty should be, what duty is,

Why day is day, night night, and time is time,

Were nothing but to waste night, day and time.

Therefore since brevity is the soul of wit,

And tediousness the limbs and outward flourishes,

I will be brief. Your noble son is mad,

Mad call I it, for to define true madness,

What is't but to be nothing else but mad?

前立誓决不兴兵侵犯陛下。老王看见他诚心悔过，非常欢喜，当下就给他三千克朗的年俸，并且委任他统率他所征募的那些兵士，去向波兰人征伐；同时他叫我把这封信呈上陛下，（以书信呈上）请求陛下允许他的军队借道通过陛下的领土，他已经在信里提出若干条件，保证决不扰乱地方的安宁。

国　　王　这样很好，等我们有空的时候，还要仔细考虑一下，然后答复。你们远道跋涉，不辱使命，很是劳苦了，先去休息休息，今天晚上我们还要在一起欢宴。欢迎你们回来！
（伏提曼德、考尼律斯同下。）

波洛涅斯　这件事情总算圆满结束了。王上，娘娘，要是我向你们长篇大论地解释君上的尊严，臣下的名分，白昼何以为白昼，黑夜何以为黑夜，时间何以为时间，那不过徒然浪费了昼、夜、时间；所以，既然简洁是智慧的灵魂，冗长是肤浅的藻饰，我还是把话说得简单一些吧。你们的那位殿下是疯了；我说他疯了，因为假如再说明什么才是真疯，那就只有发疯，此外还有什么可说的呢？可是那也

But let that go.

QUEEN	More matter, with less art.
POLONIUS	Madam, I swear I use no art at all.

That he is mad 'tis true, 'tis true, 'tis pity,

And pity ' tis ' tis true: a foolish figure,

But farewell it, for I will use no art.

Mad let us grant him then, and now remains

That we find out the cause of this effect,

Or rather say, the cause of this defect,

For this effect defective comes by cause:

Thus it remains, and the remainder thus.

Perpend. I have a daughter, have while she is mine,

Who in her duty and obedience, mark,

Hath given me this, now gather and surmise,

'To the celestial, and my soul's idol, the most beautified

Ophelia, —'

That's an ill phrase, a vile phrase, 'beautified' is a vile

phrase, but you shall hear. Thus:

'In her excellent white bosom, these, etc. —'

QUEEN	Came this from Hamlet to her?
POLONIUS	Good madam, stay awhile, I will be faithful

'Doubt thou the stars are fire,

Doubt that the sun doth move,

Doubt truth to be a liar,

But never doubt I love.

O dear Ophelia, I am ill at these numbers, I have not art to

reckon my groans, but that I love thee best, O most best,

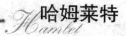
不用说了。

王　　后　多谈些实际，少弄些玄虚。

波洛涅斯　娘娘，我发誓我一点不弄玄虚。他疯了，这是真的；惟其
　　　　　是真的，所以才可叹，它的可叹也是真的——蠢话少说，
　　　　　因为我不愿弄玄虚。好，让我们同意他已经疯了；现在我
　　　　　们就应该求出这一个结果的原因，或者不如说，这一种病
　　　　　态的原因，因为这个病态的结果不是无因而至的，这就是
　　　　　我们现在要做的一步工作。我们来想一想吧。我有一个女
　　　　　儿——当她还不过是我的女儿的时候，她是属于我的——
　　　　　难得她一片孝心，把这封信给了我；现在请猜一猜这里面
　　　　　说些什么话。"给那天仙化人的，我的灵魂的偶像，最艳
　　　　　丽的奥菲利娅——"这是一个粗俗的说法，下流的说法；
　　　　　"艳丽"两字用得非常下流；可是你们听下去吧；"让这
　　　　　几行诗句留下在她的皎洁的胸中——"

王　　后　这是哈姆莱特写给她的吗？

波洛涅斯　好娘娘，等一等，我要老老实实地照原文念：

　　　　　　　"你可以疑心星星是火把；

　　　　　　　　你可以疑心太阳会移转；

　　　　　　　　你可以疑心真理是谎话；

　　　　　　　　可是我的爱永没有改变。

　　　　　亲爱的奥菲利娅啊！我的诗写得太坏。我不会用诗句来抒

believe it. Adieu.

Thine evermore, most dear lady, whilst this machine is to

him, Hamlet. '

This in obedience hath my daughter shown me;

And more above hath his solicitings,

As they fell out by time, by means, and place,

All given to mine ear.

KING   But how hath she

Received his love?

POLONIUS   What do you think of me?

KING   As of a man faithful and honourable.

POLONIUS   I would fain prove so. But what might you think

When I had seen this hot love on the wing,

As I perceived it——I must tell you that,

Before my daughter told me, what might you,

Or my dear majesty your queen here think——

If I had played the desk or table-book,

Or given my heart a working mute and dumb,

Or looked upon this love with idle sight,

What might you think? No, I went round to work,

And my young mistress thus I did bespeak,

'Lord Hamlet is a prince out of thy star,

This must not be! and then I prescripts gave her

That she should lock herself from his resort,

Admit no messengers, receive no tokens.

Which done, she took the fruits of my advice.

And he repelled, a short tale to make,

Fell into a sadness, then into a fast,

写我的愁怀；可是相信我，最好的人儿啊！我最爱的是你。再会！最亲爱的小姐，只要我一息尚存，我就永远是你的，哈姆莱特。"这一封信是我的女儿出于孝顺之心拿来给我看的；此外，她又把他一次次求爱的情形，在什么时候，用什么方法，在什么所在，全都讲给我听了。

国　　王	可是她对于他的爱情抱着怎样的态度呢？
波洛涅斯	陛下以为我是怎样的一个人？
国　　王	一个忠心正直的人。
波洛涅斯	但愿我能够证明自己是这样一个人。可是假如我看见这场热烈的恋爱正在进行——不瞒陛下说，我在我的女儿没有告诉我以前，早就看出来了——假如我知道有了这么一回事，却在暗中促成他们的好事，或者故意视若无睹，假作痴聋，一切不闻不问，那时候陛下的心里觉得怎样？我的好娘娘，您这位王后陛下的心里又觉得怎样？不，我一点儿也不敢懈怠我的责任，立刻就对我那位小姐说："哈姆莱特殿下是一位王子，不是你可以仰望的；这种事情不能让它继续下去。"于是我把她教训一番，叫她深居简出，不要和他见面，不要接纳他的来使，也不要收受他的礼物；她听了这番话，就照着我的意思实行起来。说来话短，他遭到拒绝以后，心里就郁郁不快，于是饭也吃不下了，觉也睡不着了，他的身体一天憔悴一天，他的精神一

	Thence to a watch, thence into a weakness,
	Thence to a lightness, and by this declension,
	Into the madness wherein now he raves,
	And all we mourn tor.
KING	Do you think 'tis this?
QUEEN	It may be, very like.
POLONIUS	Hath there been such a time, I would fain know that,
	That I have positively said 'Tis so', when it proved other-
	wise?
KING	Not that I know.
POLONIUS	Take this from this, if this be otherwise;
	[*He points to his head and shoulder*]
	If circumstances lead me, I will find
	Where truth is hid, though it were hid indeed
	Within the centre.
KING	How may we try it further?
POLONIUS	You know sometimes he walks four hours together
	Here in the lobby.
QUEEN	So he does, indeed.
POLONIUS	At such a time I'll loose my daughter to him.
	Be you and I behind an arras then;
	Mark the encounter, if he love her not,
	And be not from his reason fall' n thereon,
	Let me be no assistant for a state,
	But keep a farm and carters.
KING	We will try it.
QUEEN	But look where sadly the poor wretch comes reading.

天恍惚一天，这样一步步发展下去，就变成现在他这一种为我们大家所悲痛的疯狂。

国　　王　你想是这个原因吗？

王　　后　这是很可能的。

波洛涅斯　我倒很想知道知道，哪一次我曾经肯定地说过了"这件事情是这样的"，而结果却并不这样？

国　　王　照我所知道的，那倒没有。

波洛涅斯　要是我说错了话，把这个东西从这个上面拿下来吧。（指自己的头及肩）只要有线索可寻，我总会找出事实的真相，即使那真相一直藏在地球的中心。

国　　王　我们怎么可以进一步试验试验？

波洛涅斯　您知道，有时候他会接连几个钟头在这儿走廊里踱来踱去。

王　　后　他真的常常这样踱来踱去。

波洛涅斯　乘他踱来踱去的时候，我就让我的女儿去见他，你我可以躲在帷幕后面注视他们相会的情形；要是他不爱她，他的理智不是因为恋爱而丧失，那么不要叫我管理国家的政务，让我去做个耕田赶牲口的农夫吧。

国　　王　我们要试一试。

王　　后　可是瞧，这可怜的孩子忧忧愁愁地念着一本书来了。

POLONIUS	Away, I do beseech you both away,
	I'll board him presently, O give me leave.

[*Exeunt the King and Queen and Attendants.*]

[*Enter Hamlet reading.*]

POLONIUS	How does my good Lord Hamlet?
HAMLET	Well, God-a-mercy.
POLONIUS	Do you know me, my lord?
HAMLET	Excellent well, you are a fishmonger.
POLONIUS	Not I, my lord.
HAMLET	Then I would you were so honest a man.
POLONIUS	Honest, my lord?
HAMLET	Ay sir, to be honest as this world goes, is to be one man picked out of ten thousand.
POLONIUS	That's very true, my lord.
HAMLET	For if the sun breed maggots in a dead dog, being a good kissing carrion. Have you a daughter?
POLONIUS	I have, my lord.
HAMLET	Let her not walk i'th'sun. Conception is a blessing, but as your daughter may conceive, friend look to't.
POLONIUS	[*Aside*] How say you by that? Still harping on my daughter, yet he knew me not at first, he said I was a fishmonger. He is far gone, far gone, and truly in my youth I suffered much extremity for love. very near this. I'll speak to him again. What do you read, my lord?
HAMLET	Words, words, words.
POLONIUS	What is the matter, my lord?
HAMLET	Between who?
POLONIUS	I mean the matter that you read, my lord.

波洛涅斯	请陛下和娘娘避一避；让我走上去招呼他。（国王、王后
	及侍从等下。）

（哈姆莱特读书上。）

波洛涅斯	啊，恕我冒昧。您好，哈姆莱特殿下？
哈姆莱特	呃，上帝怜悯世人！
波洛涅斯	您认识我吗，殿下？
哈姆莱特	认识认识，你是一个卖鱼的贩子。
波洛涅斯	我不是，殿下。
哈姆莱特	那么我但愿你是一个和鱼贩子一样的老实人。
波洛涅斯	老实，殿下！
哈姆莱特	嗯，先生；在这世上，一万个人中间只不过有一个老
	实人。
波洛涅斯	这句话说得很对，殿下。
哈姆莱特	要是太阳能在一条死狗尸体上孵育蛆虫，因为它是一块可
	亲吻的臭肉——你有一个女儿吗？
波洛涅斯	我有，殿下。
哈姆莱特	不要让她在太阳光底下行走；肚子里有学问是幸福，但不
	是像你女儿肚子里会有的那种学问。朋友，留心哪。
波洛涅斯	（旁白）你们瞧，他念念不忘地提我的女儿；可是最初他
	不认识我，他说我是一个卖鱼的贩子。他的疯病已经很深
	了，很深了。说句老实话，我在年轻的时候，为了恋爱也
	曾大发其疯，那样子也跟他差不多哩。让我再去对他说
	话。——您在读些什么，殿下？
哈姆莱特	都是些空话，空话，空话。
波洛涅斯	讲的是什么事，殿下？
哈姆莱特	谁同谁的什么事？
波洛涅斯	我是说您读的书里讲到些什么事，殿下。

HAMLET	Slanders, sir; tbr the satirical rogue says here mat old men have grey beards, that their faces are wrinkled, their eyes purging thick amber and plum-tree gum, and that they have a plentiful lack of wit, together with most weak hams; all which, sir, though I most powerfully and potently believe, yet I hold it not honesty esty to have it thus set down, for yourself, sir, shall grow old as I am, if like a crab you could go backward.
POLONIUS	[*Aside*] Though this be madness, yet there is method in't——Will you walk out of the air, my lord?
HAMLET	Into my grave.
POLONIUS	Indeed, that's out of the air; [*Aside*] how pregnant some-times his replies are! A happiness that often madness hits on, which reason and sanity could not so prosperously be delivered of. I will leave him, and suddenly contrive the means of meeting between him and my daughter. —— My honnurable lord, I will most humbly take my leave of you.
HAMLET	You cannot, sir, take from me anything that I will more willingly part withal; except my life, except my lite, ex-cept my life.
POLONIUS	Fare you well, my lord.
HAMIET	These tedious old fools!

[*Enter Rosencrantz and Guildenstern.*]

POLONIUS	You go to seek the Lord Hamlet, there he is.
ROSENC'Z	God save you, sir! [*Exit Polonius.*]
GUILD' RN	My honoured lord!
ROSENC'Z	My most dear lord!
HAMLET	My excellent good friends! How dost thou,

哈姆莱特

哈姆莱特 一派诽谤，先生；这个专爱把人讥笑的坏蛋在这儿说着，老年人长着灰白的胡须，他们的脸上满是皱纹，他们的眼睛里黏满了眼屎，他们的头脑是空空洞洞的，他们的两腿是摇摇摆摆的；这些话，先生，虽然我十分相信，可是照这样写在书上，总有些有伤厚道；因为就是拿您先生自己来说，要是您能够像一只蟹一样向后倒退，那么您也应该跟我一样年轻了。

波洛涅斯 （旁白）这些虽然是疯话，却有深意在内。——您要走进里边去吗，殿下？别让风吹着！

哈姆莱特 走进我的坟墓里去？

波洛涅斯 那倒真是风吹不着的地方。（旁白）他的回答有时候是多么深刻！疯狂的人往往能够说出理智清明的人所说不出来的话。我要离开他，立刻就去想法让他跟我的女儿见面。——殿下，我要向您告别了。

哈姆莱特 先生，那是再好没有的事；但愿我也能够向我的生命告别，但愿我也能够向我的生命告别，但愿我也能够向我的生命告别。

波洛涅斯 再会，殿下。（欲去。）

哈姆莱特 这些讨厌的老傻瓜！

（罗森格兰兹及吉尔登斯吞重上。）

波洛涅斯 你们要找哈姆莱特殿下，那儿就是。

罗森格兰兹 上帝保佑您，大人！（波洛涅斯下。）

吉尔登斯吞 我的尊贵的殿下！

罗森格兰兹 我的最亲爱的殿下！

哈姆莱特 我的好朋友们！你好，吉尔登斯吞？啊，罗森格兰兹！好

	Guildenstern?
	Ah, Rosencrantz! Godd! lads, how do you both?
ROSENC'Z	As the indifferent children of the earth.
GUILD'RN	Happy, in that we are not over-happy,
	On Fortune's cap we are not the very button.
HAMLET	Nor the soles of her shoe?
ROSENC'Z	Neither, my lord.
HAMLET	Then you live about her waist or in the middle of her favours?
GUILD'RN	Faith, her privates we.
HAMLET	In the secret parts of fortune? O most true, she is a strumpet. What's the news?
ROSENC'Z	None, my lord, but that the world's grown honest.
HAMLET	Then is doomsday near. But your news is not true. let me question more in particular; what have you, my good friends, deserved at the hands of Fortune, that she sends you to prison hither?
GUILD'RN	Prison, my lord !
HAMLET	Denmark's a prison.
ROSENC'Z	Then is the world one.
HAMLET	A goodly one, in which there are many confines, wards and dungeons; Denmark being one o'th'worst.
ROSENC'Z	We think not so, my lord.
HAMLET	Why, then'tis none to you; for there is nothing either good or bad, but thinking makes it so; to me it is a prison.
ROSENC'Z	Why, then your ambition makes it one: 'tis too narrow for your mind.
HAMLET	O God! I could be bounded in a nut-shell, and count myself a king of infinite space; were it not that I have bad dreams.

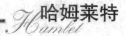

	孩子们，你们两人都好？
罗森格兰兹	不过像一般庸庸碌碌之辈，在这世上虚度时光而已。
吉尔登斯吞	无荣无辱便是我们的幸福；我们高不到命运女神帽子上的纽扣。
哈姆莱特	也低不到她的鞋底吗？
罗森格兰兹	正是，殿下。
哈姆莱特	那么你们是在她的腰上，或是在她的怀抱之中吗？
吉尔登斯	说老实话，我们是在她的私处。
哈姆莱特	在命运身上秘密的那部分吗？啊，对了；她本来是一个娼妓。你们听到什么消息没有？
罗森格兰兹	没有，殿下，我们只知道这世界变得老实起来了。
哈姆莱特	那么世界末日快到了；可是你们的消息是假的。让我再仔细问问你们；我的好朋友们，你们在命运手里犯了什么案子，她把你们送到这儿牢狱里来了？
古尔登斯吞	牢狱，殿下！
哈姆莱特	丹麦是一所牢狱。
罗森格兰兹	那么世界也是一所牢狱。
哈姆莱特	一所很大的牢狱，里面有许多监房、囚室、地牢；丹麦是其中最坏的一间。
罗森格兰兹	我们倒不这样想，殿下。
哈姆莱特	啊，那么对于你们它并不是牢狱；因为世上的事情本来没有善恶，都是各人的思想把它们分别出来的；对于我它是一所牢狱。
罗森格兰兹	啊，那是因为您的雄心太大，丹麦是个狭小的地方，不够给您发展，所以您把它看成一所牢狱啦。
哈姆莱特	上帝啊！倘不是因为我总作噩梦，那么即使把我关在一个果壳里，我也会把自己当作一个拥有着无限空间的君王的。

莎士比亚经典戏剧

GUILD'RN	Which dreams, indeed, are ambition; for the very substance of the ambitious is merely the shadow of a dream.
HAMLET	A dream itself is but a shadow.
ROSENC'Z	Truly, and I hold ambition of so airy and light a quality, that it is but a shadow's shadow.
HAMLET	Then are our beggars bodies, and our monarchs and outstretched heroes the beggars' shadows, shall we to th' court? For, by my fay, I cannot reason.
ROSENC'Z **GUILD'RN**	We'll wait upon you.
HAMLET	No such matter. I will not sort you with the rest of my servants; for to speak to you like an honest man, I am most dreadfully attended. But, in the beaten way of friendship, what make you at Elsinore?
ROSENC'Z	To visit you, my lord, no other occasion.
HAMLET	Beggar that I am, I am even poor in thanks, but I thank you: and sure, dear friends, my thanks are too dear a halfpenny; were you not sent for? Is it your own inclining? Is it a free visitation? Come, come, deal justly with me, come, come, nay speak.
GUILD'RN	What should we say, my lord?
HAMLET	Why, anything but to th'purpose. You were sent for, and there is a kind of confession in your looks, which your modesties have not craft enough to colour. I know the good king and queen have sent for you.
ROSENC'Z	To what end, my lord?
HAMLET	That you must teach me. but let me conjure you, by the rights of our fellowship, by the consonancy of our youth,

吉尔登斯吞	那种噩梦便是您的野心；因为野心家本身的存在，也不过是一个梦的影子。
哈姆莱特	一个梦的本身便是一个影子。
罗森格兰兹	不错，因为野心是那么空虚轻浮的东西，所以我认为它不过是影子的影子。
哈姆莱特	那么我们的乞丐是实体，我们的帝王和大言不惭的英雄，却是乞丐的影子了。我们进宫去好不好？因为我实在不能陪着你们谈玄说理。
罗森格兰兹 吉尔登斯吞	我们愿意侍候殿下。
哈姆莱特	没有的事，我不愿把你们当作我的仆人一样看待；老实对你们说吧，在我旁边侍候我的人全很不成样子。可是，凭着我们多年的交情，老实告诉我，你们到艾尔西诺来有什么贵干？
罗森格兰兹	我们是来拜访您来的，殿下；没有别的原因。
哈姆莱特	像我这样一个叫花子，我的感谢也是不值钱的，可是我谢谢你们；我想，亲爱的朋友们，你们专程而来，只换到我的一声不值半文钱的感谢，未免太不值得了。不是有人叫你们来的吗？果然是你们自己的意思吗？真的是自动的访问吗？来，不要骗我。来，来，快说。
吉尔登斯吞	叫我们说些什么话呢，殿下？
哈姆莱特	无论什么话都行，只要不是废话。你们是奉命而来的；瞧你们掩饰不了你们良心上的惭愧，已经从你们的脸色上招认出来了。我知道是我们这位好国王和好王后叫你们来的。
罗森格兰兹	为了什么目的呢，殿下？
哈姆莱特	那可要请你们指教我了。可是凭着我们朋友间的道义，凭着我们少年时候亲密的情谊，凭着我们始终不渝的友好的

by the obligation of our ever-preserved love, and by what more dear a better proposer can charge you withal, be even and direct with me whether you were sent for or no?

ROSENC'Z [*Aside to Guildenstern*] What say you?

HAMLET [*Aside*] Nay then, I have an eye of you!
—If you love me, hold not off.

GUILD'RN My lord, we were sent for.

HAMLET I will tell you why, so shall my anticipation prevent your discovery, and your secrecy to the king and queen moult no feather. I have of late, but wherefore I know not, lost all my mirth, forgone all custom of exercises: and indeed it goes so heavily with my disposition, that this goodly frame the earth, seems to me a sterile promontory, this most excellent canopy the air, look you, this brave o'er-hanging firmament, this majestical roof fretted with golden fire, why it appeareth nothing to me but a foul and pestilent congregation of vapours. What a piece of work is a man, how noble in reason! how infinite in faculties! in form and moving, how express and admirable in action, how like an angel in apprehension! how like a god! the beauty of the world! the paragon of animals! and yet to me, what is this quintessence of dust? Man delights not me, no, nor woman neither, though by your smiling you seem to say so.

ROSENC'Z My lord, there was no such stuff in my thoughts.

HAMLET Why did ye laugh then, when I said 'man delights not me'?

ROSENC'Z To think, my lord, if you delight not in man, what lenten entertainment the players shall receive from you. We coted them on the way, and hither are they coming to offer you service.

精神,凭着比我口才更好的人所能提出的其他一切更有力量的理由,让我要求你们开诚布公,告诉我究竟你们是不是奉命而来的?

罗森格兰兹 (向吉尔登斯吞旁白)你怎么说?

哈姆莱特 (旁白)好,那么我看透你们的行动了。——要是你们爱我,别再抵赖了吧。

吉尔登斯吞 殿下,我们是奉命而来的。

哈姆莱特 让我代你们说明来意,免得你们泄漏了自己的秘密,有负国王、王后的托付。我近来不知为了什么缘故,一点兴致都提不起来,什么游乐的事都懒得过问;在这一种抑郁的心境之下,仿佛负载万物的大地,这一座美好的框架,只是一个不毛的荒岬;这个覆盖众生的苍穹,这一顶壮丽的帐幕,这个金黄色的火球点缀着的庄严的屋宇,只是一大堆污浊的瘴气的集合。人类是一件多么了不得的杰作!多么高贵的理性!多么伟大的力量!多么优美的仪表!多么文雅的举动!在行为上多么像一个天使!在智慧上多么像一个天神!宇宙的精华!万物的灵长!可是在我看来,这一个泥土塑成的生命算得了什么?人类不能使我发生兴趣;不,女人也不能使我发生兴趣,虽然从你现在的微笑之中,我可以看到你在这样想。

罗森格兰兹 殿下,我心里并没有这样的思想。

哈姆莱特 那么当我说"人类不能使我发生兴趣"的时候,你为什么笑起来?

罗森格兰兹 我想,殿下,要是人类不能使您发生兴趣,那么那班戏子们恐怕要来自讨一场没趣了;我们在路上赶过了他们,他们是要到这儿来向您献技的。

HAMLET	He that plays the King shall be welcome, his majesty shall have tribute on me, the adventurous Knight shall use his foil and target, the Lover shall not sigh gratis, the Humorous Man shall end his part in peace, the Clown shall make those laugh whose lungs are tickle o'th'sere, and the Lady shall say her mind freely, or the blank verse shall. halt for't. What players are they?
ROSENC'Z	Even those you were wont to take such delight in, the tragedians of the city.
HAMLET	How chances it they travel? Their residence both in reputation and profit was better both ways.
ROSENC'Z	I think their inhibition comes by the means of the late innovation.
HAMLET	Do they hold the sane estimation they did when I was in the city? Are they so followed?
ROSENC'Z	No, indeed, are they not.
HAMLET	How comes it? do they grow rusty?
ROSENC'Z	Nay, their endeavour keeps in the wonted pace; but there is, sir, an eyrie of children, little eyases, that cry out on the top of question, and are most tyrannically clapped for' t: these are now the fashion, and so berattle the common stages so they call them that many wearing rapiers are afraid of goose quills, and dare scarce come thither.
HAMLET	What, are they children? Who maintains'em? How are they escoted? Will they pursue the quality no longer than they can sing? will they not say afterwards if they should grow themselves to common players as it is like most will if their means are not b etter

Hamlet

哈 姆 莱 特　扮演国王的那个人将要得到我的欢迎，我要在他的御座之前致献我的敬礼；冒险的骑士可以挥舞他的剑盾；情人的叹息不会没有酬报；躁急易怒的角色可以平安下场；小丑将要使那班善笑的观众捧腹；我们的女主角可以坦白诉说她的心事，不用怕那无韵诗的句子脱去板眼。他们是一班什么戏子？

罗森格兰兹　就是您向来所欢喜的那一个班子，在城里专演悲剧的。

哈 姆 莱 特　他们怎么走起江湖来了呢？固定在一个地方演戏，在名誉和进益上都要好得多哩。

罗森格兰兹　我想他们不能在一个地方立足，是为了时势的变化。

哈 姆 莱 特　他们的名誉还是跟我在城里那时候一样吗？他们的观众还是那么多吗？

罗森格兰兹　不，他们现在已经大非昔比了。

哈 姆 莱 特　怎么会这样的？他们的演技退步了吗？

罗森格兰兹　不，他们还是跟从前一样努力；可是，殿下，他们的地位已经被一群羽毛未丰的黄口小儿占夺了去。这些娃娃们的嘶叫博得了台下疯狂的喝彩，他们是目前流行的宠儿，他们的声势压倒了所谓普通的戏班，以至于许多腰佩长剑的上流顾客，都因为惧怕批评家鹅毛管的威力，而不敢到那边去。

哈 姆 莱 特　什么！是一些童伶吗？谁维持他们的生活？他们的薪工是怎么计算的？他们一到不能唱歌的年龄，就不再继续他们的本行了吗？要是他们赚不了多少钱，长大起来多半还是要做普通戏子的，那时候难道他们不会抱怨写戏词的人把

their writers do them wrong, to make them exclaim against their own succession?

ROSENC'Z   Faith, there has been much to do on both sides: and the nation holds it no sin to tarre them to controversy. There was, for a while, no money bid for argument, unless the Poet and the Player went to cuffs in the question.

HAMLET   Is't possible?

GUILD'RN   O, there has been much throwing about of brains.

HAMLET   Do the boys carry it away?

ROSENC'Z   Ay, that they do my lord, Hercules and his load too.

HAMLET   It is not very strange, for my uncle is king of Denmark, and those that would make mows at him while my father lived, give twenty, forty, fifty, a hundred ducats apiece for his picture in little. 'Sblood, there is something in this more than natural, if philosophy could find it out.

[*Flourish of trumpets within*]

GUILD'RN   There are the players.

HAMLET   Gentlemen, you are welcome to Elsinore.

Your hands? Come then, th'appurtenance of welcome is fashion and ceremony; let me comply with you in this garb lest my extent to the players, which I tell you must show fairly outwards, should more appear like entertainment than yours. You are welcome; but my utile-father, and aunt-mother, are deceived.

GUILD'RN   In what, my dear lord?

HAMLET   I am but mad north-north-west; when the wind is souther-ly, I know a hawk from a handsaw.

[*Re-enter Polonius.*]

他们害了，因为原先叫他们挖苦备至的不正是他们自己的未来前途吗？

罗森格兰兹 真的，两方面闹过不少的纠纷，全国的人都站在旁边恬不为意地呐喊助威，怂恿他们互相争斗。曾经有一个时期，一个脚本非得插进一段编剧家和演员争吵的对话，不然是没有人愿意出钱购买的。

哈姆莱特 有这等事？

吉尔登斯吞 是啊，在那场交替里，许多人都投入了大量心血。

哈姆莱特 结果是娃娃们打赢了吗？

罗森格兰兹 正是，殿下；连赫刺克勒斯和他背负的地球都成了他们的战利品。

哈姆莱特 那也没有什么稀奇；我的叔父是丹麦的国王，那些当我父亲在世的时候对他扮鬼脸的人，现在都愿意拿出二十、四十、五十、一百块金洋来买他的一幅小照。哼，这里面有些不是常理可解的地方，要是哲学能够把它推究出来的话。（内喇叭奏花腔。）

吉尔登斯吞 这班戏子们来了。

哈姆莱特 两位先生，欢迎你们到艾尔西诺来。把你们的手给我；欢迎总要讲究这些礼节、俗套；让我不要对你们失礼，因为这些戏子们来了以后，我不能不敷衍他们一番，也许你们见了会发生误会，以为我招待你们还不及招待他们殷勤。我欢迎你们；可是我的叔父父亲和婶母母亲可弄错啦。

吉尔登斯吞 弄错了什么，我的好殿下？

哈姆莱特 天上刮着西北风，我才发疯；风从南方吹来的时候，我不会把一只鹰当作了一只鹭鸶。

（波洛涅斯重上。）

POLONIUS   Well be with you, gentlemen!

HAMLET   Hark you Guildenstem, and you too, at each ear a hearer: that great baby you see there is not yet out of his swathling-clouts.

ROSENC'Z   Happily he is the second time come to them, for they say an old man is twice a child.

HAMLET   I will prophesy, he comes to tell me of the players, mark it. You say right sir, a Monday morning' twas then indeed.

POLONIUS   My lord, I have news to tell you.

HAMLET   My lord, I have news to tell you. Wnen Roscius was an actor in Rome —

POLONIUS   The actors are come hither, my lord.

HAMLET   Buz, buz!

POLONIUS   Upon my honour —

HAMLET   'Then came each actor on his ass'—

OLONIUS   The best actors in the world, either for tragedy, comedy, history, pastoral, pastoral-comical, historical, pastoral, tragical-historical, tragical-comical-historical-pastoral, scene individable, or poem unlimited. Seneca cannot be too heavy nor Plautus too light. For the law of writ and the liberty, these are the only men.

HAMLET   O jephthah, judge of Israel, what a treasure hadst thou!

POLONIUS   What a treasure had he, my lord?

HAMLET   Why,

'One fair daughter, and no more,
The which he loved passing well.'

POLONIUS   [*Aside*] Still on my daughter.

哈姆莱特
Hamlet

波 洛 涅 斯　祝福你们，两位先生！

哈 姆 莱 特　听着，吉尔登斯吞；你也听着；一只耳朵边有一个人听：你们看见的那个大孩子，还在襁褓之中，没有学会走路哩。

罗森格兰兹　也许他是第二次裹在襁褓里，因为人家说，一个老年人是第二次做婴孩。

哈 姆 莱 特　我可以预言他是来报告我戏子们来到的消息的；听好。——你说得不错；在星期一早上；正是正是。

波 洛 涅 斯　殿下，我有消息要来向您报告。

哈 姆 莱 特　大人，我也有消息要向您报告。当罗歇斯在罗马演戏的时候——

波 洛 涅 斯　那班戏子们已经到这儿来了，殿下。

哈 姆 莱 特　嗤！嗤！

波 洛 涅 斯　凭着我的名誉起誓——

哈 姆 莱 特　那时每一个伶人都骑着驴子而来——

波 洛 涅 斯　他们是全世界最好的伶人，无论悲剧、喜剧、历史剧、田园剧、田园喜剧、田园史剧、历史悲剧、历史田园悲喜剧、场面不变的正宗戏或是摆脱拘束的新派戏，他们无不拿手；塞内加的悲剧不嫌其太沉重，普鲁图斯的喜剧不嫌其太轻浮。无论在演出规律的或是自由的剧本方面，他们都是唯一的演员。

哈 姆 莱 特　以色列的士师耶弗他啊，你有一件怎样的宝贝！

波 洛 涅 斯　他有什么宝贝，殿下？

哈 姆 莱 特　嗨，

他有一个独生娇女，

爱她胜过掌上明珠。

波 洛 涅 斯　（旁白）还在提我的女儿。

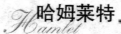

HAMLET	Am I not i' th' right, old Jephthah?
POLONIUS	If you call me Jephthah, my lord, I have a daughter that I love passing well.
HAMLET	Nay, that follows not.
POLONIUS	What follows then, my lord?
HAMLET	Why,

'As by lot, God wot',

and then you know

'It came to pass, as most like it was.'
The first row of the pious chanson will show you
more, for look where my abridgement comes.

[*Enter four or five Players.*]

You are welcome masters, welcome all. I am glad to see thee well——Welcome, good friends——O, my old friend! Why, thy face is valanced since I saw thee last, com'st thou to beard me in Denmark? What, my young lady and mistress! By'r lady, your ladyship is nearer to heaven than when I saw you last by the altitude of a chopine. Pray God your voice, like a piece of uncurrent gold, be not cracked within the ring. Masters, you are all welcome. We'll e'en to't like Frenchfalconers, fly at anything we see, we'll have a speech straight. Come give us a taste of your quality, come, a passionate speech.

1 PLAYER	What speech, my good lord?
HAMLET	I heard thee speak me a speech once, but it was never acted, or if it was, not above once, for the play I remember pleased not the million, 'twas caviary to the general, but it was as I received it, and others, whose judgments in such matters

哈 姆 莱 特	我念得对不对，耶弗他老头儿？
波 洛 涅 斯	要是您叫我耶弗他，殿下，那么我有一个爱如明珠的娇女。
哈 姆 莱 特	不，下面不是这样的。
波 洛 涅 斯	那么应当是怎样的呢，殿下？
哈 姆 莱 特	嗨，

上天不佑，劫数临头。

下面你知道还有，

偏偏凑巧，谁也难保——

要知道全文，请查这支圣歌的第一节，因为，你瞧，有人来把我的话头打断了。

　　　（优伶四五人上。）

欢迎，各位朋友，欢迎欢迎！——我很高兴看见你这样健康。——欢迎，列位。——啊，我的老朋友！你的脸上比我上次看见你的时候，多长了几根胡子，格外显得威武啦；你是要到丹麦来向我挑战吗？啊，我的年轻的姑娘！凭着圣母起誓，您穿上了一双高底木靴，比我上次看见您的时候更苗条得多啦；求求上帝，但愿您的喉咙不要沙嗄得像一面破碎的铜锣才好！各位朋友，欢迎欢迎！我们要像法国的鹰师一样，不管看见什么就撒出鹰去；让我们立刻就来念一段剧词。来，试一试你们的本领，来一段激昂慷慨的剧词。

| 伶　　　甲 | 殿下要听的是哪一段？ |
| 哈 姆 莱 特 | 我曾经听见你向我背诵过一段台词，可是它从来没有上演过；即使上演，也不会有一次以上，因为我记得这本戏并不受大众的欢迎。它是不合一般人口味的鱼子酱；可是照 |

cried in the top of mine an excellent play, well digested in the scenes, set down with as much modesty as cunning. I remember one said there were no sallets in the lines, to make the matter savoury, nor no matter in the phrase that might indict the author of affection, but called it an honest method, as wholesome as sweet, and by very much more handsome than fine: one speech in't I chiefly loved,' twas Aeneas' tale to Dido, and thereabout of it especially where he speaks of Priam's slaughter. If it live in your memory begin at this line, let me see, let me see:

'The rugged Pyrrhus, like th'Hyrcanian beast.

'tis not so, it begins with Pyrrhus.

'The rugged Pyrrhus, he whose sable arms,

Black as his purpose, did the night resemble

When he lay couched in th' ominous horse,

Hath now this dread and black complexion smeared

With heraldry more dismal: head to foot

Now is he total gules, horridly tricked

With blood of fathers, mothers, daughters, sons,

Baked and impasted with the parching streets,

That lend a tyrannous and a damned light

To their lord's murder. Roasted in wrath and fire,

And thus o' er-sized with coagulate gore,

With eyes like carbuncles, the hellish Pyrrhus

Old grandsire Priam seeks. '

So proceed you.

POLONIUS Fore God, my lord, well spoken, with good accent and good discretion.

我的意思看来，还有其他在这方面比我更有权威的人也抱着同样的见解，它是一本绝妙的戏剧，场面支配得很是适当，文字质朴而富于技巧。我记得有人这样说过：那出戏里没有滥加提味的作料，字里行间毫无矫揉造作的痕迹；他把它称为一种老老实实的写法，兼有刚健与柔和之美，壮丽而不流于纤巧。其中有一段话是我最喜爱的，那就是埃涅阿斯对狄多讲述的故事，尤其是讲到普里阿摩斯被杀的那一节。要是你们还没有把它忘记，请从这一行念起；让我想想，让我想想：——

野蛮的皮洛斯像猛虎一样——

不，不是这样；但是的确是从皮洛斯开始的；——

野蛮的皮洛斯蹲伏在木马之中，

黝黑的手臂和他的决心一样，

像黑夜一般阴森而恐怖；

在这黑暗狰狞的肌肤之上，

现在更染上令人惊怖的纹章，

从头到脚，他全身一片殷红，

溅满了父母子女们无辜的血；

那些燃烧着熊熊烈火的街道，

发出残忍而惨恶的凶光，

照亮敌人去肆行他们的杀戮，

也焙干了到处横流的血泊；

冒着火焰的熏炙，像恶魔一般，

全身胶黏着凝结的血块，

圆睁着两颗血红的眼睛，

来往寻找普里阿摩斯老王的踪迹。

你接下去吧。

波洛涅斯　上帝在上，殿下，您念得好极了，真是抑扬顿挫，曲尽其妙。

119

1 PLAYER   'Anon be finds him
Striking too short at Greeks; his antique sword,
Rebellious to his arm, lies where it falls,
Repugnant to command; unequal matched,
Pyrrhus at Priam drives, in rage strikes wide,
But with the whiff and wind of his fell sword
Th' unnerved father falls: then senseless Ilium,
Seeming to feel this blow, with flaming top
Stoops to his base; and with a hideous crash
Takes prisoner Pyrrhus' ear. For lo! his sword,
Which was declining on the milky head
Of reverend Priam, seemed i' th' air air to stick,
So as a painted tyrant Pyrrhus stood,
And like a neutral to his will and matter,
Did nothing:
But as we often see, against some storm,
A silence in the heavens, the rack stand still,
The bold winds speechless, and the orb below
As hush as death, anon the dreadful thunder
Doth rend the region, so after Pyrrhus' pause,
A roused vengeance sets him new awork,
And never did the Cyclops' hammers fall
On Mars's armour, forged for proof eterne,
With less remorse than Pyrrhus' bleeding sword
Now falls on Priam.
Out, out, thou strumpet Fortune! All you gods,
In general synod take away her power,
Break all the spokes and fellies from her wheel,

伶　　甲　那老王正在苦战，
　　　　　　但是砍不着和他对敌的希腊人；
　　　　　　一点不听他手臂的指挥，
　　　　　　他的古老的剑锵然落地；
　　　　　　皮洛斯瞧他孤弱可欺，
　　　　　　疯狂似的向他猛力攻击，
　　　　　　凶恶的利刃虽然没有击中，
　　　　　　一阵风却把那衰弱的老王推倒。
　　　　　　这一下打击有如天崩地裂，
　　　　　　惊动了没有感觉的伊利恩，
　　　　　　冒着火焰的城楼霎时坍下，
　　　　　　那轰然的巨响像一个霹雳，
　　　　　　震聋了皮洛斯的耳朵；瞧！
　　　　　　他的剑还没砍下普里阿摩斯
　　　　　　白发的头颅，却已在空中停住；
　　　　　　像一个涂朱抹彩的暴君，
　　　　　　对自己的行为漠不关心，
　　　　　　他兀立不动。
　　　　　　在一场暴风雨未来以前，
　　　　　　天上往往有片刻的宁静，
　　　　　　一块块乌云静悬在空中，
　　　　　　狂风悄悄地收起它的声息，
　　　　　　死样的沉默笼罩整个大地；
　　　　　　可是就在这片刻之内，
　　　　　　可怕的雷鸣震裂了天空。
　　　　　　经过暂时的休止，杀人的暴念
　　　　　　重新激起了皮洛斯的精神；
　　　　　　库克罗普斯为战神铸造甲胄，
　　　　　　那巨力的锤击，还不及皮洛斯
　　　　　　流血的剑向普里阿摩斯身上劈下
　　　　　　那样凶狠无情。
　　　　　　去，去，你娼妇一样的命运！
　　　　　　天上的诸神啊！剥去她的权力，
　　　　　　不要让她僭窃神明的宝座；

And bowl the round nave down the hill of heaven

As low as to the fiends.'

POLONIUS   This is too long.

HAMLET   It shall to the barber's with your beard; prithee say on: he's for a jig, or a tale of bawdry, or be sleeps. Say on, come to Hecuba.

1 PLAYER   *'But who, ah woe! had seen the mobled queen-'*

HAMLET   'The mobled queen'?

POLONIUS   That's good, 'mobled queen' is good.

1 PLAYER   *'Run barefoot up and down, threat'ning the flames*

With bisson rheum, a clout upon that head

Where late the diadem stood, and for a robe,

About her lank and all o'er-teemed loins,

A blanket in the alarm of fear caught up.

Who this had seen, with tongue in venom steeped,

'Gainst Fortune's state would treason have pronounced;

But if the gods themselves did see her then,

When she saw Pyrrhus make malicious sport

In mincing with his sword her husband's limbs,

The instant burst of clamour that she made,

Unless things mortal move them not at all,

Would have made milch the burning eyes of heaven.

And passion in the gods.'

POLONIUS   Look whe'r he has not turned his colour, and has tears in's eyes. Prithee no more.

HAMLET   Tis well, I'll have thee speak out the rest of this soon. Good my lord, will you see the players well bestowed; do you hear, let them be well used, for they are the abstracts and

拆毁她的车轮，把它滚下神山，
直到地狱的深渊。

波洛涅斯 这一段太长啦。

哈姆莱特 它应当跟你的胡子一起到理发匠那儿去薙一薙念下去吧。
他只爱听俚俗的歌曲和淫秽的故事，否则他就要瞌睡的。
念下去；下面要讲到赫卡柏了。

伶　　甲 可是啊！谁看见那蒙脸的王后——

哈姆莱特 "那蒙脸的王后"？

波洛涅斯 那很好；"蒙脸的王后"是很好的句子。

伶　　甲 满面流泪，在火焰中赤脚奔走，
一块布覆在失去宝冕的头上，
也没有一件蔽体的衣服，
只有在惊惶中抓到的一幅毡巾，
裹住她瘦削而多产的腰身；
谁见了这样伤心惨目的景象，
不要向残酷的命运申申毒詈？
她看见皮洛斯以杀人为戏，
正在把她丈夫的肢体脔割，
忍不住大放悲声，那凄凉的号叫——
除非人间的哀乐不能感动天庭——
即使天上的星星也会陪她流泪，
假使那时诸神曾在场目击，
他们的心中都要充满悲愤。

波洛涅斯 瞧，他的脸色都变了，他的眼睛里已经含着眼泪！不要念
下去了吧。

哈姆莱特 很好，其余的部分等会儿再念给我听吧。大人，请您去找
一处好好的地方安顿这一班伶人。听着，他们是不可怠慢的，

brief chronicles of the time; after your death you were better have a bad epitaph than their ill report while you live.

POLONIUS   My lord, I will use them according to their desert.

HAMLET   God's bodkin, man, much better! Use every man after
his desert, and who shall 'scape whipping? Use them after
your own honour and dignity. The less they deserve the
more merit is in your bounty. Take them in.

POLONIUS   Come, sirs.

HAMLET   Follow him, friends, we'll hear a play tomorrow. [*Exit Polonius and Players except the First Player*] Dost thou hear
me, old friend, can you play The Murder of Gonzago?

1 PLAYER   Ay, my lord.

HAMLET   We'll ha't tomorrow night. Yon could for a need study a
speech of some dozen or sixteen lines, which I would set
down and insert in't, could you not?

1 PLAYER   Ay, my lord.

HAMLET   Very well. Follow that lord, and look you mock him not.
[*To Rosencrantz and Guildenstern*] My good friends, I'll
leave you fill night. You are welcome to Elsinore.

ROSENC'Z   Good my lord.   [*Exeunt Rosencrantz and Guildenstern.*]

HAMLET   Ay, so, God bye to you! Now I am alone.
O, what a rogue and peasant slave am I!
Is it not monstrous that this player here,
But in a fiction, in a dream of passion,
Could force his soul so to his own conceit
That from her working all his visage wanned,
Tears in his eyes, distraction in his aspect,
A broken voice, and his whole function suiting

因为他们是这一个时代的缩影；宁可在死后得到一首恶劣的墓铭，不要在生前受他们一场刻毒的讥讽。

波 洛 涅 斯 殿下，我按着他们应得的名分对待他们就是了。

哈 姆 莱 特 哎哟，朋友，还要客气得多哩！要是照每一个人应得的名分对待他，那么谁逃得了一顿鞭子？照你自己的名誉地位对待他们；他们越是不配受这样的待遇，越可以显出你的谦虚有礼。领他们进去。

波 洛 涅 斯 来，各位朋友。

哈 姆 莱 特 跟他去，朋友们；明天我们要听你们唱一本戏。（波洛涅斯偕众伶下，伶甲独留）听着，老朋友，你会演《贡扎古之死》吗？

伶　　　甲 会演的，殿下。

哈 姆 莱 特 那么我们明天晚上就把它上演。也许我为了必要的理由，要另外写下约莫十几行句子的一段剧词插进去，你能够把它预先背熟吗？

伶　　　甲 可以，殿下。

哈 姆 莱 特 很好。跟着那位老爷去；留心不要取笑他。（伶甲下。向罗森格兰兹、吉尔登斯吞）我的两位好朋友，我们今天晚上再见；欢迎你们到艾尔西诺来！

吉 尔 登 斯 吞 再会，殿下！（罗森格兰兹、吉尔登斯吞同下。）

哈 姆 莱 特 好，上帝和你们同在！现在我只剩一个人了。啊，我我是一个多么不中用的蠢材！这一个伶人不过在一本虚构的故事、一场激昂的幻梦之中，却能够使他的灵魂融化在他的意象里，在它的影响之下，他的整个的脸色变成惨白，他的眼中洋溢着热泪，他的神情流露着仓皇，他的声音是这么呜咽凄凉，他的全部动作都表现得和他的意象一致，这

With forms to his conceit; and all for nothing!

For Hecuba! What's Hecuba to him, or he to Hecuba,

That he should weep for her? What would he do,

Had he the motive and the cue for passion

That I have? He would drown the stage with tears,

And cleave the general ear with horrid speech,

Make mad the guilty and appal the free,

Confound the ignorant, and amaze indeed

The very faculties of eyes and ears; yet I,

A dull and muddy-mettled rascal, peak

Like John-a-dreams, unpregnant of my cause,

And can say nothing; no, not for a king,

Upon whose property and most dear life

A danmed defeat was made, am I a coward?

Who calls me villain, breaks my pate across,

Plucks off my beard and blows it in my face

Tweaks me by the nose, gives me the lie i' th' throat

As deep as to the lungs? who does me this,

Ha? Why, I should take it, for it cannot be

But I am pigeon-livered, and lack

To make oppression bitter, or ere this

I should ha' fatted all the region kites

With this slave's offal. Bloody, hardy villain!

Remorseless, treacherous, lecherous, kindless villain!

O, vengeance! Why, what an ass am I. This is most brave,

That I, the son of a dear father murdered,

Prompted to my revenge by heaven and hell,

Must like a whore unpack my heart with words,

不是极其不可思议的吗？而且一点也不为了什么！为了赫卡柏！赫卡柏对他有什么相干，他对赫卡柏又有什么相干，他却要为她流泪？要是他也有了像我所有的那样使人痛心的理由，他将要怎样呢？他一定会让眼泪淹没了舞台，用可怖的字句震裂了听众的耳朵，使有罪的人发狂，使无罪的人惊骇，使愚昧无知的人惊惶失措，使所有的耳目迷乱了它们的功能。可是我，一个糊涂颠顶的家伙，垂头丧气，一天到晚像在做梦似的，忘记了杀父的大仇；虽然一个国王给人家用万恶的手段掠夺了他的权位，杀害了他的最宝贵的生命，我却始终哼不出一句话来。我是一个懦夫吗？谁骂我恶人？谁敲破我的脑壳？谁拔去我的胡子，把它吹在我的脸上？谁扭我的鼻子？谁当面指斥我胡说？谁对我做这种事？嘿！我应该忍受这样的侮辱，因为我是一个没有心肝、逆来顺受的怯汉，否则我早已用这奴才的尸肉，喂肥了满天盘旋的乌鸢了。嗜血的、荒淫的恶贼！狠心的、奸诈的、淫邪的、悖逆的恶贼！啊！复仇！——嗨，我真是个蠢材！我的亲爱的父亲被人谋杀了，鬼神都在鞭策我复仇，我这做儿子的却像一个下流女

And fall a-cursing like a very drab;

A stallion! Fie upon' t! Foh!

About, my brains; hum, I have heard

That guilty creatures sitting at a play

Have by the very cunning of the scene

Been struck so to the soul, that presently

They have proclaimed their malefactions;

For murder, though it have no tongue, will speak

With most miraculous organ: I'll have these players

Play something like the murder of my father

Before mine uncle, I'll observe his looks,

I'll tent him to the quick; if'a do blench

I know my course. The spirit that I have seen

May be a devil, and the devil hath power

T'assume a pleasing shape, yea, and perhaps

Out of my weakness and my melancholy,

As he is very potent with such spirits,

Abuses me to damn me; I'll have grounds

More relative than this: the play's the thing

Wherein I'll catch the conscience of the king.　　[*Exit.*]

人似的，只会用空言发发牢骚，学起泼妇骂街的样子来，在我已经是了不得的了！呸！呸！活动起来吧，我的脑筋！我听人家说，犯罪的人在看戏的时候，因为台上表演的巧妙，有时会激动天良，当场供认他们的罪恶；因为暗杀的事情无论干得怎样秘密，总会借着神奇的喉舌泄露出来。我要叫这班伶人在我的叔父面前表演一本跟我的父亲的惨死情节相仿的戏剧，我就在一旁窥察他的神色；我要探视到他的灵魂的深处，要是他稍露惊骇不安之态，我就知道我应该怎么办。我所看见的幽灵也许是魔鬼的化身，借着一个美好的形状出现，魔鬼是有这一种本领的；对于柔弱忧郁的灵魂，他最容易发挥他的力量；也许他看准了我的柔弱和忧郁，才来向我作祟，要把我引诱到沉沦的路上。我要先得到一些比这更切实的证据；凭着这一本戏，我可以发掘国王内心的隐秘。（下。）

ACT 3 SCENE 1

A room in the castle

[*Enter King , Queen , Polonius , Ophelia , Rosencrantz and Guildenstern.*]

KING	And can you by no drift of conference
	Get from him why he puts on this confusion ,
	Grating so harshly all his days of quiet
	With turbulent and dangerous lunacy?
ROSENC'Z	He does confess he feels himself distracted ,
	But from what cause he will by no means speak.
GUILD'RN	Nor do we find him forward to be sounded ,
	But with a crafty madness keeps aloof
	When we would bring him on to some confession
	Of his true state.
QUEEN	Did he receive you well?
ROSENC'Z	Most like a gentleman.
GUILD'RN	But with much forcing of his disposition.
ROSENC'Z	Niggard of question , but of our demands
	Most free in his reply.
QUEEN	Did you assay him to any pastime?
ROSENC'Z	Madam , it so fell out that certain players
	We o'er-raught on the way. Of these we told him ,
	And there did seem in him a kind of joy

第 三 幕

第一场　城堡中一室

（国王、王后、波洛涅斯、奥菲利娅、罗森格兰兹及吉尔登斯吞上。）

国　　王　你们不能用迂回婉转的方法，探出他为什么这样神魂颠倒，让紊乱而危险的疯狂困扰他的安静的生活吗？

罗森格兰兹　他承认他自己有些神经迷惘，可是绝口不肯说为了什么缘故。

吉尔登斯吞　他也不肯虚心接受我们的探问；当我们想要引导他吐露他自己的一些真相的时候，他总是用假作痴呆的神气故意回避。

王　　后　他对待你们还客气吗？

罗森格兰兹　很有礼貌。

吉尔登斯吞　可是不大自然。

罗森格兰兹　他很吝惜自己的话，可是我们问他话的时候，他回答起来却是毫无拘束。

王　　后　你们有没有劝诱他找些什么消遣？

罗森格兰兹　娘娘，我们来的时候，刚巧有一班戏子也要到这儿来，给我们赶过了；我们把这消息告诉了他，他听了好像很高

	To hear of it. they are here about the court,
	And as I think, they have already order
	This night to play before him.
POLONIUS	'Tis most true,
	And he beseeched me to entreat your majesties
	To hear and see the matter.
KING	With all my heart, and it doth much content me
	To hear him so inclined, good gentlemen, give him a fur-
	theredge, And drive his purpose into these delights.
ROSENC'Z	We shall, my lord.

                             [*Exeunt Rosencrantz and Guildenstern.*]

KING	Sweet Gertrude, leave us too,
	For we have closely sent for Hamlet hither,
	That he, as' twere by accident, may here
	Affront Ophelia; her father and myself, lawful espials,
	Will so bestow ourselves, that seeing unseen,
	We may of their encounter frankly judge,
	And gather by him as he is behaved,
	If' t be th' affliction of his love or no that thus he
	suffers for.
QUEEN	I shall obey you and for your part, Ophelia, I do wish
	That your good beauties be the happy cause
	Of Hamlet's wildness, so shall I hope your virtues
	Will bring him to his wonted way again, to both your
	honours.
OPHELIA	Madam, I wish it may.

                                            [*Exit the Queen.*]

兴。现在他们已经到了宫里，我想他已经吩咐他们今晚为他演出了。

波洛涅斯 一点不错；他还叫我来请两位陛下同去看看他们演得怎样哩。

国　　王 那好极了；我非常高兴听见他在这方面感兴趣。请你们两位还要更进一步鼓起他的兴味，把他的心思移转到这种娱乐上面。

罗森格兰兹 是，陛下。（罗森格兰兹、吉尔登斯吞同下。）

国　　王 亲爱的乔特鲁德，你也暂时离开我们；因为我们已经暗中差人去唤哈姆莱特到这儿来，让他和奥菲利娅见见面，就像他们偶然相遇一般。她的父亲跟我两人将要权充一下密探，躲在可以看见他们，却不能被他们看见的地方，注意他们会面的情形，从他的行为上判断他的疯病究竟是不是因为恋爱上的苦闷。

王　　后 我愿意服从您的意旨。奥菲利娅，但愿你的美貌果然是哈姆莱特疯狂的原因；更愿你的美德能够帮助他恢复原状，使你们两人都能安享尊荣。

奥菲利娅 娘娘，但愿如此。（王后下。）

POLONIUS   Ophelia, walk you here. Gracious, so please you,

We will bestow ourselves. [*To Ophelia*] Read on this book,

That show of such an exercise may colour

Your loneliness; we are oft to blame in this,

'Tis too much proved, that with devotion's visage

And pious action we do sugar o' er the devil himself.

KING   [*Aside*] O, ' tis too true,

How smart a lash that speech doth give my conscience.

The harlot's cheek, beautied with plast' ring art,

Is not more ugly to the thing that helps it,

Than is my deed to my most painted word; O heavy burden!

POLONIUS   I hear him coming, let's withdraw, my lord.

[*Exeunt the King and Polonius.*]

[*Enter Hamlet.*]

HAMLET   To be, or not to be, that is the question,

Whether ' tis nobler in the mind to suffer

The slings and arrows of outrageous fortune,

Or to take arms against a sea of troubles,

And by opposing, end them. To die, to sleep

No more, and by a sleep to say we end

The heart-ache, and the thousand natural shocks

That flesh is heir to; ' tis a consummation

Devoutly to be wished to die to sleep!

To sleep, perchance to dream, ay there's the rub,

For in that sleep of death what dreams may come

When we have shuffled off this mortal coil

Must give us pause. There's the respect

That makes calamity of so long life;

哈姆莱特

波洛涅斯 奥菲利娅,你在这儿走走。陛下,我们就去躲起来吧。(向奥菲利娅)你拿这本书去读,他看见你这样用功,就不会疑心你为什么一个人在这儿了。人们往往用至诚的外表和虔敬的行动,掩饰一颗魔鬼般的内心,这样的例子是太多了。

国　　王 (旁白)啊,这句话是太真实了!它在我的良心上抽了多么重的一鞭!涂脂抹粉的娼妇的脸,还不及掩藏在虚伪的言辞后面的我的行为更丑恶。难堪的重负啊!

波洛涅斯 我听见他来了;我们退下去吧,陛下。(国王及波洛涅斯下。)

(哈姆莱特上。)

哈姆莱特 生存还是毁灭,这是一个值得考虑的问题;默然忍受命运的暴虐的毒箭,或是挺身反抗人世的无涯的苦难,通过斗争把它们扫清,这两种行为,哪一种更高贵?死了;睡着了;什么都完了;要是在这一种睡眠之中,我们心头的创痛,以及其他无数血肉之躯所不能避免的打击,都可以从此消失,那正是我们求之不得的结局。死了;睡着了;睡着了也许还会做梦;嗯,阻碍就在这儿:因为当我们摆脱了这一具朽腐的皮囊以后,在那死的睡眠里,究竟将要做些什么梦,那不能不使我们踌躇顾虑。人们甘心久困于患难之

For who would bear the whips and scorns of time,

Th'oppressor's wrong, the proud man's contumely,

The pangs of disprized love, the law's delay,

The insolence of office, and the spurns

That patient merit of th'unworthy takes,

When he himself might his quietus make

With a bare bodkin; who would fardels bear,

To grunt and sweat under a weary life,

But that the dread of something after death,

The undiscovered country, from whose bourn

No traveller returns, puzzles the will,

And makes us rather bear those ills we have,

Than fly to others that we know not of?

Thus conscience does make cowards of us all,

And thus the native hue of resolution

Is sieldied o'er with the pale east of thought,

And enterprises of great pitch and moment

With this regard their currents turn awry,

And lose the name of action. Soft you now,

The fair Ophelia — Nymph, in thy orisons

Be all my sins remembered.

OPHELIA	Good my lord, how does your honour for this many a day?
HAMLET	I humbly thank you, well, well, well
OPHELIA	My lord, I have remembrances of yours,
	That I have longed long to re-deliver.
	I pray you now receive them.
HAMLET	No, not I, I never gave you aught.
OPHELIA	My honoured lord, you know right well you did,

中，也就是为了这个缘故；谁愿意忍受人世的鞭挞和讥嘲、压迫者的凌辱、傲慢者的冷眼、被轻蔑的爱情的惨痛、法律的迁延、官吏的横暴和费尽辛勤所换来的小人的鄙视，要是他只要用一柄小小的刀子，就可以清算他自己的一生？谁愿意负着这样的重担，在烦劳的生命的压迫下呻吟流汗，倘不是因为惧怕不可知的死后，惧怕那从来不曾有一个旅人回来过的神秘之国，是它迷惑了我们的意志，使我们宁愿忍受目前的磨折，不敢向我们所不知道的痛苦飞去？这样，重重的顾虑使我们全变成了懦夫，决心的赤热的光彩，被审慎的思维盖上了一层灰色，伟大的事业在这一种考虑之下，也会逆流而退，失去了行动的意义。且慢！美丽的奥菲利娅！——女神，在你的祈祷之中，不要忘记替我忏悔我的罪孽。

奥菲利娅	我的好殿下，您这许多天来贵体安好吗？
哈姆莱特	谢谢你，很好，很好，很好。
奥菲利娅	殿下，我有几件您送给我的纪念品，我早就想把它们还给您；请您现在收回去吧。
哈姆莱特	不，我不要；我从来没有给你什么东西。
奥菲利娅	殿下，我记得很清楚您把它们送给了我，那时候您还向我

And with them words of so sweet breath composed

As made the things more rich. Their perfume lost,

Take these again, for to the noble mind

Rich gifts wax poor when givers prove unkind.

There, my lord.

HAMLET Ha, ha! Are you honest?

OPHELIA My lord?

HAMLET Are you fair?

OPHELIA What means your lordship?

HAMLET That if you be honest and fair, your honesty should admit no discourse to your beauty.

OPHELIA Could beauty, my lord, have better commerce than with honesty?

HAMLET Ay truly, for the power of beauty will sooner transform honesty from what it is to a bawd, than the force of honesty can translate beauty into his likeness. This was sometime a paradox, but now the time gives it proof. I did love you once.

OPHELIA Indeed, my lord, you made me believe so.

HAMLET You should not have believed me, for virtue cannot so inoculate our old stock, but we shall relish of it. I loved you not.

OPHELIA I was the more deceived.

HAMLET Get thee to a nunnery, why wouldst thou be a breeder of sinners? I am myself indifferent honest, but yet I could accuse me of such things, that it were better my mother had not borne me: I am very proud, revengeful, ambitious, with more offences at my beck, than I have thoughts to put them in, imagination to give them shape, or time to act them

说了许多甜言蜜语，使这些东西格外显得贵重；现在它们
的芳香已经消散，请您拿回去吧，因为在有骨气的人看
来，送礼的人要是变了心，礼物虽贵，也会失去了价值。
拿去吧，殿下。

哈姆莱特 哈哈！你贞洁吗？

奥菲利娅 殿下！

哈姆莱特 你美丽吗？

奥菲利娅 殿下是什么意思？

哈姆莱特 要是你既贞洁又美丽，那么你的贞洁应该断绝跟你的美丽
来往。

奥菲利娅 殿下，难道美丽除了贞洁以外，还有什么更好的伴侣吗？

哈姆莱特 嗯，真的；因为美丽可以使贞洁变成淫荡，贞洁却未必能
使美丽受它自己的感化；这句话从前像是怪诞之谈，可是
现在时间已经把它证实了。我的确曾经爱过你。

奥菲利娅 真的，殿下，您曾经使我相信您爱我。

哈姆莱特 你当初就不应该相信我，因为美德不能熏陶我们罪恶的本
性；我没有爱过你。

奥菲利娅 那么我真是受了骗了。

哈姆莱特 进尼姑庵去吧；为什么你要生一群罪人出来呢？我自己还
不算是一个顶坏的人；可是我可以指出我的许多过失，一
个人有了那些过失，他的母亲还是不要生下他来的好。我
很骄傲，有仇必报，富于野心，我的罪恶是那么多，连我
的思想也容纳不下，我的想象也不能给它们形象，甚至于
我都没有充分的时间可以把它们实行出来。像我这样的家

in：what should such fellows as I do crawling between earth and heaven? We are arrant knaves all, believe none of us. Go thy ways to a nunnery.

Where's your father?

OPHELIA	At home, my lord.
HAMLET	Let the doors be shut upon him, that he may play the fool nowhere but in's own house. Farewell.
OPHELIA	O help him, you sweet heavens!
HAMLET	If thou dost many, I'll give thee this plague for thy dowry. Be thou as chaste as ice, as pure as snow, thou shalt not escape calumny; get thee to a nunnery, go, farewell. Or if thou wilt needs marry, marry a fool, for wise men know well enough what monsters you make of them. to a nunnery, go, and quickly too, farewell.
OPHELIA	O heavenly powers, restore him!
HAMLET	I have heard of your paintings too, well enough. God hath given you one face and you make yourselves another, you jig, you amble, and you lisp, you nickname God's creatures, and make your wantonness your ignorance; go to, I'll no more on't, it hath made me mad. I say we will have no mo marriage. Those that are married already, all but one, shall live, the rest shall keep as they are; to a nunnery, go.

[*Exit.*]

OPHELIA O, what a noble mind is here o' erthrown!

The courtier's, soldier's, scholar's, eye, tongue, sword,

Th'expectancy and rose of the fair state,

The glass of fashion, and the mould of form,

伙，匍匐于天地之间，有什么用处呢？我们都是些十足的坏人；一个也不要相信我们。进尼姑庵去吧。你的父亲呢？

奥菲利娅 在家里，殿下。

哈姆莱特 把他关起来，让他只好在家里发发傻劲。再会！

奥菲利娅 哎哟，天哪！救救他！

哈姆莱特 要是你一定要嫁人，我就把这一个诅咒送给你做嫁奁：尽管你像冰一样坚贞，像雪一样纯洁，你还是逃不过谗人的诽谤。进尼姑庵去吧，去；再会！或者要是你必须嫁人的话，就嫁给一个傻瓜吧；因为聪明人都明白你们会叫他们变成怎样的怪物。进尼姑庵去吧，去；越快越好。再会！

奥菲利娅 天上的神明啊，让他清醒过来吧！

哈姆莱特 我也知道你们会怎样涂脂抹粉；上帝给了你们一张脸，你们又替自己另外造了一张。你们掩饰媚行，淫声浪气，替上帝造下的生物乱取名字，卖弄你们不懂事的风骚。算了吧，我再也不敢领教了；它已经使我发了狂。我说，我们以后再不要结什么婚了；已经结过婚的，除了一个人以外，都可以让他们活下去；没有结婚的不准再结婚，进尼姑庵去吧，去。（下。）

奥菲利娅 啊，一颗多么高贵的心是这样陨落了！朝臣的眼睛、学者的辩舌、军人的利剑、国家所瞩望的一朵娇花；时流的明镜、人伦的雅范、举世瞩目的中心，这样无可挽回地陨落

Th'observed of all observers, quite quite down,

And I of ladies most deject and wretched,

That sucked the honey of his music vows,

Now see that noble and most sovereign reason

Like sweet bells jangled, out of tune and harsh,

That unmatched form and reature of blown youth,

Blasted with ecstasy! O, woe is me!

T' have seen what I have seen, see what I see!

[*Re-enter the King and Polonius.*]

KING   Love! his affections do not that way tend,

Nor what he spake, thought it lacked form a little,

Was not like madness. There's something in his soul

O'er which his melancholy sits on brood,

And I do doubt the hatch and the disclose

Will be some danger; which for to prevent,

I have in quick determination

Thus set it down: he shall with speed to England,

For the demand of our neglected tribute.

Haply the seas, and countries different,

With variable objects, shall expel

This something-settled matter in his heart,

Whereon his brains still beating puts him thus

From fashion of himself. What think you on't?

POLONIUS   It shall do well. But yet do I believe

The origin and commencement of his grief

Sprung from neglected love. How now, Ophelia?

You need not tell us what Lord Hamlet said,

We heard it all. My lord, do as you please,

了！我是一切妇女中间最伤心而不幸的，我曾经从他音乐一般的盟誓中吮吸芬芳的甘蜜，现在却眼看着他的高贵无上的理智，像一串美妙的银铃失去了谐和的音调，无比的青春美貌，在疯狂中凋谢！啊！我好苦，谁料过去的繁华，变作今朝的泥土！

（国王及波洛涅斯重上。）

国　　王　恋爱！他的精神错乱不像是为了恋爱；他说的话虽然有些颠倒，也不像是疯狂。他有些什么心事盘踞在他的灵魂里，我怕它也许会产生危险的结果。为了防止万一，我已经当机立断，决定了一个办法：他必须立刻到英国去，向他们追索延宕未纳的贡物；也许他到海外各国游历一趟以后，时时变换的环境，可以替他排解去这一桩使他神思恍惚的心事。你看怎么样？

波洛涅斯　那很好；可是我相信他的烦闷的根本原因，还是为了恋爱上的失意。啊，奥菲利娅！你不用告诉我们哈姆莱特殿下说些什么话；我们全都听见了。陛下，照您的意思办吧；

But if you hold it fit, after the play,

Let his queen-mother all alone entreat him

To show his grief, let her be round with him,

And I'll be placed so please you in the ear

Of all their conference. If she find him not,

To England send him; or confine him where

Your wisdom best shall think.

KING   It shall be so,

Madness in great ones must not unwatched go. 　[*Exeunt.*]

SCENE 2

A hall in the castle

[*Enter Hamlet, and two or three of the Players.*]

HAMLET   Speak the speech I pray you as I pronounced it to you, trippingly on the tongue, but if you mouth it as many of your players do, I had as lief the town-crier spoke my lines. Nor do not saw the air too much with your hand thus, but use all gently, for in the very torrent, tempest, and as I may say whirlwind of your passion, you must acquire and beget a temperance that may give it smoothness. O, it offends me to the soul, to hear a robustious periwig-pated fellow tear a passion to tatters, to very rags, to split the ears of the groundlings, who for the most part are capable of nothing but inexplicable dumb-shows and noise: I would have such a fellow whipped for o' erdoing Termagant, it out-herods Herod, pray you avoid it.

1 PLAYER   I warrant your honour.

可是您要是认为可以的话，不妨在戏剧终场以后，让他的母后独自一人跟他在一起，恳求他向她吐露他的心事；她必须很坦白地跟他谈谈，我就找一个所在听他们说些什么。要是她也探听不出他的秘密来，您就叫他到英国去，或者凭着您的高见，把他关禁在一个适当的地方。

国　　王　就这样吧；大人物的疯狂是不能听其自然的。（同下。）

第二场　城堡中的厅堂

（哈姆莱特及若干伶人上。）

哈姆莱特　请你念这段剧词的时候，要照我刚才读给你听的那样子，一个字一个字打舌头上很轻快地吐出来；要是你也像多数的伶人们一样，只会拉开了喉咙嘶叫，那么我宁愿叫那宣布告示的公差念我这几行词句。也不要老是把你的手在空中这么摇挥；一切动作都要温文，因为就是在洪水暴风一样的感情激发之中，你也必须取得一种节制，免得流于过火。啊！我顶不愿意听见一个披着满头假发的家伙在台上乱嚷乱叫，把一段感情片片撕碎，让那些只爱热闹的低级观众听了出神，他们中间的大部分是除了欣赏一些莫名其妙的手势以外，什么都不懂。我可以把这种家伙抓起来抽一顿鞭子，因为他把妥玛刚特形容过分，希律王的凶暴也要对他甘拜下风。请你留心避免才好。

伶　　甲　我留心着就是了，殿下。

HAMLET   Be not too tame neither, but let your own discretion be your tutor, suit the action to the word, the word to the action, with this special observance, that you o' erstep not the modesty of nature; for anything so o' erdone is from the purpose of playing, whose end both at the first, and now, was and is, to hold as ' twere the mirror up to nature, to show virtue her own feature, scorn her own image, and the very age and body of the time his form and pressure. Now this overdone, or come tardy off, though it make the unskilful laugh, cannot but make the judicious grieve, the censure of the which one must in your allowance o' erweigh a whole theatre of others. O there be players that I have seen play, and heard others praise, and that highly (not to speak it profanely) that neither having th' accent of Christians, nor the gait of Christian, pagan, nor man, have so strutted and bellowed, that I have thought some of nature's journeymen had made men, and not made them well, they imitated humanity so abominably.

1 PLAYER   I hope we have reformed that indifferently with us, sir.

HAMLET   O reform it altogether and let those that play your clowns speak no more than is set down for them, for there be of them that will themselves laugh, to set on some quantity of barren spectators to laugh too, though in the mean time some necessary question of the play be then to be considered. That's villainous, and shows a most pitiful ambition in the fool that uses it. Go, make you ready.   [*Exeunt Players.*]

[*Enter Polonius, Rosencrantz and Guildenstern.*]

How now, my lord? Will the king hear this piece of work?

哈姆莱特　　可是太平淡了也不对，你应该接受你自己的常识的指导，把动作和言语互相配合起来；特别要注意到这一点，你不能越过自然的常道；因为任何过分的表现都是和演剧的原意相反的，自有戏剧以来，它的目的始终是反映自然，显示善恶的本来面目，给它的时代看一看它自己演变发展的模型。要是表演得过分了或者太懈怠了，虽然可以博外行的观众一笑，明眼之士却要因此而皱眉；你必须看重这样一个卓识者的批评甚于满场观众盲目的毁誉。啊！我曾经看见有几个伶人演戏，而且也听见有人把他们极口捧场，说一句比喻不伦的话，他们既不会说基督徒的语言，又不会学着基督徒、异教徒或者一般人的样子走路，瞧他们在台上大摇大摆，使劲叫喊的样子，我心里就想一定是什么造化的雇工把他们造了下来：造得这样拙劣，以至于全然失去了人类的面目。

伶　　　甲　　我希望我们在这方面已经有了相当的纠正了。

哈姆莱特　　啊！你们必须彻底纠正这一种弊病。还有你们那些扮演小丑的，除了剧本上专为他们写下的台词以外，不要让他们临时编造一些话加上去。往往有许多小丑爱用自己的笑声，引起台下一些无知的观众的哄笑，虽然那时候全场的注意力应当集中于其他更重要的问题上；这种行为是不可恕的，它表示出那丑角的可鄙的野心。去，准备起来吧。（伶人等同下。）

　　　　　（波洛涅斯、罗森格兰兹及吉尔登斯吞上。）

　　啊，大人，王上愿意来听这一本戏吗？

POLONIUS	And the queen too, and that presently.
HAMLET	Bid the players make haste. *[Exit Polonius.]*
	Will you two help to hasten them?
ROSENC'Z	Ay, my lord. *[Exeunt Rosencrantz and Guildenstern.]*
HAMLET	What, ho! Horatio!
	[Enter Horatio.]
HORATIO	Here, sweet lord, at your service.
HAMLET	Horatio, thou art e' en as just a man
	As e' er my conversation coped withal.
HORATIO	O, my dear lord.
HAMLET	Nay, do not think I flatter,

For what advancement may I hope from thee,

That no revenue hast but thy good spirits

To feed and clothe thee? Why should the poor be flattered?

No, let the candied tongue lick absurd pomp,

And crook the pregnant hinges of the knee

Where thrift may follow fawning. Dost thou hear?

Since my dear soul was mistress of her choice,

And could of men distinguish her election,

Sh'hath sealed thee for herself, for thou hast been

As one in suff' ring all that suffers nothing,

A man that Fortune's buffets and rewards

Hast ta'en with equal thanks; and blest are those

Whose blood and judgment are so well commingled,

That they are not a pipe for Fortune's finger

To sound what stop she please; give me that man

That is not passion' s slave, and I will wear him

In my heart's core, ay in my heart of heart,

波 洛 涅 斯	他跟娘娘都就要来了。
哈 姆 莱 特	叫那些戏子们赶紧点儿。（波洛涅斯下。）你们两人也去帮着催催他们。
罗森格兰兹	是，殿下。（罗森格兰兹、吉尔登斯吞下。）
哈 姆 莱 特	喂！霍拉旭！
	（霍拉旭上。）
霍 拉 旭	有，殿下。
哈 姆 莱 特	霍拉旭，你是我所交接的人们中间最正直的一个人。
霍 拉 旭	啊，殿下！——
哈 姆 莱 特	不，不要以为我在恭维你；你除了你的善良的精神以外，身无长物，我恭维了你又有什么好处呢？为什么要向穷人恭维？不，让蜜糖一样的嘴唇去吮舐愚妄的荣华，在有利可图的所在屈下他们生财有道的膝盖来吧。听着。自从我能够辨别是非、察择贤愚以后，你就是我灵魂里选中的一个人，因为你虽然经历一切的颠沛，却不曾受到一点伤害，命运的虐待和恩宠，你都是受之泰然；能够把感情和理智调整得那么适当，命运不能把他玩弄于指掌之间，那样的人是有福的。给我一个不为感情所奴役的人，我愿意把他珍藏在我

As I do thee. Something too much of this

There is a play tonight before the king,

One scene of it comes near the circumstance

Which I have told thee of my father's death.

I prithee when thou seest that act afoot,

Even with the very comment of thy soul

Observe my uncle, if his occulted guilt

Do not itself unkennel in one speech,

It is a damned ghost that we have seen,

And my imaginations are as foul

As Vulcan's stithy; give him heedful note,

For I mine eyes will rivet to his face,

And after we will both our judgments join

In censure of his seeming.

HORATIO   Well, my lord,

If 'a steal aught the whilst this play is playing,

And 'scape detecting, I will pay the theft.

HAMLET   They are coming to the play. I must be idle. Get you a place.

[*Danish march. A flourish. Enter the King and Queen,*
Polonius, Ophelia, Rosencraniz, Guildenstern, and others.]

KING   *How fares our cousin Hamlet?*

HAMLET   *Excellent i' faith, of the chameleon's dish, I eat the air,*
promise-crammed, you cannot feed capons so.

KING   *I have nothing with this answer, Hamlet. These words are*
not mine.

HAMLET   *No, nor mine now.* [*To Polonius*] My lord, you played
once i' th' university, you say?

的心坎，我的灵魂的深处，正像我对你一样。这些话现在也不必多说了。今晚我们要在国王面前演一出戏，其中有一场的情节跟我告诉过你的我的父亲的死状颇相仿佛；当那幕戏正在串演的时候，我要请你集中你的全副精神，注视我的叔父，要是他在听到了那一段戏词以后，他的隐藏的罪恶还是不露出一丝痕迹来，那么我们所看见的那个鬼魂一定是个恶魔，我的幻想也就像铁匠的砧石那样黑漆一团了。留心看他；我也要把我的眼睛看定他的脸上；过后我们再把各人观察的结果综合起来，给他下一个判断。

霍　拉　旭　很好，殿下；在演这出戏的时候，要是他在容色举止之间，有什么地方逃过了我们的注意，请您唯我是问。

哈姆莱特　他们来看戏了；我必须装出一副糊涂样子。你去拣一个地方坐下。

（奏丹麦进行曲，喇叭奏花腔。国王、王后、波洛涅斯、奥菲利娅、罗森格兰兹、吉尔登斯吞及余人等上。）

国　　　王　你过得好吗，哈姆莱特贤侄？

哈姆莱特　很好，好极了；我过的是变色蜥蜴的生活，整天吃空气，肚子让甜言蜜语塞满了；这可不是你们填鸭子的办法。

国　　　王　你这种话真是答非所问，哈姆莱特；我不是那个意思。

哈姆莱特　不，我现在也没有那个意思。（向波洛涅斯）大人，您说您在大学里念书的时候，曾经演过一回戏吗？

POLONIUS	That did I, my lord, and was accounted a good actor.
HAMLET	What did you enact?
POLONIUS	I did enact Julius Caesar. I was killed i'th'Capitol, Brutus killed me.
HAMLET	It was a brute part of him to kill so capital a calf there. Be the players ready?
ROSENC'Z	Ay, my lord, they stay upon your patience.
QUEEN	Come hither, my dear Hamlet, sit by me.
HAMLET	No, good mother, here's metal more attractive.
POLONIUS	[*To the King*] O ho! Do you mark that?
HAMLET	Lady, shall I lie in your lap?
OPHELIA	No, my lord.
HAMLET	I mean, my head upon your lap?
OPHELIA	Ay, my lord.
HAMLET	Do you think I meant country matters?
OPHELIA	I think nothing, my lord.
HAMLET	That's a fair thought to lie between maids' legs.
OPHELIA	What is, my lord?
HAMLET	Nothing.
OPHELIA	You are merry, my lord.
HAMLET	Who, I?
OPHELIA	Ay, my lord.
HAMLET	O God, your only jig-maker. What should a man do but be merry, for look you how cheerfully my mother looks, and my father died within's two hours.
OPHELIA	Nay, 'tis twice two months, my lord.
HAMLET	So long? Nay, then let the devil wear black, for I'll have a suit of sables; O heavens, die two months ago, and not

哈姆莱特

Hamlet

波洛涅斯	是的，殿下，他们都称赞我是一个很好的演员哩。
哈姆莱特	您扮演什么角色呢？
波洛涅斯	我扮的是裘力斯·恺撒；勃鲁托斯在朱庇特神殿里把我杀死。
哈姆莱特	他在神殿里杀死了那么好的一头小牛，真太残忍了。那班戏子已经预备好了吗？
罗森格兰兹	是，殿下，他们在等候您的旨意。
王　　后	过来，我的好哈姆莱特，坐在我的旁边。
哈姆莱特	不，好妈妈，这儿有一个更迷人的东西哩。
波洛温斯	（向国王）啊哈！您看见吗？
哈姆莱特	小姐，我可以睡在您的怀里吗？
奥菲利娅	不，殿下。
哈姆莱特	我的意思是说，我可以把我的头枕在您的膝上吗？
奥菲利娅	嗯，殿下。
哈姆莱特	您以为我在转着下流的念头吗？
奥菲利娅	我没有想到，殿下。
哈姆莱特	睡在姑娘大腿的中间，想起来倒是很有趣的。
奥菲利娅	什么，殿下？
哈姆莱特	没有什么。
奥菲利娅	您在开玩笑哩，殿下。
哈姆莱特	谁，我吗？
奥菲利娅	嗯，殿下。
哈姆莱特	上帝啊！要说玩笑，那就得属我了。一个人为什么不说说笑笑呢？您瞧，我的母亲多么高兴，我的父亲还不过死了两个钟头。
奥菲利娅	不，已经四个月了，殿下。
哈姆莱特	这么久了吗？哎哟，那么让魔鬼去穿孝服吧，我可要去做一身貂皮的新衣啦。天啊！死了两个月，还没有把他忘记

forgotten yet? Then there's hope a great man's memory may outlive his life half a year, but by'r lady' a must build churches then, or else shall' a suffer not thinking on, with the hobby-horse, whose epitaph is 'For O! for O! the hobby horse is forgot.'

[*Hautboys play. the dumb-show enters.*]

(Enter a King and a Queen, very lovingly, the Queen embracing him and he her, she kneels and makes show of protestation unto him, he takes her up and declines his head open her neck, he lies him down upon a bank of flowers, she seeing him he lies him doun upon a bank of flowers, she seeing him asleep leaves him: anon comes in another man, takes off his crown, kisses it, and pours poison in the sleeper's ears and leaves him. The Queen returns, finds the King dead, and makes passionate action. The poisoner with some three or four mutes comes in again, seeming to condole with her. The dead body is carried away. The poisoner woos the Queen with gifts, she seems harsh awhile, but in the end accepts his love.)　　　　[Exeunt.]

OPHELIA	What means this, my lord?
HAMLET	Marry, this is miching mallecho, it means mischief.
OPHELIA	Belike this show imports the argument of the play.

[*Enter Prologue.*]

HAMLET	We shall know by this fellow. The players cannot keep counsel, they'll tell all.
OPHELIA	Will he tell us what this show meant?
HAMLET	Ay, or any show that you will show him. Be not you ashamed to show, he'll not shame to tell you what it means.
OPHELIA	You are naught, you are naught, I'll mark the play.

吗？那么也许一个大人物死了以后，他的记忆还可以保持半年之久；可是凭着圣母起誓，他必须造下几所教堂，否则他就要跟那被遗弃的木马一样，没有人再会想念他了。

> 高音笛奏乐。哑剧登场。

> （一国王及一王后上，状极亲热，互相拥抱。后跪地，向王做宣誓状，王扶后起，俯首后颈上。王就花坪上睡下；后见王睡熟离去。另一人上，自王头上去冠，吻冠，注毒药于王耳，下。后重上，见王死，作哀恸状。下毒者率其他二、三人重上，佯作陪后悲哭状。从者舁王尸下。下毒者以礼物赠后，向其乞爱；后先作憎恶不愿状，卒允其请。同下。）

奥 菲 利 娅	这是什么意思，殿下？
哈 姆 莱 特	呃，这是阴谋诡计、不干好事的意思。
奥 菲 利 娅	大概这一场哑剧就是全剧的本事了。

> （致开场词者上。）

哈 姆 莱 特	这家伙可以告诉我们一切；演戏的都不能保守秘密，他们什么话都会说出来。
奥 菲 利 娅	他也会给我们解释方才那场哑剧有什么奥妙吗？
哈 姆 莱 特	是啊；这还不算，只要你做给他看什么，他也能给你解释什么；只要你做出来不害臊，他解释起来也决不害臊。
奥 菲 利 娅	殿下真是淘气，真是淘气。我还是看戏吧。

PROLOGUE   For us and for our tragedy,

Here stooping to your clemency,

We beg your hearing patiently.   [*Exit.*]

HAMLET   Is this a prologue, or the posy of a ring?

OPHELIA   'Tis brief, my lord.

HAMLET   As woman's love.

[*Enter two Players, King and Queen.*]

PL. KING   *Full thirty times hath Phoebus' cart gone round*

Neptune's salt wash, and Tellus' orbed ground,

And thirty dozen moons with borrowed sheen

About the world have times twelve thirties been,

Since love our hearts and Hymen did our hands

Unite commutual in mose sacred bands.

PL. QUEEN   *So many journeys may the sun and moon*

Make us again count o' er ere love be done!

But woe is me, you are so sick of late,

So far from cheer, and from your former state,

That I distrust you. Yet though I distrust,

Discomfort you, my lord, it nothing must,

For women fear too much, even as they love,

And women's fear and love hold quantity,

In neither aught, or in extremity.

Now what my love is proof hath made you know,

And as my love is sized, my fear is so.

Where love is great, the littlest doubts are fear,

Where little fears grow great, great love grows there.

PL. KING   *Faith, I must leave thee, love, and shortly too.*

My operant powers their functions leave to do,

哈姆莱特
Hamlet

开 场 词	这悲剧要是演不好, 要请各位原谅指教, 小的在这厢有礼了。(致开场词者下。)
哈 姆 莱 特	这算开场词呢,还是指环上的诗铭?
奥 菲 利 娅	它很短,殿下。
哈 姆 莱 特	正像女人的爱情一样。

(二伶人扮国王、王后上。)

伶　　王	日轮已经盘绕三十春秋 那茫茫海水和滚滚地球, 月亮吐耀着借来的晶光, 三百六十回向大地环航, 自从爱把我们缔结良姻, 许门替我们证下了鸳盟。
伶　　后	愿日月继续他们的周游, 让我们再厮守三十春秋! 可是唉,你近来这样多病, 郁郁寡欢,失去旧时高兴, 好教我满心里为你忧惧。 可是,我的主,你不必疑虑; 女人的忧伤像爱情一样, 不是太少,就是超过分量; 你知道我爱你是多么深, 所以才会有如此的忧心。 越是相爱,越是挂肚牵胸; 不这样哪显得你我情浓?
伶　　王	爱人,我不久必须离开你, 我的全身将要失去生机;

And thou shalt live in this fair world behind,

Honoured, beloved, and haply one as kind

For husband shalt thou —

PL. QUEEN O, confound the rest!

Such love must needs be treason in my breast,

In second husband let me be accurst,

None wed the second, but who killed the first.

HAMLET [Aside] That's wormwood, wormwood.

PL QUEEN The instances that second marriage move

Are base respects of thrift, but none of love.

A second time I kill my husband dead,

When second husband kisses me in bed.

PL. KING I do believe you think what now you speak,

But what we do determine, oft we break.

Purpose is but the slave to memory,

Of violent birth but poor validity,

Which now like fruit unripe sticks on the tree,

But fall unshaken when they mellow be.

Most necessary' tis that we forget

To pay ourselves what to ourselves is debt.

What to ourselves in passion we propose,

The passion ending, doth the purpose lose.

The violence of either grief or joy

Their own enactures with themselves destroy,

Where joy most revels, grief doth most lament,

Grief joys, joy grieves, on slender accident.

This world is not for aye, nor ' tis not strange

That even our loves should with our fortunes change:

Shakespeare Classics

留下你在这繁华的世界
安享尊荣，受人们的敬爱：
也许再嫁一位如意郎君——

伶　　后　啊！我断不是那样薄情人；
我倘忘旧迎新，难邀天恕，
再嫁的除非是杀夫淫妇。

哈 姆 莱 特　（旁白）苦恼，苦恼！

伶　　后　妇人失节大半贪慕荣华，
多情女子决不另抱琵琶；
我要是与他人共枕同衾，
怎么对得起地下的先灵！

伶　　王　我相信你的话发自心田，
可是我们往往自食前言。
志愿不过是记忆的奴隶，
总是有始无终，虎头蛇尾，
像未熟的果子密布树梢，
一朝红烂就会离去枝条。
我们对自己所负的债务，
最好把它丢在脑后不顾；
一时的热情中发下誓愿，
心冷了，那意志也随云散。
过分的喜乐，剧烈的哀伤，
反会毁害了感情的本常。
人世间的哀乐变幻无端，
痛哭转瞬早变成了狂欢。
世界也会有毁灭的一天，
何怪爱情要随境遇变迁；

For' tis a question lett us, yet to prove,

Whether love lead fortune, or else fortune love.

The great man down, you mark his favourite flies,

The poor advanced makes friends of enemies,

And hitherto doth love on fortune tend,

For who not needs shall never lack a friend,

And who in want a hallow friend doth try,

Direcdy seasons him his enemy.

But orderly to end where I begun,

Our wills and fates do so contrary run,

That our devices still are overthrown,

Our thoughts are ours, their ends none of our own.

So think thou wilt no second husband wed,

But die thy thoughts when thy first lord is dead.

PL. QUEEN   *Nor earth to me give food not heaven light,*

Sport and repose lock from me day and night,

To desperation turn my trust and hope,

An anchor's cheere in prison be my scope,

Each opposite that blanks the face of joy

Meet what I would have well and it destroy,

Both here and hence pursue me lasting strife,

If once a widow, ever I be wife!

HAMLET   If she should break it now!

PL. KING   *'Tis deeply sworn. Sweet, leave me here awhile,*

My spirits grow dull, and fain I would beguile

The tedious day with sleep.   [*He sleeps.*]

PL. QUEEN   Sleep rock thy brain,

And never come mischance between us twain!   [*Exit.*]

莎士比亚经典戏剧

有谁能解答这一个哑谜，
是境由爱造？是爱逐境移？
失财势的伟人举目无亲；
走时运的穷酸仇敌逢迎。
这炎凉的世态古今一辙：
富有的门庭挤满了宾客；
要是你在穷途向人求助，
即使知交也要情同陌路。
把我们的谈话拉回本题，
意志命运往往背道而驰，
决心到最后会全部推倒，
事实的结果总难符预料。
你以为你自己不会再嫁，
只怕我一死你就要变卦。

伶　　后　　地不要养我，天不要亮我！
昼不得游乐，夜不得安卧！
毁灭了我的希望和信心；
铁锁囚门把我监禁终身！
每一种恼人的飞来横逆，
把我一重重的心愿摧折！
我倘死了丈夫再作新人，
让我生前死后永陷沉沦！

哈 姆 莱 特　　要是她现在背了誓！

伶　　王　　难为你发这样重的誓愿。
爱人，你且去；我神思昏倦，
想要小睡片刻。（睡。）

伶　　后　　愿你安睡；
上天保佑我俩永无灾悔！（下。）

HAMLET	Madam, how like you this play?
QUEEN	The lady doth protest too much, methinks.
HAMLET	O, but she'll keep her word.
KING	Have you heard the argument? Is there no offence in't?
HAMLET	No, no, they do but jest, poison in jest, no offence i' th' world.
KING	What do you call the play?
HAMLET	The Mouse-trap. Marry, how? Tropically: this play is the image of a murder done in Vienna. Gonzago is the duke's name, his wife Baptista, you shall see anon, 'tis a knavish piece of work, but what of that? Your majesty, and we that have free souls, it touches us not; let the galled jade wince, our withers are unwrung.

[*Enter 1 Player for Lucianus.*]

HAMLET	This is one Lucianus, nephew to the king.
OPHELIA	You are as good as a chorus, my lord.
HAMLET	I could interpret between you and your love, if I could see the puppets dallying.
OPHELIA	You are keen, my lord, you are keen.
HAMLET	It would cost you a groaning to take off mine edge.
OPHELIA	Still better and worse.
HAMLET	So you must take husbands. Begin, murderer. Pox! Leave thy damnable faces and begin! Come, the croaking raven doth bellow for revenge.
LUCIANUS	*Thoughts black, hands apt, druge fit, and time agreeing,* *Confederate season, else no creature seeing,* *Thou mixture rank, of midnight weeds collected,* *With Hecate's ban thrice blasted, thrice infected,*

哈姆莱特

Hamlet

哈 姆 莱 特　母亲，您觉得这出戏怎样？

王　　　后　我觉得那女人在表白心迹的时候，说话过火了一些。

哈 姆 莱 特　啊，可是她会守约的。

国　　　王　这本戏是怎么一个情节？里面没有什么要不得的地方吗？

哈 姆 莱 特　不，不，他们不过开玩笑毒死了一个人；没有什么要不
　　　　　　得的。

国　　　王　戏名叫什么？

哈 姆 莱 特　《捕鼠机》。呃，怎么？这是一个象征的名字。戏中的的
　　　　　　故事影射着维也纳的一件谋杀案。贡扎古是那公爵的名
　　　　　　字；他的妻子叫做白娅蒂丝姐。您看下去就知道是怎么一
　　　　　　回事啦。这是个很恶劣的作品，可是那有什么关系？它不
　　　　　　会对您陛下跟我们这些灵魂清白的人有什么相干；让那有
　　　　　　毛病的马儿去惊跳退缩吧，我们的肩背都是好好的。

　　　　　　　　（一伶人扮琉西安纳斯上。）

哈 姆 莱 特　这个人叫做琉西安纳斯，是那国王的侄子。

奥 菲 利 娅　您很会解释剧情，殿下。

哈 姆 莱 特　要是我看见傀儡戏扮演您跟您爱人的故事，我也会替你们
　　　　　　解释的。

奥 菲 利 娅　您的嘴真厉害，殿下，您的嘴真厉害。

哈 姆 莱 特　我要是真厉害起来，你非得哼哼不可。

奥 菲 利 娅　说好就好，说糟就糟。

哈 姆 莱 特　女人嫁丈夫也是一样。动手吧，凶手！混账东西，别扮鬼
　　　　　　脸了，动手吧！来；哇哇的乌鸦发出复仇的啼声。

琉西安纳斯　黑心快手，遇到妙药良机；

　　　　　　趁着没人看见事不宜迟。

　　　　　　你夜半采来的毒草炼成，

　　　　　　赫卡忒的咒语念上三巡，

Thy natural magic and dire property

On wholesome life usurps immediately.

[*Pours the poison into his ears*]

HAMLET　He poisons him i' th' garden for's estate, his name's Gonzago, the story is extant, and written in very choice Italian, you shall see anon how the murderer gets the love of Gonzago' s wife.

OPHELIA　The king rises.

HAMLET　What, frighted with false fire!

QUEEN　How fares my lord?

POLONIUS　Give o'er the play.

KING　Give me some light. Away!

POLONIUS　Lights, lights, lights! [*Exeunt all but Hamlet and Horatio.*]

HAMLET　Why, let the stricken deer go weep, the hart ungalled play, for some must watch while some must sleep,

Thus runs the world away.

Would not this, sir, and a forest of feathers, if the rest of my fortunes turn Turk with me, with two Provincial roses on my razed shoes, get me a fellowship in a cry of players, sir?

HORATIO　Half a share.

HAMLET　A whole one, I.

For thou dost know, O Damon dear,

This realm dismantled was

Of Jove himself, and now reigns here

A very, very — peacock.

HORATIO　You might have rhymed.

HAMLET　O good Horatio, I'll take the ghost' s word for a thousand pound. Didst perceive?

赶快发挥你凶恶的魔力，

让他的生命速归于幻灭。（以毒药注入睡者耳中。）

哈姆莱特 他为了觊觎权位，在花园里把他毒死。他的名字叫贡扎古；那故事原文还存在，是用很好的意大利文写成的。底下就要做到那凶手怎样得到贡扎古的妻子的爱了。

奥菲利娅 王上站起来了！

哈姆莱特 什么！给一响空枪吓怕了吗？

王　　后 陛下怎么样啦？

波洛涅斯 不要演下去了！

国　　王 给我点起火把来！去！

众　　人 火把！火把！火把！（除哈姆莱特、霍拉旭外均下。）

哈姆莱特 嗨，让那中箭的母鹿掉泪，

没有伤的公鹿自去游玩；

有的人失眠，有的人酣睡，

世界就是这样循环轮转。

老兄，要是我的命运跟我作起对来，凭着我这念词的本领，头上插上满头的羽毛，开缝的靴子上再缀上两朵绢花，你想我能不能在戏班子里插足？

霍　拉　旭 也许他们可以让您领半额包银。

哈姆莱特 我可要领全额的。

因为你知道，亲爱的朋友，

这一个荒凉破碎的国土

原本是乔武统治的雄邦，

而今王位上却坐着——孔雀。

霍　拉　旭 您该押韵才是。

哈姆莱特 啊，好霍拉旭！那鬼魂真的没有骗我。你看见吗？

HORATIO	Very well, my lord.
HAMLET	Upon the talk of the poisoning?
HORATIO	I did very well note him.
HAMLET	Ah, ha! Come, some music!
	Come, the recorders!
	For if the king like not the comedy,
	Why then, belike he likes it not, perdy.
	Come, some music!

[*Re-enter Rosencrantz and Guildenstern.*]

GUILD'RN	Good my lord, vouchsafe me a word with you.
HAMLET	Sir, a whole history.
GUILD'RN	The king, sir ——
HAMLET	Ay, sir, what of him?
GUILD'RN	Is in his retirement marvellous distempered.
HAMLET	With drink, sir?
GUILD'RN	No my lord, rather with choler.
HAMLET	Your wisdom should show itself more richer to signify this to the doctor. For, for me to put him to his purgation, would perhaps plunge him into more choler.
GUILD'RN	Good my lord, put your discourse into some frame, and start not so wildly from my affair.
HAMLET	I am tame, sir, pronounce.
GUILD'RN	The queen your mother, in most great affliction of spirit, hath sent me to you.
HAMLET	You are welcome.
GUILD'RN	Nay, good my lord, this courtesy is not of the right breed. If it shall please you to make me a wholesome answer, I will do your mother's commandment, If not, your pardon and my

哈姆莱特

Hamlet

霍 拉 旭	看见的，殿下。
哈 姆 莱 特	在那演戏的一提到毒药的时候？
霍 拉 旭	我看得他很清楚。
哈 姆 莱 特	啊哈！来，奏乐！来，那吹笛子的呢？
	要是国王不爱这出喜剧，
	那么他多半是不能赏识。来，奏乐！

（罗森格兰兹及吉尔登斯吞重上。）

吉尔登斯吞	殿下，允许我跟您说句话。
哈 姆 莱 特	好，你对我讲全部历史都可以。
吉尔登斯吞	殿下，王上——
哈 姆 莱 特	嗯，王上怎么样？
吉尔登斯吞	他回去以后，非常不舒服。
哈 姆 莱 特	喝醉了吗？
吉尔登斯吞	不，殿下，他在发脾气。
哈 姆 莱 特	你应该把这件事告诉他的医生，才算你的聪明；因为叫我去替他诊视，恐怕反而更会激动他的脾气的。
吉尔登斯吞	好殿下，请您说话检点些，别这样拉扯开去。
哈 姆 莱 特	好，我是听话的，你说吧。
吉尔登斯吞	您的母后心里很难过，所以叫我来。
哈 姆 莱 特	欢迎得很。
吉尔登斯吞	不，殿下，这一种礼貌是用不着的。要是您愿意给我一个好好的回答，我就把您母亲的意旨向您传达；不然的话，请您

return shall be the end of my business.

HAMIET	Sir, I cannot.
ROSENC'Z	What, my lord?
HAMLET	Make you a wholesome answer: my wit's diseased.
	But, sir, such answer as I can make, you shall command, or rather as you say, my mother. Therefore no more, but to the matter. My mother, you say —
ROSEN'Z	Then thus she says, your behaviour hath struck her into amazement and admiration.
HAMLET	O wonderful son that can so stonish a mother! But is there no sequel at the heels of this mother's admiration? Impart.
ROSENC'Z	She desires to speak with you in her closet ere you go to bed.
HAMLET	We shall obey, were she ten times our mother, Have you any further trade with us?
ROSENC'Z	My lord, you once did love me.
HAMLET	And do still, by these pickers and stealers.
ROSENC'Z	Good my lord, what is your cause of distemper? You do surely bar the door upon your own liberty, if you deny your griefs to your friend.
HAMLET	Sir, I lack advancement.
ROSENC'Z	How can that be, when you have the voice of the king himself for your succession in Denmark?
HAMLET	Ay, but 'While the grass grows', the proverb is something musty.

[*Players bring in recorders*]

O, the recorders, let me see one. To withdraw with you, why do you go about to recover the wind of me, as if you would drive me into a toil?

GUILD'RN	O, my lord if my duty be too bold, my love is too

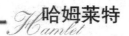
原谅我，让我就这么回去，我的事情就算完了。

哈姆莱特　我不能。

吉尔登斯吞　您不能什么，殿下？

哈姆莱特　我不能给你一个好好的回答，因为我的脑子已经坏了；可是我所能够给你的回答，你——我应该说我的母亲——可以要多少有多少。所以别说废话，言归正传吧；你说我的母亲——

罗森格兰兹　她这样说：您的行为使她非常吃惊。

哈姆莱特　啊，好儿子，居然会叫一个母亲吃惊！可是在这母亲的吃惊的后面，还有些什么话呢？说吧。

罗森格兰兹　她请您在就寝以前，到她房间里去跟她谈谈。

哈姆莱特　即使她十次是我的母亲，我也一定服从她。你还有什么别的事情？

罗森格兰兹　殿下，我曾经蒙您错爱。

哈姆莱特　凭着我这双扒手起誓，我现在还是欢喜你的。

罗森格兰兹　好殿下，您心里这样不痛快，究竟为了什么原因？要是您不肯把您的心事告诉您的朋友，那恐怕会害您自己失去自由。

哈姆莱特　我不满足我现在的地位。

罗森格兰兹　怎么！王上自己已经亲口把您立为王位的继承者了，您还不能满足吗？

哈姆莱特　嗯，可是"要等草儿青青——"这句老话也有点儿发了霉啦。

　　　　　（乐工等持笛上。）

啊！笛子来了；拿一支给我。跟你们退后一步说话；为什么你们总这样千方百计地绕到我下风的一面，好像一定要把我逼进你们的圈套？

吉尔登斯吞　啊！殿下，要是我有太冒昧放肆的地方，那都是因为我对

unmannerly.

HAMLET	I do not well understand that. Will you play upon this pipe?
GUILD'RN	My lord, I cannot.
HAMLET	I pray you.
GUILD'RN	Believe me, I cannot.
HAMLET	I do beseech you.
GUILD'RN	I know no touch of it, my lord.
HAMLET	It is as easy as lying; govern these ventages with your fingers and thumb, give it breath with your mouth, and it will discourse most eloquent music. Look you, these are the stops.
GUILD' RN	But these cannot I command to any utt'rance of harmony, I have not the skill.
HAMLET	Why, look you now, how unworthy a thing you make of me! You would play upon me, you would seem to know my stops, you would pluck out the heart of my mystery, you would sound me from my lowest note to the top of my compass: and there is much music, excellent voice, in this little organ, yet cannot you make it speak Why, do you think I am easier to be played on than a pipe? Call me what instrument you will, though you can fret me, you cannot play upon me.

[*Re-enter Polonius.*]

God bless you, sir!

POLONIUS	My lord, the queen would speak with you, and presently.
HAMLET	Do you see yonder cloud that's almost in shape of a camel?
POLONIUS	By th' mass and' tis, like a camel indeed.
HAMLET	Methinks it is like a weasel.
POLONIUS	It is backed like a weasel.
HAMLET	Or, like a whale?

于您敬爱太深的缘故。

哈 姆 莱 特　我不大懂得你的话。你愿意吹吹这笛子吗？

吉尔登斯吞　殿下，我不会吹。

哈 姆 莱 特　请你吹一吹。

吉尔登斯吞　我真的不会吹。

哈 姆 莱 特　请你不要客气。

吉尔登斯吞　我真的一点不会，殿下。

哈 姆 莱 特　那是跟说谎一样容易的；你只要用你的手指按着这些笛孔，把你的嘴放在上面一吹，它就会发出最好听的音乐来。瞧，这些是音栓。

吉尔登斯吞　可是我不会从它里面吹出谐和的曲调来；我不懂那技巧。

哈 姆 莱 特　哼，你把我看成了什么东西！你会玩弄我；你自以为摸得到我的心窍；你想要探出我的内心的秘密；你会从我的最低音试到我的最高音；可是在这支小小的乐器之内，藏着绝妙的音乐，你却不会使它发出声音来。哼，你以为玩弄我比玩弄一支笛子容易吗？无论你把我叫做什么乐器，你也只能撩拨我，不能玩弄我。

　　　　　　（波洛涅斯重上。）

　　　　　　上帝祝福你，先生！

波 洛 涅 斯　殿下，娘娘请您立刻就去见她说话。

哈 姆 莱 特　你看见那片像骆驼一样的云吗？

波 洛 涅 斯　哎哟，它真的像一头骆驼。

哈 姆 莱 特　我想它还是像一头鼬鼠。

波 洛 涅 斯　它拱起了背，正像是一头鼬鼠。

哈 姆 莱 特　还是像一条鲸鱼吧？

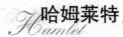
POLONIUS	Very like a whale.
HAMLET	Then I will come to my mother by and by. [*Aside*]
	They fool me to the top of my bent. I will come by and by.
POLONIUS	I will say so. [*Exit Polonius.*]
HAMLET	'By and by' is easily said. Leave me, friends.

[*Exeunt all but Hamlet.*]

'Tis now the very witching time of night,

When churchyards yawn, and hell itself breathes out

Contagion to this world: now could I drink hot blood,

And do such bitter business as the day

Would quake to look on: soft, now to my mother.

O heart, lose not thy nature, let not ever

The soul of Nero enter this firm bosom,

Let me be cruel not unnatural.

I will speak daggers to her, but use none.

My tongue and soul in this be hypocrites,

How in my words somever she be shent,

To give them seals never, my soul, consent!   [*Exit.*]

SCENE 3

A room in the castle

[*Enter the King, Rosencrantz and Guildenstern.*]

KING	I like him not, nor stands it safe with us
	To let his madness range. Therefore prepare you,
	I your commission will forthwith dispatch,
	And he to England shall along with you.
	The terms of our estate may not endure

波 洛 涅 斯	很像一条鲸鱼。
哈 姆 莱 特	那么等一会儿我就去见我的母亲。（旁白）我给他们愚弄得再也忍不住了。（高声）我等一会儿就来。
波 洛 涅 斯	我就去这么说。（下。）
哈 姆 莱 特	说等一会儿是很容易的。离开我，朋友们。（除哈姆莱特外均下）现在是一夜之中最阴森的时候，鬼魂都在此刻从坟墓里出来，地狱也要向人世吐放疠气；现在我可以痛饮热腾腾的鲜血，干那白昼所不敢正视的残忍的行为。且慢！我还要到我母亲那儿去一趟。心啊！不要失去你的天性之情，永远不要让尼禄的灵魂潜入我这坚定的胸怀；让我做一个凶徒，可是不要做一个逆子。我要用利剑一样的说话刺痛她的心，可是决不伤害她身体上一根毛发；我的舌头和灵魂要在这一次学学伪善者的样子，无论在言语上给她多么严厉的谴责，在行动上却要做得丝毫不让人家指摘。（下。）

第三场　城堡中一室

（国王、罗森格兰兹及吉尔登斯吞上。）

国　　王	我不喜欢他；纵容他这样疯闹下去，对于我是一个很大的威胁。所以你们快去准备起来吧；我马上叫人办好你们要递送的文书，同时打发他跟你们一块儿到英国去。就我的

Hazard so near' s as doth hourly grow out of his brows.

GUILD'RN We will ourselves provide.

Most holy and religious fear it is

To keep those many many bodies safe

That live and feed upon your majesty.

ROSENC'Z The single and peculiar life is bound

With all the strength and armour of the mind

To keep itself from noyance, but much more

That spirit upon whose weal depends and rests

The lives of many. The cess of majesty

Dies not alone; but like a gulf doth draw

What's near it with it. O, 'tis a massy wheel

Fixed on the summit of the highest mount,

To whose huge spokes ten thousand lesser things

Are mortised and adjoined, which when it falls,

Each small annexment, petty consequence,

Attends the boist'rous ruin. Never alone

Did the king sigh, but with a general groan.

KING Arm you, I pray you, to this speedy voyage,

For we will fetters put about this fear

Which now goes too flee-footed.

GLILD' RN
ROSENC'Z We will haste us. [*Exeunt Rosencranta and Guildenstern.*]

[*Enter Polonius.*]

POLONIUS My lord, he's going to his mother's closet:

Behind the arras I'll convery myself

To hear the process. I'll warrant she'll tax him home,

And as you said, and wisely was it said,

地位而论，他的疯狂每小时都可以危害我的安全，我不能让他留在我的近旁。

吉尔登斯吞 我们就去准备起来；许多人的安危都寄托在陛下身上，这一种顾虑是最圣明不过的。

罗森格兰兹 每一个庶民都知道怎样远祸全身，一个身负天下重寄的人，尤其应该时刻不懈地防备危害的袭击。君主的薨逝不仅是个人的死亡，它像一个漩涡一样，凡是在它近旁的东西，都要被它卷去同归于尽；又像一个矗立在最高山峰上的巨轮，它的轮辐上连附着无数的小物件，当巨轮轰然崩裂的时候，那些小物件也跟着它一齐粉碎。国王的一声叹息，总是随着全国的呻吟。

国　　王 请你们准备立刻出发，因为我们必须及早制止这一种公然的威胁。

吉尔登斯吞
罗森格兰兹 我们就去赶紧预备。（罗森格兰兹、吉尔登斯吞同下。）

（波洛涅斯上。）

波洛涅斯 陛下，他到他母亲房间里去了。我现在就去躲在帏幕后面，听他们怎么说。我可以断定她一定会把他好好教训一

'Tis meet that some more audience than a mother,

Since nature makes them partial, should o' erhear

The speech of vantage; fare you well, my liege,

I'll call upon you ere you go to bed,

And tell you what I know.

KING   Thanks, dear my lord.   *[Exit Polonius.]*

O, my offence is rank, it smells to heaven,

It hath the primal eldest curse upon' t,

A brother's murder! Pray can I not,

Though inclination be as sharp as will.

My stronger guilt defeats my strong intent,

And like a man to double business bound,

I stand in pause where I shall first begin,

And both neglect. What if this cursed hand

Were thicker than itself with brother' s blood,

Is there not rain enough in the sweet heavens

To wash it white as snow? Whereto serves mercy

But to confront the visage of offence?

And what's in prayer but this twofold force,

To be forestalled ere we come to fall,

Or pardoned being down? Then I'll look up.

My fault is past, but O, what form of prayer

Can serve my turn? ' Forgive mo my foul murder'?

That cannot be since I am still possessed

Of those effects for which I did the murder;

My crown, mine own ambition, and my queen;

May one be pardoned and retain th'offence?

In the corrupted currents of this world

顿的。您说得很不错，母亲对于儿子总有几分信心，所以最好有一个第三者躲在旁边偷听他们的谈话。再会，陛下；在您未睡以前，我还要来看您一次，把我所探听到的事情告诉您。

国　王　谢谢你，贤卿。（波洛涅斯下）啊！我的罪恶的戾气已经上达于天；我的灵魂上负着一个元始以来最初的诅咒，杀害兄弟的暴行！我不能祈祷，虽然我的愿望像决心一样强烈；我的更坚强的罪恶击败了我的坚强的意愿。像一个人同时要做两件事情，我因为不知道应该先从什么地方下手而徘徊歧途，结果反弄得一事无成。要是这一只可诅咒的手上染满了一层比它本身还厚的兄弟的血，难道天上所有的甘霖，都不能把它洗涤得像雪一样洁白吗？慈悲的使命，不就是宽宥罪恶吗？祈祷的目的，不是一方面预防我们的堕落，一方面救拔我们于已堕落之后吗？那么我要仰望上天；我的过失已经犯下了。可是唉！哪一种祈祷才是我所适用的呢？"求上帝赦免我的杀人重罪"吗？那不能，因为我现在还占有着那些引起我的犯罪动机的目的物，我的王冠、我的野心和我的王后。非分攫取的利益还在手里，就可以幸邀宽恕吗？在这贪污的人世，罪恶的镀金的

Offence's gilded hand may shove by jusice,

And oft 'tis seen the wicked prize itself

Buys out the law. But' tis not so above,

There is no shuffling, there the action lies

In his true nature, and we ourselves compelled

Even to the teeth and forehead of our faults

To give in evidence. What then? What rests?

Try what repentance can. What can it not?

Yet What can it, when one can not repent?

O wretched state! O bosom black as death!

O limed soul, that struggling to be free,

Art more engaged; help, angels! Make assay,

Bow stubborn knees, and heart, with strings of steel,

Be soft as sinews of the new-bom babe,

All may be well.   [*Retires and kneels.*]

　　[*Enter Hamlet.*]

HAMLET　　Now might I do it pat, now he is a praying,

And now I'll do' t, and so he goes to heaven, and so am I

revenged, That would be scanned:

A Villain kills my father, and for that

I his sole son do this same villain send to heaven.

Why, this is bait and salary, not revenge.

He took my father grossly, full of bread,

With all his crimes broad blown, as flush as May,

And how his audit stands who knows save heaven?

But in our circumstance and comse of thought,

'Tis heavy with him: and am I then revenged

To take him in the purging of his soul,

手也许可以把公道推开不顾，暴徒的赃物往往成为枉法的贿赂；可是天上却不是这样的，在那边一切都无可遁避，任何行动都要显现它的真相，我们必须当面为我们自己的罪恶作证。那么怎么办呢？还有什么法子好想呢？试一试忏悔的力量吧。什么事情是忏悔所不能做到的？可是对于一个不能忏悔的人，它又有什么用呢？啊，不幸的处境！啊，像死亡一样黑暗的心胸！啊，越是挣扎，越是不能脱身的胶住了的灵魂！救救我，天使们！试一试吧：屈下来，顽强的膝盖；钢丝一样的心弦，变得像新生之婴的筋肉一样柔嫩吧！但愿一切转祸为福！（退后跪祷。）

（哈姆莱特上。）

哈 姆 莱 特　他现在正在祈祷，我正好动手；我决定现在就干，让他上天堂去，我也算报了仇了。不，那还要考虑一下：一个恶人杀死我的父亲；我，他的独生子，却把这个恶人送上天堂。啊，这简直是以恩报怨了。他用卑鄙的手段，在我父亲满心俗念、罪孽正重的时候乘其不备把他杀死；虽然谁也不知道在上帝面前，他的生前的善恶如何相抵，可是照我们一般的推想，他的孽债多半是很重的。现在他正在洗涤他的灵魂，要是我在这时候结果了他的性命，那么天国

When be is fit and seasoned fot his passage?

No. up, sword, and know thou a more horrid hent,

When he is drunk asleep, or in his rage,

Or in th'incestuous pleasure of his bed,

At gaming, swearing, or about some act

That has no relish of salvation in' t,

Then trip him that his heels may kick at heaven,

And that his soul may be as damned and black

As hell whereto it goes; my mother stays,

This physic but prolongs thy sickly days.   [*Exit.*]

KING   My words fly up, my thoughts remain below.

Words without thoughts never to heaven go.   [*Exit.*]

SCENE 4

The Queen's Closet

[*Enter lite Queen and Polonius.*]

POLONIUS   He will come straight. Look you lay home to him,

Tell him his pranks have been too broad to bear with,

And that your grace hath screened and stood between

Much heat and him. I'll silence me even here.

Pray you be round with him.

HAMLET   [*Within*] Mother, mother, mother!

QUEEN   I'll war'nt you.

Fear me not. Withdraw, I hear him coming.

[*Polonius hides behind the arras.*]

[*Enters Hamlet.*]

HAMLET   Now, mother, what' s the matter?

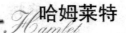

的路是为他开放着，这样还算是复仇吗？不！收起来，我的剑，等候一个更惨酷的机会吧；当他在酒醉以后，在愤怒之中，或是在乱伦纵欲的时候，有赌博、咒骂或是其他邪恶的行为的中间，我就要叫他颠踬在我的脚下，让他幽深黑暗不见天日的灵魂永堕地狱。我的母亲在等我。这一服续命的药剂不过延长了你临死的痛苦。（下。）

（国王起立上前。）

国　　王　我的言语高高飞起，我的思想滞留地下；没有思想的言语永远不会上升天界。（下。）

第四场　王后寝宫

（王后及波洛涅斯上。）

波 洛 涅 斯　他就要来了。请您把他着实教训一顿，对他说他这种狂妄的态度，实在叫人忍无可忍，倘没有您娘娘替他居中回护，王上早已对他大发雷霆了。我就悄悄地躲在这儿。请您对他讲得着力一点。

哈 姆 莱 特　（在内）母亲，母亲，母亲！

王　　后　都在我身上，你放心吧。下去吧，我听见他来了。

（波洛涅斯匿帏后。）

（哈姆莱特上。）

哈 姆 莱 特　母亲，您叫我有什么事？

QUEEN	Hamlet, thou hast thy father much offended.
HAMLET	Mother, you have my father much offended.
QUEEN	Come, come, you answer with an idle tongue.
HAMLET	Go, go, you question with a wicked tongue.
QUEEN	Why, how now, Hamlet?
HAMLET	What's the matter now?
QUEEN	Have you forgot me?
HAMLET	No, by the rood not so.
	You are the queen, your husband's brother's wife,
	And would it were not so, you are my mother.
QUEEN	Nay then, I'll set those to you that can speak.
HAMLET	Come, come, and sit you down, you shall not budge,
	You go not till I set you up a glass
	Where you may see the inmost part of you.
QUEEN	What wilt thou do? thou wilt not murder me?
	Help, help, ho!
POLONIUS	[*Behind the arras*] What, ho! help, help, help!
HAMLET	[*Braws*] How now! A rat? Dead, for a ducat, dead.
	[*He makes a pass through the arras.*]
POLONIUS	O, I am slain!
QUEEN	O me, what hast thou done?
HAMLET	Nay, I know not, is it the king?
QUEEN	O what a rash and bloody deed is this!
HAMLET	A bloody deed, almost as bad, good mother,
	As kill a king, and marry with his brother.
QUEEN	As kill a king!
HAMLET	Ay, lady, it was my word.
	[*Lifts up the array and discovers*] Thou wretched, rash,

哈姆莱特

Hamlet

王　　后	哈姆莱特，你已经大大得罪了你的父亲啦。
哈姆莱特	母亲，您已经大大得罪了我的父亲啦。
王　　后	来，来，不要用这种胡说八道的话回答我。
哈姆莱特	去，去，不要用这种胡说八道的话问我。
王　　后	啊，怎么，哈姆莱特！
哈姆莱特	现在又是什么事？
王　　后	你忘记我了吗？
哈姆莱特	不，凭着十字架起誓，我没有忘记你；你是王后，你的丈夫的兄弟的妻子，你又是我的母亲——但愿你不是！
王　　后	哎哟，那么我要去叫那些会说话的人来跟你谈谈了。
哈姆莱特	来，来，坐下来，不要动；我要把一面镜子放在你的面前，让你看一看你自己的灵魂。
王　　后	你要干什么呀？你不是要杀我吗？救命！救命呀！
波洛涅斯	（在后）喂！救命！救命！救命！
哈姆莱特	（拔剑）怎么！是哪一个鼠贼？准是不要命了，我来结果你。（以剑刺穿帏幕。）
波洛涅斯	（在后）啊！我死了！
王　　后	嗳哟！你干了什么事啦？
哈姆莱特	我也不知道；那不是国王吗？
王　　后	啊，多么鲁莽残酷的行为！
哈姆莱特	残酷的行为！好妈妈。简直就跟杀了一个国王再去嫁给他的兄弟一样坏。
王　　后	杀了一个国王！
哈姆莱特	嗯，母亲，我正是这样说。（揭帏见波洛涅斯）你这倒运

intruding fool, farewell!

I took thee for thy better, take thy fortune,

Thou find'st to be too busy is some danger.——

Leave wringing of your hands, peace, sit you down,

And let ne wring your heart, for so I shall

If it be made of penetrable stuff,

If damned custom have not brassed it so,

That it be proof and bulwark against sense.

QUEEN   What have I done, that thou dar'st wag thy tongue

In noise so rude against ne?

HAMLET   Such an act that blurs the grace and blush of modesty,

Calls virtue hypocrite, takes off the rose

Form the fair forehead of an innocent love

And sets a blister there, makes marriage vows

As false as dicers' oaths, O such a deed

As from the body of contraction plucks

The very soul, and sweet religion makes

A rhapsody of words; heaven's face does glow,

And this solidity and compound mass

With heated visage, as against the doom,

Is thonght-sick at the act.

QUEEN   Ay me, what act,

That roars so loud, and thunders in the index?

HAMLET   Look here, upon this picture, and on this,

The counterfeit presenment of two brothers.

See what a grace was seated on this brow,

Hyperion's curls, the front of Jove himself,

An eye like Mars to threaten and command,

的、粗心的、爱管闲事的傻瓜，再会！我还以为是一个在你上面的人哩。也是你命不该活；现在你可知道爱管闲事的危险了。——别尽扭着你的手。静一静，坐下来，让我扭你的心；你的心倘不是铁石打成的，万恶的习惯倘不曾把它硬化得透不进一点感情，那么我的话一定可以把它刺痛。

王　　后　我干了些什么错事，你竟敢这样肆无忌惮地向我摇唇弄舌？

哈姆莱特　你的行为可以使贞节蒙污，使美德得到了伪善的名称；从纯洁的恋情的额上取下娇艳的蔷薇，替它盖上一个烙印；使婚姻的盟约变成赌徒的誓言一样虚伪；啊！这样一种行为，简直使盟约成为一个没有灵魂的躯壳，神圣的婚礼变成一串谵妄的狂言；苍天的脸上也为它带上羞色，大地因为痛心这样的行为，也罩上满面的愁容，好像世界末日就要到来一般。

王　　后　唉！究竟是什么极恶重罪，你把它说得这样惊人呢？

哈姆莱特　瞧这一幅图画，再瞧这一幅；这是两个兄弟的肖像。你看这一个的相貌多么高雅优美：太阳神的鬈发，天神的前额，像战神一样威风凛凛的眼睛，像降落在高吻穹苍的山

As station like the herald Mercury,

New-lighted on a heaven-kissing hill,

A combination and a form indeed,

Where every god did seem to set his seal

To give the world assurance of a man.

This was your husband. Look you now what follows.

Here is your husband, like a mildewed ear.

Blasting his wholesome brother. Have you eyes?

Could you on this fair mountain leave to feed,

And batten on this moor? Ha! Have you eyes?

You cannot call it love, for at your age

The heyday in the blood is tame, it's humble,

And waits upon the judgment, and what judgment

Would step from this to this? Sense sure you have

Else could you not have motion, but sure that sense

Is apoplexed, for madness would not err,

Nor sense to ecstasy was ne'er so thralled,

But it reserved some quantity of choice

To serve in such a difference. What devil was't

That thus hath cozened you at hoodman-blind?

Eyes without feeling, feeling without sight,

Ears without hands or eyes, smelling sans all,

Or but a sickly part of one true sense

Could not so mope. O shame, where is thy blush?

Rebellious hell,

If thou eaust murine in a matron's bones,

To flaming youth let virtue be as wax

And melt in her own fire. Proclaim no shame,

巅的神使一样矫健的姿态；这一个完善卓越的仪表，真像每一个天神都曾在那上面打下印记，向世间证明这是一个男子的典型。这是你从前的丈夫。现在你再看这一个：这是你现在的丈夫，像一株霉烂的禾穗，损害了他的健硕的兄弟。你有眼睛吗？你甘心离开这一座大好的高山，靠着这荒野生活吗？嘿！你有眼睛吗？你不能说那是爱情，因为在你的年纪，热情已经冷淡下来，变驯服了，肯听从理智的判断；什么理智愿意从这么高的地方，降落到这么低的所在呢？知觉你当然是有的，否则你就不会有行动；可是你那知觉也一定已经麻木了；因为就是疯人也不会犯那样的错误，无论怎样丧心病狂，总不会连这样悬殊的差异都分辨不出来。那么是什么魔鬼蒙住了你的眼睛，把你这样欺骗呢？有眼睛而没有触觉、有触觉而没有视觉、有耳朵而没有眼或手、只有嗅觉而别的什么都没有，甚至只剩下一种官觉还出了毛病，也不会糊涂到你这步田地。羞啊！你不觉得惭愧吗？要是地狱中的孽火可以在一个中年妇人的骨髓里煽起了蠢动，那么在青春的烈焰中，让贞操像蜡一样融化了吧。当无法阻遏的情欲大举进攻的时候，用不着喊什

When the compulsive ardour gives the charge,

Since frost itself as actively doth burn,

And reason pandars will.

QUEEN O Hamlet, speak no more.

Thou turn' st my eyes into my very soul,

And there I see such black and grained spots

As will not leave their tinct.

HAMLET Nay, but to live

In the rank sweat of an enseamed bed

Stewed in corrupfion, honeying and making love

Over the nasty sty.

QUEEN O speak to me no more,

These words like daggers enter in mine ears,

No more, sweet Hamlet.

HAMLET A murderer and a villain,

A slave that is not twentieth part the tithe

Of your precedent lord, a vice of kings,

A cutpurse of the empire and the rule,

That from a shelf the precious diadem stole

And put it in his pocket.

QUEEN No more.

HAMLET A King of shreds and patches.

[*Enter the Ghost.*]

Save me and hover o' er me with your wings,

You heavenly guards! — What would your gracious figure?

QUEEN Alas, he' s mad.

HAMLET Do you not come your tardy son to chide,

That lapsed in time and passion lets go by

么羞耻了，因为霜雪都会自动燃烧，理智都会做情欲的奴隶呢。

王　　后　啊，哈姆莱特！不要说下去了！你使我的眼睛看进了我自己灵魂的深处，看见我灵魂里那些洗拭不去的黑色的污点。

哈姆莱特　嘿，生活在汗臭垢腻的眠床上，让淫邪熏没了心窍，在污秽的猪圈里调情弄爱——

王　　后　啊，不要再对我说下去了！这些话像刀子一样戳进我的耳朵里；不要说下去了，亲爱的哈姆莱特！

哈姆莱特　一个杀人犯、一个恶徒、一个不及你前夫二百分之一的庸奴、一个冒充国王的丑角、一个盗国窃位的扒手，从架子上偷下那顶珍贵的王冠，塞在自己的腰包里！

王　　后　别说了！

哈姆莱特　一个下流褴褛的国王——

　　　　　（鬼魂上。）

　　　　　天上的神明啊，救救我，用你们的翅膀覆盖我的头顶！——陛下英灵不昧，有什么见教？

王　　后　哎哟，他疯了！

哈姆莱特　您不是来责备您的儿子不该消磨时间和热情，把您煌煌的

	Th' important ac ting of your dread command?
	O, say!
GHOST	Do not forget! this visitation
	Is but to whet thy almost blunted purpose.
	But look, amazement on thy mother sits,
	O step between her and her fighting soul;
	Conceit in weakest bodies strongest works,
	Speak to her, Hamlet.
HAMLET	How is it with you, lady?
QUEEN	Alas, how it's with you,
	That you do bend your eye on vacancy,
	And with th' incorporal air do hold discourse?
	Forth at your eyes your spirits wildly peep,
	And as the sleeping soldiers in th' alarm,
	Your bedded hairs like life in excrements
	Start up and stand an end. O gentle son,
	Upon the heat and flame of thy distemper
	Sprinkle cool patience. Whereon do you look?
HAMLET	On him! on him! Look you, how pale he glares!
	His form and cause conjoined, preaching to stones,
	Would make them capable. ——Do not look upon me,
	Lest with this piteous action you convert
	My stem effects, then what I have to do
	Will want tme colour, tears perchance for blood.
QUEEN	To whom do you speak this?
HAMLET	Do you see nothing there?
QUEEN	Nothing at all, yet all that is I see.
HAMLET	Nor did you nothing hear?

　　　　　　命令搁在一旁，耽误了应该做的大事吗？啊，说吧！

鬼　　魂　　不要忘记。我现在是来磨砺你的快要蹉跎下去的决心。可是瞧！你的母亲那副惊愕的表情。啊，快去安慰安慰她的正在交战中的灵魂吧！最柔弱的人最容易受幻想的激动。去对她说话，哈姆莱特。

哈 姆 莱 特　　您怎么啦，母亲？

王　　后　　唉！你怎么啦？为什么你把眼睛睁视着虚无，向空中喃喃说话？你的眼睛里射出狂乱的神情；像熟睡的兵士突然听到警号一般，你的整齐的头发一根根都像有了生命似的竖立起来。啊，好儿子！在你的疯狂的热焰上，浇洒一些清凉的镇静吧！你瞧什么？

哈 姆 莱 特　　他，他！您瞧，他的脸色多么惨淡！看见了他这一种形状，要是再知道他所负的沉冤，即使石块也会感动的。——不要瞧着我，免得你那种可怜的神气反会妨碍我的冷酷的决心；也许我会因此而失去勇气，让挥泪代替了流血。

王　　后　　你这番话是对谁说的？

哈 姆 莱 特　　您没有看见什么吗？

王　　后　　什么也没有；要是有什么东西在那边，我不会看不见的。

哈 姆 莱 特　　您也没有听见什么吗？

王　　后　　不，除了我们两人的说话以外，我什么也没有听见。

QUEEN	No, nothing but ourselves.
HAMLE	Why, look you there! Look how it steals away!
	My father in his habit as he lived,
	Look where he goes, even now, out at the portal.

[Exit the Ghost.]

QUEEN　This is the very coinage of your brain!
This bodiless creation ecstasy is very cunning in.

HAMLET　Ecstasy! my pulse as yours doth temperately keep time,
And makes as healthful music. It is not madness
That I have uttered; bring me to the test
And I the matter will re-word, which madness
Would gambol from. Mother, for love of grace,
Lay not that flattering unction to your soul,
That not your trespass but my madness speaks,
It will but skin and film the ulcerous place,
Whiles rank corruption mining all within
Infects unseen. Confess yomself to heaven,
Repent what's past, avoid what is to come,
And do not spread the compost on the weeds
To make them ranker. Forgive me this my virtue,
For in the fatness of these pursy times
Virtue itself of vice must pardon beg,
Yea curb and woo for leave to do him good.

QUEEN　O Hamlet, thou hast cleft my heart in twain.

HAMLET　O throw away the worser part of it,
And live the purer with the other half.
Good night, but go not to my uncle's bed,
Assume a virtue if you have it not.

Shakespeare Classics

哈 姆 莱 特 啊，您瞧！瞧，它悄悄地去了！我的父亲，穿着他生前所穿的衣服！瞧！他就在这一刻，从门口走出去了！（鬼魂下。）

王　　　后 这是你脑中虚构的意象；一个人在心神恍惚之中，最容易发生这种幻妄的错觉。

哈 姆 莱 特 心神恍惚！我的脉搏跟您的一样，在按着正常的节奏跳动哩。我所说的并不是疯话；要是您不信，不妨试试，我可以把话一字不漏地复述一遍，一个疯人是不会记忆得那样清楚的。母亲，为了上帝的慈悲，不要自己安慰自己，以为我这一番说话，只是出于疯狂，不是真的对您的过失而发；那样的思想不过是骗人的油膏，只能使您溃烂的良心上结起一层薄膜，那内部的毒疮却在底下愈长愈大。向上天承认您的罪恶吧，忏悔过去，警戒未来；不要把肥料浇在莠草上，使它们格外蔓延起来。原谅我这一番正义的劝告；因为在这种万恶的时世，正义必须向罪恶乞恕，它必须俯首屈膝，要求人家接纳他的善意的箴规。

王　　　后 啊，哈姆莱特！你把我的心劈为两半了！

哈 姆 莱 特 啊！把那坏的一半丢掉，保留那另外的一半，让您的灵魂清净一些。晚安！可是不要上我叔父的床；即使您已经失节，也得勉力学做一个贞节妇人的样子。习惯虽然是一个

That monster custom, who all sense doth eat
Of habits evil, is angel yet in this,
That to the use of actions fair and good
He likewise gives a frock or livery
That aptly is put on. Refrain tonight,
And that shall lend a kind of easiness
To the next abstinence, the next more easy:
For use almost can change the stamp of nature,
And either··· the devil, or throw him out,
With wondrous potency: once more, good night,
And when you are desirous to be blessed,
I'll blessing beg of you. For this same lord,

    [*Pointing to Polonius*]

I do repent; but heaven hath pleased it so,
To punish me with this, and this with me,
That I must be their scourge and minister.
I will bestow him and will answer well
The death I gave him; so, again, good night.
I must be cruel only to be kind.
This bad begins, and worse remains behind.
One word more, good lady,

QUEEN   What shall I do?

HAMLET   Not this by no means that I bid you do:
Let the bloat king tempt you again to bed,
Pinch wanton on your cheek, call you his mouse,
And let him for a pair of reechy kisses,
Or paddling in your neck with his damned fingers,
Make you to ravel all this matter out

可以使人失去羞耻的魔鬼，但是它也可以做一个天使，对于勉力为善的人，它会用潜移默化的手段，使他弃恶从善。您要是今天晚上自加抑制，下一次就会觉得这一种自制的功夫并不怎样为难，慢慢地就可以习以为常了；因为习惯简直有一种改变气质的神奇的力量，它可以制服魔鬼，并且把他从人们心里驱逐出去。让我再向您道一次晚安；当您希望得到上天祝福的时候，我将求您祝福我。至于这一位老人家，（指波洛涅斯）我很后悔自己一时鲁莽把他杀死；可是这是上天的意思，要借着他的死惩罚我，同时借着我的手惩罚他，使我成为代天行刑的凶器和使者。我现在先去把他的尸体安顿好了，再来承担这个杀人的过咎。晚安！为了顾全母子的恩慈，我不得不忍情暴戾；不幸已经开始，更大的灾祸还在接踵而至。再有一句话，母亲。

王　　　后　我应当怎么做？

哈 姆 莱 特　我不能禁止您不再让那肥猪似的僭王引诱您和他同床，让他拧您的脸，叫您做他的小耗子；我也不能禁止您因为他给了您一两个恶臭的吻，或是用他万恶的手指抚摩您的颈项，就把您所知道的事情一起说了出来，告诉他我实在是

That I essentially am not in madness,

But mad in craft. 'Twere good you let him know,

For who that's but a queen, fair, sober, wise,

Would from a paddock, from a bat, a gib,

Such dear concernings hide? Who would do so?

No, in despite of sense and secrecy,

Unpeg the basket on the house's top,

Let the birds fly, and like the famous ape,

To try conclusions in the basket creep,

And break your own neck down.

QUEEN Be thou assured, if words be made of breath,

And breath of life, I have no life to breathe

What thou hast said to me.

HAMLET I must to England, you know that?

QUEEN Alack,

I had forgot, 'tis so concluded on.

HAMLET There's letters sealed, and my two school-fellows,

Whom I will trust as I will adders fanged,

They bear the mandate, they must sweep my way

And marshal me to knavery; let it work,

For 'tis the sport to have the engineer

Hoist with his own petar, and' t shall go hard

But I will delve one yard below their mines,

And blow them at the moon: O, 'tis most sweet

When in one line two crafts directly meet.

This man shall set me packing,

I'll lug the guts into the neighbour room;

Mother, good night in deed. This counsellor

莎士比亚经典戏剧

装疯，不是真疯。您应该让他知道的；因为哪一个美貌聪明懂事的王后，愿意隐藏着这样重大的消息，不去告诉一只蛤蟆、一只蝙蝠、一只老雄猫知道呢？不，虽然理性警告您保守秘密，您尽管学那寓言中的猴子，因为受了好奇心的驱使，到屋顶上去开了笼门，把鸟儿放走，自己钻进笼里去，结果连笼子一起掉下来跌死吧。

王　　后　你放心吧，要是言语来自呼吸，呼吸来自生命，只要我一息犹存，就决不会让我的呼吸泄漏了你对我所说的话。

哈姆莱特　我必须到英国去；您知道吗？

王　　后　唉！我忘了；这事情已经这样决定了。

哈姆莱特　公文已经封好，打算交给我那两个同学带去，对这两个家伙我要像对待两条咬人的毒蛇一样随时提防；他们将要做我的先驱，引导我钻进什么圈套里去。我倒要瞧瞧他们的能耐。开炮的要是给炮轰了，也是一件好玩的事；他们会埋地雷，我要比他们埋得更深，把他们轰到月亮里去。啊！用诡计对付诡计，不是顶有趣的吗？这家伙一死，多半会提早了我的行期；让我把这尸体拖到隔壁去。母亲，晚安！这一位大臣生前

Is now most still, most secret, and most grave,

Who was in life a foolish prating knave

Come, sir, to draw toward an end with you.

Good night mother.

[*Exeunt severally. Hamlet dragging in Polonius.*]

是个愚蠢饶舌的家伙，现在却变成非常谨严庄重的人了。来，老先生，该是收场的时候了。晚安，母亲！（各下。哈姆莱特曳波洛涅斯尸入内。）

ACT 4   SCENE 1

A room in the castle

[*Enter the King, Queen, Rosencrantz and Guildenstern.*]

KING   There's matter in these sighs, these profound heaves, you

must translate, 'tis fit we understand them.

Where is your son?

QUEEN   [*To Rosencrantz and Guildenstern*] Bestow this place on us

a little while.   [*Exeunt Rosencrantz and Guildenstern.*]

Ah, mine own lord, what have I seen tonight!

KING   What, Gertrude? How does Hamlet?

QUEEN   Mad as the sea and wind when both contend

Which is tile mightier: in his lawless fit,

Behind the arras hearing, something stir,

Whips out his rapier, eries 'A rat, a rat!'

And in this brainish apprehension kills

The unseen good old man.

KING   O heavy deed!

It had been so with us had we been there.

His liberty is full of threats to all,

To you yourself, to us, to everyone.

Alas, how shall this bloody deed be answered?

It will be laid to us, whose providence

Should have kept short, restrained, and ont of haunt

This mad young man; but so much was our love,

We would not understand what was most fit,

第 四 幕

第一场 城堡中一室

（国王、王后、罗森格兰兹及吉尔登斯吞上。）

国　王　这些长吁短叹之中，都含着深长的意义，你必须明说出
来，让我知道。你的儿子呢？

王　后　（向罗森格兰兹、吉尔登斯吞）请你们暂时退开。（罗森格
兰兹、吉尔登斯吞下。）啊，陛下！今晚我看见了多么惊
人的事情！

国　王　什么，乔特鲁德？哈姆莱特怎么啦？

王　后　疯狂得像彼此争强斗胜的天风和海浪一样。在他野性发作
的时候，他听见帏幕后面有什么东西爬动的声音，就拔出
剑来，嚷着，"有耗子！有耗子！"于是在一阵疯狂的恐
惧之中，把那躲在幕后的好老人家杀死了。

国　王　啊，罪过罪过！要是我在那儿，我也会照样死在他手里
的；放任他这样胡作非为，对于你、对于我、对于每一
个人，都是极大的威胁。唉！这一件流血的暴行应当由
谁负责呢？我是不能辞其咎的，因为我早该防患未然，
把这个发疯的孩子关禁起来，不让他到处乱走；可是我
太爱他了，以至于不愿想一个适当的方策，正像一个害

But like the owner of a foul disease,

To keep it from divulging, let it feed

Even on the pith of life: where is he gone?

QUEEN To draw apart the body he hath killed,

O'er whom his very madness, hke sane ore

Among a mineral of metals base,

Shows itself pure; he weeps for what is done.

KING O, Gertrude, come away!

The sun no sooner shall the mountains touch,

But we will ship him hence, and this vile deed

We must with all our majesty and skill

Both countenance and excuse. Ho! Guildenstern!

[*Re-enter Rosencrantz and Guildenstern.*]

Friends both, go join you with some further aid.

Hamlet in madness hath Polonius slain,

And from his mother's closet hath he dragged him.

Go, seek him out, speak fair, and bring the body

Into the chapel; I pray you, haste in this.

[*Exeunt Rosenceantz and Guildenstern.*]

Come, Gertrude, we'll call up our wisest friends,

And let them know both what we mean to do

And what's untimely done:

Whose whisper o'er the world's diameter,

As level ! as the cannon to his blank

Transports his poisoned shot, may miss our name,

And hit the woundless air. O, come away!

My soul is full of discord and dismay. [*Exeunt.*]

着恶疮的人，因为不让它出毒的缘故，弄到毒气攻心，无法救治一样。他到哪儿去了？

王　后　拖着那个被他杀死的尸体出去了。像一堆下贱的铅铁，掩不了黄金的光彩一样，他知道他自己做错了事，他的纯良的本性就从他的疯狂里透露出来，他哭了。

国　王　啊，乔特鲁德！来！太阳一到了山上，我就赶紧让他登船出发。对于这一件罪恶的行为，我只有尽量利用我的权威和手腕，替他掩饰过去。喂！吉尔登斯呑！

（罗森格兰兹及吉尔登斯呑重上。）

两位朋友，你们去多找几个人帮忙。哈姆莱特在疯狂之中，已经把波洛涅斯杀死；他现在把那尸体从他母亲的房间里拖出去了。你们去找他来，对他说话要和气一点；再把那尸体搬到教堂里去。请你们快去把这件事情办好。（罗森格兰兹、吉尔登斯呑下。）来，乔特鲁德，我要去召集我那些最有见识的朋友们，把我的决定和这一件意外的变故告诉他们，免得外边无稽的谰言牵涉到我身上，它的毒箭从低声的密语中间散放出去，是像弹丸从炮口射出去一样每发必中的，现在我们这样做后，它或许会落空了。啊，来吧！我的灵魂里充满着混乱和惊愕。（同下。）

SCENE 2

Another room in the castle

[*Enter Hamlet.*]

HAMLEF	Safely stowed.
ROSENC'Z **GUILD' RN**	[*within*] Hamlet! Lord Hamlet!
HAMLET	But soft, what noise, who calls on Hamlet?
	O, here they come!

[*Enter Rosencrantz and Guildenstern.*]

ROSENC'Z	What have you done, my lord, with the dead body?
HAMLET	Compounded it with dust whereto ' tis kin.
ROSENC'Z	Tell us where ' tis that we may take it thence,
	And bear it to the chapel.
HAMLET	Do not believe it.
ROSENC'Z	Believe what?
HAMLET	That I can keep your counsel and not mine own. Besides, to be demanded of a sponge, what replication should be made by the son of a king?
ROSENC'Z	Take you me for a sponge, my lord?
HAMLET	Ay, sir, that soaks up the king's countenance, his rewards, his authorities. But such officers do the king best service in the end, he keeps them like an apple, in the corner of his jaw, first mouthed to be last swallowed, when he needs what you have gleaned, it is but squeezing you, and, sponge, you shall be dry again.
ROSENC'Z	I understand you not, my lord.

第二场　城堡中另一室

（哈姆莱特上。）

哈 姆 莱 特　藏好了。

罗森格兰兹　（在内）哈姆莱特！哈姆莱特殿下！
吉尔登斯吞

哈 姆 莱 特　什么声音？谁在叫哈姆莱特？啊，他们来了。

（罗森格兰兹及吉尔登斯吞上。）

罗森格兰兹　殿下，您把那尸体怎么样啦？

哈 姆 莱 特　它本来就是泥土，我仍旧让它回到泥土里去。

罗森格兰兹　告诉我们它在什么地方，让我们把它搬到教堂里去。

哈 姆 莱 特　不要相信。

罗森格兰兹　不要相信什么？

哈 姆 莱 特　不要相信我会说出我的秘密，倒替你们保守秘密。而且，
一块海绵也敢问起我来！一个堂堂王子应该用什么话去回
答它呢？

罗森格兰兹　您把我当作一块海绵吗，殿下？

哈 姆 莱 特　嗯，先生，一块吸收君王的恩宠、利禄和官爵的海绵。可
是这样的官员要到最后才会显出他们对于君王的最大用处
来；像猴子吃硬壳果一般，他们的君王先把他们含在嘴里
舐弄了好久，然后再一口咽了下去。当他需要被你们所吸
收去的东西的时候，他只要把你们一挤，于是，海绵，你
又是一块干巴巴的东西了。

罗森格兰兹　我不懂您的话，殿下。

HAMLET	I am glad of it: a knavish speech sleeps in a foolish ear.
ROSENC'Z	My lord, you must tell us where the body is, and go with us to the king.
HAMLET	The body is with the king, but the king is not with the body.
	The king is a thing —
GUILD'RN	A thing, my lord!
HAMLET	Of nothing, bring me to him. Hide fox, and all after.

[Exeunt.]

SCENE 3

Another room in the castle

[*Enter the King, attended.*]

KING	I have sent to seek him, and to find the body.
	How dangerous is it that this man goes loose!
	Yet must not we put the strong law on him,
	He's loved of the distracted multitude,
	Who like not in their judgment but their eyes,
	And where ' tis so, th'offender's scourge is weighed
	But never the offence: to bear all smooth and even,
	This sudden sending him away must seem
	Deliberate pause. Diseases desperate grown
	By desperate appliance are relieved, or not at all.
	[*Enter Rosencrantz.*]
KING	How now! What hath befallen?
ROSENC'Z	Where the dead body is bestowed, my lord,
	We cannot get from him.

哈 姆 莱 特　那很好，下流的话正好让它埋葬在一个傻瓜的耳朵里。

罗森格兰兹　殿下，您必须告诉我们那尸体在什么地方，然后跟我们见
　　　　　　王上去。

哈 姆 莱 特　他的身体和国王同在，可是那国王并不和他的身体同在。
　　　　　　国王是一件东西——

吉尔登斯吞　一件东西，殿下！

哈 姆 莱 特　一件虚无的东西。带我去见他。狐狸躲起来，大家追上
　　　　　　去。（同下。）

第三场　城堡中另一室

（国王上，侍从后随。）

国　　　王　我已经叫他们找他去了，并且叫他们把那尸体寻出来。让
　　　　　　这家伙任意胡闹，是一件多么危险的事情！可是我们又不
　　　　　　能把严刑峻法加在他的身上，他是为糊涂的群众所喜爱
　　　　　　的，他们喜欢一个人，只凭眼睛，不凭理智；我要是处罚
　　　　　　了他，他们只看见我的刑罚的苛酷，却不想到他犯的是什
　　　　　　么重罪。为了顾全各方面的关系，这样叫他迅速离国，必
　　　　　　须显得像是深思熟虑的结果。应付非常的变故，只有用非
　　　　　　常的手段，不然是不中用的。

（罗森格兰兹上。）

国　　　王　啊！事情怎样啦？

罗森格兰兹　陛下，他不肯告诉我们那尸体在什么地方。

KING	But where is he?
ROSENC'Z	Without, my lord, guarded, to know your pleasure.
KING	Bring him before us.
ROSENC'Z	Ho! bring in the lord.
	[*Enter Hamlet and Guildldenstern.*]
KING	Now, Hamlet, where's Polonius?
HAMLET	At supper.
KING	At supper? Where?
HAMLET	Not where he eats, but where he is eaten, a certain convocation of pohlitic worms are e'en at him; your worm is your only emperor for diet, we fat all creatures else to fat us, and we fat ourselves for maggots. Your fat king and your lean beggar is but variable service, two dishes, but to one table; that's the end.
KING	Alas, alas!
HAMLET	A man may fish with the worm that hath eat of a king, and eat of the fish that hath fed of that worm.
KING	What dost thou mean by this?
HAMLET	Nothing but to show you how a king may go a progress through the guts of a beggar.
KING	Where is Polonius?
HAMLET	In heaven, send thither to see, if your messenger find him not there, seek him i'th'other place yourself. But if indeed you find him not within this month, you shall nose him as you go up the stairs into the lobby.
KING	[*To Attendants*] Go seek him there.
HAMLET	He will stay till you come. [*Exeunt Attendants.*]
KING	Hamlet, this deed, for thine especial safety,

国　　　王	可是他呢？
罗森格兰兹	在外面，陛下；我们把他看起来了，等候您的旨意。
国　　　王	带他来见我。
罗森格兰兹	喂，吉尔登斯吞！带殿下进来。

　　　　　　　　（哈姆莱特及吉尔登斯吞上。）

国　　　王	啊，哈姆莱特，波洛涅斯呢？
哈 姆 莱 特	吃饭去了。
国　　　王	吃饭去了！在什么地方？
哈 姆 莱 特	不是在他吃饭的地方，是在人家吃他的地方；有一群精明的蛆虫正在他身上大吃特吃哩。蛆虫是全世界最大的饕餮家；我们喂肥了各种牲畜给自己受用，再喂肥了自己去给蛆虫受用。胖胖的国王跟瘦瘦的乞丐是一个桌子上两道不同的菜；不过是这么一回事。
国　　　王	唉！唉！
哈 姆 莱 特	一个人可以拿一条吃过一个国王的蛆虫去钓鱼，再吃那吃过那条蛆虫的鱼。
国　　　王	你这句话是什么意思？
哈 姆 莱 特	没有什么意思，我不过指点你一个国王可以在一个乞丐的脏腑里作一番巡礼。
国　　　王	波洛涅斯呢？
哈 姆 莱 特	在天上；你差人到那边去找他吧。要是你的使者在天上找不到他，那么你可以自己到另外一个所在去找他。可是你们在这一个月里要是找不到他的话，你们只要跑上走廊的阶石，也就可以闻到他的气味了。
国　　　王	（向若干侍从）到走廊里去找一找。
哈 姆 莱 特	他一定会恭候你们。（侍从等下。）
国　　　王	哈姆莱特，你干出这种事来，使我非常痛心。由于我很关

Which we do tender, as we dearly grieve

For that which thou hast done, must send thee hence

With fiery quickness, Therefore prepare thyself,

The bark is ready, and the wind at help,

Th'associates tend, and everything is bent for England.

HAMLET For England.

KING Ay, Hamlet.

HAMLET Good.

KING So is it if thou knew' st our purposes.

HAMLET I see a cherub that sees them. But, come, for England!

Farewell, dear mother.

KING Thy loving father, Hamlet.

HAMLET My mother: father and mother is man and wife, man and

wife is one flesh, and so my mother.

Come, for England! [*Exit.*]

KING Follow him at foot, tempt him with speed aboard,

Delay it not, I'll have him hence tonight.

Away! for everything is sealed and done

That else leans on th' affair; pray you, make haste.

[*Exeunt.*]

And, England, if my love thou hold'st at aught,

As my great power thereof may give thee sense,

Since yet thy cicatrice looks raw and red

After the Danish sword, and thy free awe

Pays homage to us; thou mayst not coldly set

Our sovereign process, which imports at full

By letters congruing to that effect,

The present death of Hamlet. Do it, England,

心你的安全，你必须火速离开国境；所以快去自己预备预备。船已经整装待发，风势也很顺利，同行的人都在等着你，一切都已经准备好向英国出发。

哈姆莱特　到英国去！

国　　王　是的，哈姆莱特。

哈姆莱特　好。

国　　王　要是你明白我的用意，你应该知道这是为了你的好处。

哈姆莱特　我看见一个明白你的用意的天使。可是来，到英国去！再会，亲爱的母亲！

国　　王　我是你慈爱的父亲，哈姆莱特。

哈姆莱特　我的母亲。父亲和母亲是夫妇两个，夫妇是一体之亲；所以再会吧，我的母亲！来，到英国去！（下。）

国　　王　跟在他后面，劝诱他赶快上船，不要耽误；我要叫他今晚离开国境。去！和这件事有关的一切公文要件，都已经密封停当了。请你们赶快一点。（罗森格兰兹、吉尔登斯吞下。）英格兰王啊，丹麦的宝剑在你的国土上还留着鲜明的创痕，你向我们纳款输诚的敬礼至今未减，要是你畏惧我的威力，重视我的友谊，你就不能忽视我的旨意；我已经在公函里要求你把哈姆莱特立即处死，照着我的意思做

For like the hectic in my blood he rages,

And thou must cure me; till I know' tis done,

Howe'er my haps, my joys were ne'er begun.　　*[Exit.]*

SCENE 4

A plain in Denmark

[Eater Fortinbras, a Captain, and Soldiers, marching.]

FORT'BRAS　Go, captain, from me greet the Danish king,

　　Tell him that by his licence Fortinbras

　　Craves the conveyance of a promised march

　　Over his kingdom. You know the rendezvous.

　　If that his majesty would aught with us,

　　We shall express our duty in his eye,

　　And let him know so.

CAPTAIN　I will do' t, my lord.

FORT'BRAS　Go softly on.

[Exeunt Fortinbras and Soldiers.]

[Enter Hamlet, Rosencrantz, Guildenstern and others.]

HAMLET　Good sir, whose powers are these?

CAPTAIN　They are of Norway, sir.

HAMLET　How purposed, sir, I pray you?

CAPTAIN　Against some part of Poland.

HAMLET　Who commands them, sir?

CAPTAIN　The nephew to old Norway, Fortinbras.

HAMLET　Goes it against the main of Poland, sir,

　　Or for some frontier?

吧，英格兰王，因为他像是我深入膏肓的痼疾，一定要借你的手把我医好。我必须知道他已经不在人世，我的脸上才会浮起笑容。（下。）

第四场　丹麦原野

（福丁布拉斯、一队长及兵士等列队行进上。）

福丁布拉斯　队长，你去替我问候丹麦国王，告诉他说福丁布拉斯因为得到他的允许，已经按照约定，率领一支军队通过他的国境，请他派人来带路。你知道我们在什么地方集合。要是丹麦王有什么话要跟我当面说，我也可以入朝晋谒；你就这样对他说吧。

队　　长　是，主将。

福丁布拉斯　慢步前进。（福丁布拉斯及兵士等下。）

（哈姆莱特、罗森格兰兹、吉尔登斯吞等同上。）

哈姆莱特　官长，这些是什么人的军队？

队　　长　他们都是挪威的军队，先生。

哈姆莱特　请问他们是开到什么地方去的？

队　　长　到波兰的某一部分去。

哈姆莱特　谁是领兵的主将？

队　　长　挪威老王的侄儿福丁布拉斯。

哈姆莱特　他们是要向波兰本土进攻呢，还是去袭击边疆？

CAPTAIN	Truly to speak, and with no addition,
	We go to gain a little patch of ground
	That hath in it no profit but the name.
	To pay five ducats, five, I would not farm it;
	Nor will it yield to Norway or the Pole
	A ranker rate should it be sold in fee.
HAMLET	Why, then the Polack never will defend it.
CAPTAIN	Yes, 'tis already garrisoned.
HAMLET	Two thousand souls and twenty thousand ducats
	Will not debate the question of this straw!
	This is th' imposthume of much wealth and peace,
	That inward breaks, and shows no cause without
	Why the man dies. I humbly thank you, sir.
CAPTAIN	God bye you, sir. [*Exit.*]
ROSENC'Z	Will' t please you go, my lord?
HAMLET	I'll be with you straight, go a little before.

                       [*Exeunt all but Hamlet.*]

How all occasions do inform against me,
And spur my dull revenge! What is a man,
If his chief good and market of his time
Be but to sleep and feed? A beast, no more:
Sure he that made us with such large discourse,
Looking before and after, gave us not
That capability and god-like reason
To fust in us unused. Now, whether it be
Bestial oblivion, or some craven scruple
Of thinking too precisely on th'event,
A thought which quartered hath but one part wisdom,

队　　长	不瞒您说，我们是要去夺一小块徒有虚名毫无实利的土地。叫我出五块钱去把它租下来，我也不要；要是把它标卖起来，不管是归挪威，还是归波兰，也不会得到更多的好处。
哈姆莱特	啊，那么波兰人一定不会防卫它的了。
队　　长	不，他们早已布防好了。
哈姆莱特	为了这一块荒瘠的土地，牺牲了二千人的生命，二万块的金元，争执也不会解决。这完全是因为国家富足升起了，晏安的积毒蕴蓄于内，虽然已经到了溃烂的程度，外表上却还一点看不出致死的原因来。谢谢您，官长。
队　　长	上帝和您同在，先生。（下。）
罗森格兰兹	我们去吧，殿下。
哈姆莱特	我就来，你们先走一步。（除哈姆莱特外均下）我所见到、听到的一切，都好像在对我谴责，鞭策我赶快进行我的蹉跎未就的复仇大愿！一个人要是把生活的幸福和目的，只看作吃吃睡睡，他还算是个什么东西？简直不过是一头畜生！上帝造下我们来，使我们能够这样高谈阔论，瞻前顾后，当然要我们利用他所赋予我们的这一种能力和灵明的理智，不让它们白白废掉。现在我明明有理由、有决心、有力量、有方法，可以动手干我所要干的事，可是我还是在大言不惭地说："这件事需要作。"可是始终不曾在行动上表现出

And ever three parts coward, I do not know

Why yet I live to say 'This thing's to do',

Sith I have cause, and will, and strength, and means,

To do't. Examples gross as earth exhort me.

Witness this army of such mass and charge,

Led by a delicate and tender prince,

Whose spirit with divine ambition puffed

Makes mouths at the invisible event,

Exposing what is mortal and unsure

To all that fortune, death and danger dare,

Even for an egg-shell. Rightly to be great

Is not to stir without great argument,

But greatly to find quarrel in a straw

When honour's at the stake. How stand I then,

Tha have a father killed, a mother stained,

Exeitements of my reason and my blood,

And let all sleep? While to my shame I see

The imminent death of twenty thousand men,

That for a fantasy and trick of fame

Go to their graves like beds, fight for a plot

Whereon the numbers cannot try the cause,

Which is not tomb enough and continent

To hide the slain? O, from this lime forth,

My thoughts be bloody, or be nothing worth!　[*Exeunt.*]

来；我不知道这是因为像鹿豕一般的健忘呢，还是因为三分懦怯一分智慧的过于审慎的顾虑。像大地一样显明的榜样都在鼓励我；瞧这一支勇猛的大军，领队的是一个娇养的少年王子，勃勃的雄心振奋了他的精神，使他蔑视不可知的结果，为了区区弹丸大小的一块不毛之地，拼着血肉之躯，去向命运、死亡和危险挑战。真正的伟大不是轻举妄动，而是在荣誉遭遇危险的时候，即使为了一根稻秆之微，也要慷慨力争。可是我的父亲给人惨杀，我的母亲给人污辱，我的理智和感情都被这种不共戴天的大仇所激动，我却因循隐忍，一切听其自然，看着这二万个人为了博取一个空虚的名声，视死如归地走下他们的坟墓里去，目的只是争夺一方还不够给他们作战场或者埋骨之所的土地，相形之下，我将何地自容呢？啊！从这一刻起，让我屏除一切的疑虑妄念，把流血的思想充满在我的脑际！（下。）

SCENE 5

Elsinore. A room in the castle

[*Enter the Queen, Horatio and a Gentleman.*]

QUEEN	I will not speak with her.
GENT'MAN	She is importnnate, indeed distract,
	Her mood will needs be pitied.
QUEEN	What would she have?
GENT'MAN	She speaks much of her father, says she hears
	There's tricks i' th' world, and hems, and beats her heart,
	Spurns enviously at straws, speaks things in doubt
	That carry but half sense. Her speech is nothing,
	Yet the unshaped use of it doth move
	The hearers to collection; they aim at it,
	And botch the words up fit to their own thoughts,
	Which as her winks and nods and gestures yield them,
	Indeed would make one think there might be thought,
	Though nothing sure, yet much unhappily.
HORATIO	'Twere good she were spoken with, for she may strew
	Dangerous conjectures in ill-breeding minds.
QUEEN	Let her come in. [*Exit Gentleman.*]
	To my sick soul, as sin's true nature is,
	Each toy seems prologue to some great amiss,
	So full of artless jealousy is guilt,
	It spills itself, in fearing to be spilt.

[*Re-enter the Gentleman with Ophelia.*]

第五场　艾尔西诺。城堡中一室

（王后、霍拉旭及一侍臣上。）

王　　后	我不愿意跟她说话。
侍　　臣	她一定要见您；她的神气疯疯癫癫，瞧着怪可怜的。
王　　后	她要什么？
侍　　臣	她不断提起她的父亲；她说她听见这世上到处是诡计；一边呻吟，一边捶她的心，对一些琐琐屑屑的事情痛骂，讲的都是些很玄妙的话，好像有意思，又好像没有意思。她的话虽然不知所云，可是却能使听见的人心中发生反应，而企图从它里面找出意义来；他们妄加猜测，把她的话断章取义，用自己的思想附会上去；当她讲那些话的时候，有时眨眼，有时点头，做着种种的手势，的确使人相信在她的言语之间，含蓄着什么意思，虽然不能确定，却可以做一些很不好听的解释。
霍　拉　旭	最好有什么人跟她谈谈，因为也许她会在愚妄的脑筋里散布一些危险的猜测。
王　　后	让她进来。（侍臣下。） 我负疚的灵魂惴惴惊惶， 琐琐细事也像预兆灾殃； 罪恶是这样充满了疑猜， 越小心越容易流露鬼胎。

（侍臣率奥菲利娅重上。）

OPHEIIA	Where is the beauteous majesty of Denmark?
QUEEN	How now, Ophelia?
OPHELIA	[*Sings*] *How should I your true love know*
	From another one?
	By his cockle hat and staff,
	And his sandal shoon.
QUEEN	Alas, sweet lady, what imports this song?
OPHELIA	Say you? Nay, pray you mark.　[*Sings*]
	He is dead and gone, lady,
	He is dead and gone,
	At his head a grass-green turf,
	At his heels a stone.
	O, ho!
QUEEN	Nay, but Ophelia —
OPHELIA	Pray you mark.　[*Sings*]
	White his shroud as the mountain snow —
	[*Enter the King.*]
QUEEN	Alas, look here, my lord.
OPHELIA	*Larded all with sweet flowers,*
	Which bewept to the grave did not go,
	With true-love showers.
KING	How do you, pretty lady?
OPHELIA	Well, God'ild you! They say the owl was a baker's daughter. Lord, we know what we are, but know not what we may be. God be at your table!
KING	Conceit upon her father.
OPHELIA	Pray you let's have no words of this, but when they ask you what it means, say you this.　[*Sings*]

奥 菲 利 娅	丹麦的美丽的王后陛下呢？
王　　　后	啊，奥菲利娅！
奥 菲 利 娅	（唱）张三李四满街走，
	谁是你情郎？
	毡帽在头杖在手，
	草鞋穿一双。
王　　　后	唉！好姑娘，这支歌是什么意思呢？
奥 菲 利 娅	您说？请您听好了。（唱）
	姑娘，姑娘，他死了，
	一去不复来；
	头上盖着青青草，
	脚下石生苔。
	嗬呵！
王　　　后	嗳，可是，奥菲利娅——
奥 菲 利 娅	请您听好了。（唱）
	殓衾遮体白如雪——
	（国王上。）
王　　　后	唉！陛下，您瞧。
奥 菲 利 娅	鲜花红似雨；
	花上盈盈有泪滴，
	伴郎坟墓去。
国　　　王	你好，美丽的姑娘？
奥 菲 利 娅	好，上帝保佑您！他们说猫头鹰是一个面包师的女儿变成的。主啊！我们都知道我们现在是什么，可是谁也不知道自己将来会变成什么。愿上帝和您同席！
国　　　王	她父亲的死激成了她这种幻想。
奥 菲 利 娅	对不起，我们再别提这件事了。要是有人问您这是什么意思，您就这样对他说：（唱）

Tomorrow is Saint Valentine's day,

All in the morning betime,

And I a maid at your window

To be your Valentine.

Then up he rose, and donned his clo'es,

And dupped the chamber door,

let in the maid, that out a maid

Never departed more.

KING   Pretty Opheha!

OPHELIA   Indeed la, without an oath, I'll make an end on't   [*Sings*]

By Gis and by Saint Charity,

Alack and fie for shame!

Young men will do' t, if they come to' t,

By Cock, they are to blame.

Quoth she, Before you tumbled me,

You promised me to wed.

So would I ha' done, by yonder sun,

And thou hadst not come to my bed.

KING   How long hath she been thus?

OPHELIA   I hope all will be well. We must be patient, but I cannot
choose but weep to think they would lay him i' th'cold
ground. My brother shall know of it, and so I thank you for
your good counsel. Come, my coach! Good night, ladies,
good night. Sweet ladies, good night, good night.

[*Exit.*]

KING   Follow her close, give her good watch, I pray you.

[*Exit Horatio.*]

O, this is the poison of deep grief, it springs

情人佳节就在明天，

我要一早起身，

梳洗齐整到你窗前，

来做你的恋人。

他下了床披了衣裳，

他开开了房门；

她进去时是个女郎，

出来变了妇人。

国　　　王　美丽的奥菲利娅！

奥菲利娅　真的，不用发誓，我会把它唱完：（唱）

凭着神圣慈悲名字，

这种事太丢脸！

少年男子不知羞耻，

一味无赖纠缠。

她说你曾答应娶我，

然后再同枕席。

——本来确是想这样做，

无奈你等不及。

国　　　王　她这个样子已经多久了？

奥菲利娅　我希望一切转祸为福！我们必须忍耐；可是我一想到他们
　　　　　把他放下寒冷的泥土里去，我就禁不住掉泪。我的哥哥必
　　　　　须知道这件事。谢谢你们很好的劝告。来，我的马车！晚
　　　　　安，太太们；晚安，可爱的小姐们；晚安，晚安！（下。）

国　　　王　紧紧跟住她；留心不要让她闹出乱子来。（霍拉旭下）啊！
　　　　　深心的忧伤把她害成这样子；这完全是为了她父亲的死。

All from her father's death.

O Gertrude, Gertrude,

When sorrows come, they come not single spies.

But in battalions: first her father slain,

Next your son gone, and he most violent author

Of his own just remove, the people muddied,

Thick and unwholesome in their thoughts and whispers

For good Polonius' death; and we have done but greenly,

In hugger-mugger to inter him. Poor Ophelia

Divided from herself and her fair judgment,

Without the which we are pictures or mere beasts,

Last, and as much containing as all these,

Her brother is in secret come from France,

Feeds on his wonder, keeps himself in clouds,

And wants not buzzers to infect his ear

With pestilent speeches of his father's death,

Wherein necessity, of matter beggared,

Will nothing stick our person to arraign

In ear and ear: O my dear Gertrude, this

Like to a murdering-piece in many places

Gives me superfluous death!   [*A tumult within.*]

QUEEN   Alack! what noise is this?

          [*Enter an Attendant.*]

KING   Attend! Where are my Switzers? let them guard the door.

          What is the matter?

ATTENDANT   Save yourself, my lord!

          The ocean, ovepeering of his list,

          Eats not the flats with more impiteous haste

啊，乔特鲁德，乔特鲁德！不幸的事情总是接踵而来：第一是她父亲的被杀；然后是你儿子的远别，他闯了这样大祸，不得不亡命异国，也是自取其咎。人民对于善良的波洛涅斯的暴死，已经群疑蜂起，议论纷纷；我这样匆匆忙忙地把他秘密安葬，更加引起了外间的疑窦；可怜的奥菲利娅也因此而伤心得失去了她的正常的理智，我们人类没有了理智，不过是画上的图形，无知的禽兽。最后，跟这些事情同样使我不安的，她的哥哥已经从法国秘密回来，行动诡异，居心叵测，他的耳中所听到的，都是那些播弄是非的人所散播的关于他父亲死状的恶意的谣言；这些谣言，由于找不到确凿的事实根据，少不得牵制到我的身上。啊，我的亲爱的乔特鲁德！这就像一尊厉害的开花炮，打得我遍体血肉横飞，死上加死。（内喧呼声。）

王　　后　哎哟！这是什么声音？

（一侍臣上。）

国　　王　我的瑞士卫队呢？叫他们把守宫门。什么事？

侍　　臣　赶快避一避吧，陛下；比大洋中的怒潮冲决堤岸、席卷平

Than young Laertes in a riotous head

O'erbears your officers: the rabble call him lord,

And as the world were now but to begin,

Antiquity forgot, custom not known,

The ratifiers and props of every word,

They cry 'Choose we, Laertes shall be kiag!'

Caps, hands, and tongues applaud it to the clouds,

'Laertes shall be king, Laertes king!'

QUEEN   How cheerfully on the false trail they cry!

O, this is counter, you false Danish dogs!

[*a noise within*]

KING   The doors are broke.

[*Enter Laertes, armed, bursts into the room with Danes following.*]

LAERTES   Where is this king? Sirs, stand you all without.

ALL   No, let's come in.

LAERTES   I pray you, give me leave.

ALL   We will, we will.   [*they retire without the door*]

LAERTES   I thank you, keep the door. O thou vile king,

Give me my father.

QUEEN   Calmly, good Laertes.

LAERTES   That drop of blood that's calm proclaims me bastard,

Cries cuckold to my father, brands the harlot,

Even here, between the chaste unsmirched brows

Of my true mother.

KING   What is the cause, Laertes,

That thy rebellion looks so giant-like? ——

Let him go, Gertrude, do not fear our person,

原还要汹汹其势，年轻的雷欧提斯带领着一队叛军，打败了您的卫士，冲进宫里来了。这一群暴徒把他称为主上；就像世界还不过刚才开始一般，他们推翻了一切的传统和习惯，自己制订规矩，擅作主张，高喊着，"我们推举雷欧提斯做国王！"他们掷帽举手，吆喝的声音响彻云霄，"让雷欧提斯做国王，让雷欧提斯做国王！"

王　后	他们这样兴高采烈，却不知道已经误入歧途！啊，你们干了错事了，你们这些不忠的丹麦狗！（内喧呼声。）
国　王	宫门都已打破了。

（雷欧提斯戎装上；一群丹麦人随上。）

雷欧提斯	国王在哪儿？弟兄们，大家站在外面。
众　人	不，让我们进来。
雷欧提斯	对不起，请你们听我的话。
众　人	好，好。（众人退立门外。）
雷欧提斯	谢谢你们；把门看守好了。啊，你这万恶的奸王！还我的父亲来！
王　后	安静一点，好雷欧提斯。
雷欧提斯	我身上要是有一点血安静下来，我就是个野生的杂种，我的父亲是个王八，我的母亲的贞洁的额角上，也要雕上娼妓的恶名。
国　王	雷欧提斯，你这样大张声势，兴兵犯上，究竟为了什么原因？——放了他，乔特鲁德；不要担心他会伤害我的身

There's such divinity doth hedge a king,

That treason can but peep to what it would,

Acts little of his will.——Tell me, laertes,

Why thou art thus incensed?——Let him go, Gertrude —

Speak, man.

LAERTES	Where is my father?
KING	Dead.
QUEEN	But not by him.
KING	Let him demand his fill.
LAERTES	How came he dead? I'll not be juggled with.

To hell allegiance, vows to the blackest devil,

Conscience and grace to the profoundest pit!

I dare damnation. To this point I stand,

That both the worlds I give to negligence,

let come what comes, only I'll be revenged

Most throughly for my father.

KING	Who shall stay you.
LAERTES	My will, not all the world's;

And for my means, I'll husband them so well,

They shall go far with little.

KING Good Laertes, if you desire to know the certainty

Of your dear father, is't writ in your revenge,

That, sweepstake, you will draw both friend and foe,

Winner and loser?

LAERTES	None but his enemies.
KING	Will you know them then?
LAERTES	To his good friends thus wide I'll ope my arms,

体，一个君王是有神灵呵护的，叛变只能在一边蓄意窥伺，作不出什么事情来。——告诉我，雷欧提斯，你有什么气恼不平的事？——放了他，乔特鲁德。——你说吧。

雷 欧 提 斯	我的父亲呢？
国　　　王	死了。
王　　　后	但是并不是他杀死的。
国　　　王	尽他问下去。
雷 欧 提 斯	他怎么会死的？我可不能受人家的愚弄。忠心，到地狱里去吧！让最黑暗的魔鬼把一切誓言抓了去！什么良心，什么礼貌，都给我滚下无底的深渊里去！我要向永劫挑战。我的立场已经坚决：今生怎样，来生怎样，我一概不顾，只要痛痛快快地为我的父亲复仇。
国　　　王	有谁阻止你呢？
雷 欧 提 斯	除了我自己的意志以外，全世界也不能阻止我；至于我的力量，我一定要使用得当，叫它事半功倍。
国　　　王	好雷欧提斯，要是你想知道你的亲爱的父亲究竟是怎样死去的话，难道你复仇的方式是把朋友和敌人都当作对象，把赢钱的和输钱的赌注都一扫而光吗？
雷 欧 提 斯	冤有头，债有主，我只要找我父亲的敌人算账。
国　　　王	那么你要知道谁是他的敌人吗？
雷 欧 提 斯	对于他的好朋友，我愿意张开我的手臂拥抱他们，像舍身

And like the kind life-rend'ring pelican,

Repast them with my blood.

KING Why, now you speak

Like a good child and a true gentleman.

That I am guiltless of your father's death,

And am most sensibly in grief for it,

It shall as level to your judgment 'pear,

As day does to your eye.

ALL [*Within*] Let her come in.

LAERTES How now! What noise is that?

[*Re-enter Ophelia.*]

O heat, dry up my brains, tears seven times salt,

Burn out the sense and viltue of mine eye!

By heaven, thy madness shall be paid with weight,

Till our scale turn the beam. O rose of May,

Dear maid, kind sister, sweet Ophelia!

O heavens, is't possible a young maid's wits

Should be as mortal as an old man's life?

Nature is fine in love, and where 'tis fine,

It sends some precious instance of itself

After the thing it loves.

OPHEIA [*Sings*] *They bore him barefaced on the bier,*

Hey non nonny, nonny, hey nonny,

And in his grave rained many a tear —

Fare you well, my dove!

LAERTES Hadst thou thy wits, and didst persuade revenge,

It could not move thus.

OPHELIA You must sing ' down a-down', and you call him a-down-a.

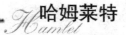
的鹈鹕一样，把我的血供他们畅饮。

国　　王　啊，现在你才说得像一个孝顺的儿子和真正的绅士。我不
但对于令尊的死不曾有份，而且为此也感觉到非常的悲
痛；这一个事实将会透过你的心，正像白昼的阳光照射你
的眼睛一样。

众　　人　（在内）放她进去！

雷 欧 提 斯　怎么！那是什么声音？

　　　　　　（奥菲利娅重上。）

啊，赤热的烈焰，炙枯了我的脑浆吧！七倍辛酸的眼泪，
灼伤了我的视觉吧！天日在上，我一定要叫那害你疯狂的
仇人重重地抵偿他的罪恶。啊，五月的玫瑰！亲爱的女
郎，好妹妹，奥菲利娅！天啊！一个少女的理智，也会像
一个老人的生命一样受不起打击吗？人类的天性由于爱情
而格外敏感，因为是敏感的，所以会把自己最珍贵的部分
舍弃给所爱的事物。

奥 菲 利 娅　（唱）

　　他们把他抬上枢架；

　　哎呀，哎呀，哎哎呀；

　　在他坟上泪如雨下；——

　　再会，我的鸽子！

雷 欧 提 斯　要是你没有发疯而激励我复仇，你的言语也不会比你现在
这样子更使我感动了。

奥 菲 利 娅　你应该唱："当啊当，还叫他啊当啊。"哦，这纺轮转动

O, how the wheel becomes it! It is the false steward that stole his master's daughter.

LAERTES This nothing's more than matter.

OPHELIA There's rosemary, that's for remembrancepray you, love, remember: and there is pansies, that's for thoughts.

LAERTES A document in madness, thoughts and remembrance fitted.

OPHELIA There's fennel for you, and columbines.

There's rue for you, and here's some for me, we may call it herb of grace o' Sundays: O, you must wear your rue with a difference. There's a daisy. I would give you some violets, but they withered all, when my father died: they say, he made a good end; [*Sings*] *For bonny sweet Rohin is all my joy.*

LAERTES Thought and affliction, passion, hell itself,

She turns to favour and to prettiness.

OPHELIA [*sings*] *And will he not come again?*

And will he not come again?

No, no, he is dead,

Go to thy death-bed,

He never will come again.

His beard was as white as snow,

All flaxen was his poll,

He is gone, he is gone,

And we cast away moan,

God ha'mercy on his soul!

And of all Christian souls I pray God. God bye you.   [*Exit.*]

LAERTES Do you see this, O God?

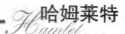
的声音配合得多么好听！唱的是那坏良心的管家把主人的女儿拐了去了。

雷欧提斯　这一种无意识的话，比正言危论还要有力得多。

奥菲利娅　这是表示记忆的迷迭香；爱人，请你记着吧：这是表示思想的三色堇。

雷欧提斯　这疯话很有道理，思想和记忆都提得很合适。

奥菲利娅　这是给您的茴香和漏斗花；这是给您的芸香；这儿还留着一些给我自己；遇到礼拜天，我们不妨叫它慈悲草。啊！您可以把您的芸香插戴得别致一点。这儿是一枝雏菊；我想要给您几朵紫罗兰，可是我父亲一死，它们全都谢了；他们说他死得很好——（唱）

可爱的罗宾是我的宝贝。

雷欧提斯　忧愁、痛苦、悲哀和地狱中的磨难，在她身上都变成了可怜可爱。

奥菲利娅　（唱）

他会不会再回来？他会不会再回来？

不，不，他死了；

你的命难保，

他再也不会回来。

他的胡须像白银，

满头黄发乱纷纷。

人死不能活，

且把悲声歇；

上帝饶赦他灵魂！

求上帝饶赦一切基督徒的灵魂！上帝和你们同在！（下。）

雷欧提斯　上帝啊，你看见这种惨事吗？

KING	Laertes, I must commune with your grief,
	Or you deny me right. Go but apart,
	Make choice of whom your wisest friends you will
	And they shall hear and judge ' twixt you and me.
	If by direct or by collateral hand
	They find us touched, we will our kingdom give,
	Our crown, our life, and all that we call ours,
	To you in satisfaction; but if not,
	Be you content to lend your patience to us,
	And we shall jointly labour with your soul
	To give it due content.
LAERTES	Let this be so. his means of death, his obscure funeral,
	No trophy, sword, nor hatchment o' er his bones,
	No noble rite, nor formal ostentation,
	Cry to be heard as ' twere from heaven to earth,
	That I must call't in question.
KING	So you shall,
	And where th 'offence is let the great axe fall.
	I pray you, go with me. *[Exeunt.]*

SCENE 6

Another room in the castle

[Enter Horatio and an Attendant.]

HORATIO	What are they that would speak with me?
ATTENDANT	Seafaring men, sir. They say they have letters for you.
HORATIO	Let them come in. *[Exit Attendant.]*
	I do not know from what part of the world

国　　王	雷欧提斯，我必须跟你详细谈谈关于你所遭逢的不幸；你不能拒绝我这一个权利。你不妨先去选择几个你的最有见识的朋友，请他们在你我两人之间做公证人：要是他们评断的结果，认为是我主动或同谋杀害的，我愿意放弃我的国土、我的王冠、我的生命以及我所有的一切，作为对你的补偿；可是他们假如认为我是无罪的，那么你必须答应助我一臂之力，让我们两人开诚合作，定出一个惩凶的方策来。
雷欧提斯	就这样吧；他死得这样不明不白，他的下葬又是这样偷偷摸摸的，他的尸体上没有一些战士的荣饰，也不曾替他举行一些哀祭的仪式，从天上到地下都在发出愤懑不平的呼声，我不能不问一个明白。
国　　王	你可以明白一切；谁是真有罪的，让斧钺加在他的头上吧。请你跟我来。（同下。）

第六场　城堡中另一室

（霍拉旭及一仆人上。）

霍　拉　旭	要来见我说话的是些什么人？
仆　　人	是几个水手，主人；他们说他们有信要交给您。
霍　拉　旭	叫他们进来。（仆人下。）倘不是哈姆莱特殿下差来的人，我

I should be greeted, if not from Lord Hamlet.

[*Enter Sailors.*]

1 SAILOR God bless you, sir.

HORATIO Let him bless thee too.

2 SAILOR He shall, sir, an' t please him. There's a letter for you, sir, it came from th' ambassador that was bound for England, if your name be Horatio, as I am let to know it is.

HORATIO [*Reads*] 'Horatio, when thou shalt have overlooked this, give these fellows some means to the king, they have letters for him. Ere we were two days old at sea, a pirate of very warlike appointment gave us chase. Finding ourselves too slow of sail, we put on a corapelled valour, and in the grapple I boarded them. On the instant they got clear of our ship, so I alone became their prisoner. They have dealt with me like thieves of mercy, but they knew what they did; I am to do a good turn for them. Let the king have the letters I have sent, and repair thou to me with as much speed as thou wouldest fly death. I have words to speak in thine ear will make thee dumb, yet are they much too light for the bore of the matter. These good fellows will bring thee where I am. Rosencrantz and Guildenstern hold their course for England of them I have much to tell thee. Farewell.

He that thou knowest thine, Hamlet. '

Come, I will give you way for these your letters,

And do' t the speedier that you may direct me

To him from whom you brought them.   [*Exeunt.*]

不知道在这世上的哪一部分会有人来看我。

（众水手上。）

水　手　甲	上帝祝福您，先生！
霍　拉　旭	愿他也祝福你。
水　手　乙	他要是高兴，先生，他会祝福我们的。这儿有一封信给您，先生——它是从那位到英国去的钦使寄来的。——要是您的名字果然是霍拉旭的话。
霍　拉　旭	（读信）"霍拉旭，你把这封信看过以后，请把来人领去见一见国王；他们还有信要交给他。我们在海上的第二天，就有一艘很凶猛的海盗船向我们追击。我们因为船行太慢，只好勉力迎敌；在彼此相持的时候，我跳上了盗船，他们就立刻抛下我们的船，扬帆而去，剩下我一个人做他们的俘虏。他们对待我很是有礼，可是他们也知道这样作对他们有利；我还要重谢他们哩。把我给国王的信交给他以后，请你就像逃命一般火速来见我。我有一些可以使你听了咋舌的话要在你的耳边说；可是事实的本身比这些话还要严重得多。来人可以把你带到我现在所在的地方。罗森格兰兹和吉尔登斯吞到英国去了；关于他们我还有许多话要告诉你。再会。你的知心朋友哈姆莱特。"来，让我立刻就带你们去把你们的信送出，然后请你们尽快领我到那把这些信交给你们的那个人的地方去。（同下。）

SCENE 7

Another room in the castle
[*Enter the King and Laertes.*]

KING	Now must your conscience my acquittance seal,
	And you must put me in your heart for friend,
	Sith you have heard and with a knowing ear
	That he which hath your noble father slain
	Pursued my life.
LAERTES	It well appears: but tell me,
	Why you proceeded not against these feats,
	So crimeful and so capital in nature,
	As by your safety, greatness, wisdom, all things else,
	You mainly were stirred up.
KING	O, for two special reasons,
	Which may to you perhaps seem much unsinewed,
	But yet to me they're strong. The queen his mother
	Lives almost by his looks, and for myself,
	My virtue or my plague, be it either which,
	She is so conjunctive to my life and soul,
	That as the star moves not but in his sphere
	I could not but by her. The other motive,
	Why to a public count I might not go,
	Is the great love the general gender bear him,
	Who dipping all his faults in their affection,
	Would like the spring that turneth wood to stone,
	Convert his gyves to graces, o that my arrows,
	Too slightly timbered for so loud a wind,

第七场 城堡中另一室

（国王及雷欧提斯上。）

国　　王　你已经用你同情的耳朵，听见我告诉你那杀死令尊的人，也在图谋我的生命；现在你必须明白我的无罪，并且把我当作你的一个心腹的友人了。

雷欧提斯　听您所说，果然像是真的；可是告诉我，您自己的安全、长远的谋虑和其他一切，都在大力推动您，为什么您对于这样罪大恶极的暴行，反而不采取严厉的手段呢？

国　　王　啊！那是因为有两个理由，也许在你看来是不成其为理由的，可是对于我却有很大的关系。王后，他的母亲，差不多一天不看见他就不能生活；至于我自己，那么不管这是我的好处或是我的致命的弱点，我的生命和灵魂是这样跟她联结在一起，正像星球不能跳出轨道一样，我也不能没有她而生活。而且我所以不能把这件案子公开，还有一个重要的顾虑：一般民众对他都有很大的好感，他们盲目的崇拜像一道使树木变成石块的魔泉一样，会把他戴的镣铐也当作光荣。我的箭太轻、太没有力了，遇到这样的狂风，一定不能

Would have reverted to my bow again,

And not where I had aimed them.

LAERTES   And so have I a noble father lost,

A sister driven into desperate terms,

Whose worth, if praises may go back again,

Stood challenger on mount of all the age

For her perfections. But my revenge will come.

KING   Break not your sleeps for that, you must not think

That we are made of stuff so flat and dull,

That we can let our beard be shook with danger

And think it pastime. You shortly shall hear more.

I loved your father, and we love ourself,

And that I hope will teach you to imagine-

[*Enter a Messenger.*]

KING   How now! what news?

MESSENGER   Letters, my lord, from Hamlet.

These to your majesty, these to the queen.

KING   From Hamlet! who brought them?

MESSENGER   Sailors, my lord, they say, I saw them not.

They were given me by Claudio, he received them

Of him that brought them.

KING   Laertes, you shall hear them.

Leave us.   [*Exit the Messenger.*]

[*Reads*] 'High and mighty, you shall know I am set naked on your kingdom. Tomorrow shall I beg leave to see your kingly eyes, when I shall, first asking your pardon thereunto, recount the occasion of my sudden and more strange return. Hamlet. '

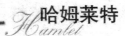

射中目的，反而给吹了转来。

雷欧提斯　那么难道我的一个高贵的父亲就这样白白死去，一个好好的妹妹就这样白白疯了不成？如果能允许我赞美她过去的容貌才德，那简直是可以傲视一世、睥睨古今的。可是我的报仇的机会总有一天会到来。

国　　王　不要让这件事扰乱了你的睡眠！你不要以为我是这样一个麻木不仁的人，会让人家揪着我的胡须，还以为这不过是开开玩笑。不久你就可以听到消息。我爱你父亲，我也爱我自己；那我希望可以使你想到——

（一使者上。）

国　　王　啊！什么消息？

使　　者　启禀陛下，是哈姆莱特寄来的信；这一封是给陛下的，这一封是给王后的。

国　　王　哈姆莱特寄来的！是谁把它们送到这儿来的？

使　　者　他们说是几个水手，陛下，我没有看见他们；这两封信是克劳狄奥交给我的，来人把信送在他手里。

国　　王　雷欧提斯，你可以听一听这封信。出去！（使者下。读信）“陛下，我已经光着身子回到您的国土上来了。明天我就要请您允许我拜谒御容。让我先向您告我的不召而返之罪，然后再向您禀告我这次突然意外回国的原因。哈姆

What should this mean? Are all the rest come back?

Or is it some abuse, and no such thing?

LAERTES Know you the hand?

KING 'Tis Hamlet' s character. 'Naked',

And in a postscript here he says ' alone'.

Can you devise me?

LAERTES I am lost in it, my lont, but let him come!

It warms the very sickness in my heart

That I shall live and tell him to his teeth

' Thus diest thou. '

KING If it be so, Laertes,

As how should it be so? How otherwise?

Will you be ruled by me?

LAERTES Ay, my lord, so you will not o'errule me to a peace.

KING To thine own peace. If he be now returned,

As chceking at his voyage, and that he means

No more to undertake it, I will work him

To an exploit, now ripe in my device,

Under the which he shall not choose but fall:

And for his death no wind of blame shall breathe,

But even his mother shall uncharge the practice,

And call it accident.

LAERTES My lord, I will be ruled, the rather if you could devise it so

That I might he the organ.

KING It falls right.

You have been talked of since your traved much,

And that in Hamlet's hearing, for a quality

Wherein they say you shine. Your sum of parts

莱特敬上。"这是什么意思？同去的人也都一起回来了吗？还是有什么人在捣鬼，事实上并没有这么一回事？

雷欧提斯 您认识这笔迹吗？

国　　王 这确是哈姆莱特的亲笔。"光着身子"！这儿还附着一笔，说是"一个人回来"。你看他是什么用意？

雷欧提斯 我可不懂，陛下。可是他来得正好；我一想到我能够有这样一天当面申斥他："你干的好事"，我的郁闷的心也热起来了。

国　　王 要是果然这样的话，可是怎么会这样呢？然而，此外又如何解释呢？雷欧提斯，你愿意听我的吩咐吗？

雷欧提斯 愿意，陛下，只要您不勉强我跟他和解。

国　　王 我是要使你自己心里得到平安。要是他现在中途而返，不预备再作这样的航行，那么我已经想好了一个计策，怂恿他去做一件事情，一定可以叫他自投罗网；而且他死了以后，谁也不能讲一句闲话，即使他的母亲也不能觉察我们的诡计，只好认为是一件意外的灾祸。

雷欧提斯 陛下，我愿意服从您的指挥；最好请您设法让他死在我的手里。

国　　王 我正是这样计划。自从你到国外游学以后，人家常常说起你有一种特长的本领，这种话哈姆莱特也是早就听到过的；虽然在我的意见之中，这不过是你所有的才艺中间最

Did not together' pluck such envy from him,

As did that one, and that in my regard

Of the unworthiest siege.

LAERTES　What part is that, my lord?

KING　A very riband in the cap of youth,

Yet needful too, for youth no less becomes

The light and careless livery that it wears,

Than settled age his sables and his weeds

Importing health and graveness; two months since,

Here was a gentleman of Normandy,

I have seen myself, and served against, the French,

And they can well on horseback; but this gallant

Had witchcraft in' t, he grew unto his seat,

And to such wondrous doing brought his horse,

As had he been incorpsed and demi-natured

With the brave beast. So far he topped my thought,

That I in forgery of shapes and tricks

Come short of what he did.

LAERTES　A Norman, was't?

KING　A Norman.

LAERTES　Upon my life, Lamord.

KING　The very same.

LAERTES　I know him well, he is the brooch indeed

And gem of all the nation.

KING　He made confession of you,

And gave you such a masterly report

For art and exercise in your defence,

And for your rapier most especial,

不足道的一种，可是你的一切才艺的总和，都不及这一种本领更能挑起他的妒忌。

雷 欧 提 斯 是什么本领呢，陛下？

国　　王 它虽然不过是装饰在少年人帽上的一条缎带，但也是少不了的；因为年轻人应该装束得华丽潇洒一些，表示他的健康活泼，正像老年人应该装束得朴素大方一些，表示他的矜严庄重一样。两个月以前，这儿来了一个诺曼绅士；我自己曾经见过法国人，和他们打过仗，他们都是很精于骑术的；可是这位好汉简直有不可思议的魔力，他骑在马上，好像和他的坐骑化成了一体似的，随意驰骤，无不出神入化。他的技术是那样远超过我的预料，无论我杜撰一些怎样夸大的词句，都不够形容它的奇妙。

雷 欧 提 斯 是个诺曼人吗？

国　　王 是诺曼人。

雷 欧 提 斯 那么一定是拉摩德了。

国　　王 正是他。

雷 欧 提 斯 我认识他；他的确是全国知名的勇士。

国　　王 他承认你的武艺很了不得，对于你的剑术尤其极口称赞，说是倘有人能够和你对敌，那一定大有可观；他发誓说他

That he cried out 'twould be a sight indeed

If one could match you; the scrimers of their nation

He swore had neither motion, guard, nor eye,

If you opposed them; sir, this report of his

Did Hamlet so envenom with his envy,

That he could nothing do but wish and beg

Your sudden coming o' er to play with him.

Now, out of this —

LAERTES   What out of this, my lord?

KING   Laertes, 'was your father dear to you?

Or are you like the painting of a sorrow,

A face without a heart?

LAERTES   Why ask you this?

KING   Not that I think you did not love your father,

But that I know love is begun by tine,

And that I see in passages of proof

Time qualifies the spark and fire of it.

There lives within the very flame of love

A kind of wick or snuff that will abate it,

And nothing is at a like goodness still,

For goodness, growing to a pleurisy,

Dies in his own too much. That we would do

We should do when we would: for this 'would' changes,

And hath abatements and delays as many

As there are tongues, are hands, are accidents,

And then this 'should' is like a spendthrift sigh,

That hurts by easing; but to the quick o' th' ulcer.

Hamlet comes back, what would you undertake

们国里的剑士要是跟你交起手来，一定会眼花缭乱，全然失去招架之功。他对你的这一番夸奖，使哈姆莱特妒恼交集，一心希望你快些回来，跟他比赛一下。从这一点上——

雷欧提斯 从这一点上怎么，陛下？

国　　王 雷欧提斯，你真爱你的父亲吗？还是不过是做作出来的悲哀，只有表面，没有真心？

雷欧提斯 您为什么这样问我？

国　　王 我不是以为你不爱你的父亲；可是我知道爱不过起于一时感情的冲动，经验告诉我，经过了相当时间，它是会逐渐冷淡下去的。爱像一盏油灯，灯芯烧枯以后，它的火焰也会由微暗而至于消灭。一切事情都不能永远保持良好，因为过度的善反会摧毁它的本身，正像一个人因充血而死去一样。我们所要做的事，应该一想到就做；因为人的想法是会变化的，有多少舌头、多少手、多少意外，就会有多少犹豫、多少迟延；那时候再空谈该做什么，只不过等于聊以自慰的长吁短叹，只能伤害自己的身体罢了。可是回到我们所要谈论的中心问题上来吧。哈姆莱特回来了；你预备

To show yourself your father's son in deed

More than in words?

LAERTES To cat his throat i' th' church.

KING No place indeed should murder sanctuarize,

Revenge should have no bounds: but, good Laertes,

Will you do this, keep close within your chamber.

Hamlet returned shall know you are come home.

We'll put on those shall praise your excellence,

And set a double varnish on the fame

The Frenchman gave you, bring you in fine together,

And wager on your heads; he being remiss,

Most generous, and free from all contriving,

Will not peruse the foils, so that with ease,

Or with a little shuffling, you may choose

A sword unbated, and in a pass of practice

Requite him for your father.

LAERTES I will do' t,and, for the purpose, I'll anoint my sword.

I bought an unction of a mountebank,

So mortal, that but dip a knife in it,

Where it draws blood, no cataplasm so rare,

Collected from all simples that have virtue

Under the moon, can save the thing from death

That is but scratched withal. I'll touch my point

With this contagion, that if I gall him slightly,

It may be death.

KING Let's further think of this,

Weigh what convenience both of time and means

May fit us to our shape, If this should fail,

怎样用行动代替言语，表明你自己的确是你父亲的孝子呢？

雷欧提斯　我要在教堂里割破他的喉咙。

国　　王　当然，无论什么所在都不能庇护一个杀人的凶手；复仇应该不受地点的限期。可是，好雷欧提斯，你要是果然志在复仇，还是住在自己家里不要出来。哈姆莱特回来以后，我们可以让他知道你也已经回来，叫几个人在他的面前夸奖你的本领，把你说得比那法国人所讲的还要了不得，怂恿他和你作一次比赛，赌个输赢。他是个粗心的人，一向厚道，想不到人家在算计他，一定不会仔细检视比赛用的刀剑的利钝；你只要预先把一柄利剑混杂在里面，趁他没有注意的时候不动声色地自己拿了，在比赛之际，看准他的要害刺了过去，就可以替你的父亲报了仇了。

雷欧提斯　我愿意这样做；为了达到复仇的目的，我还要在我的剑上涂一些毒药。我已经从一个卖药人手里买到一种致命的药油，只要在剑头上沾了一滴，刺到人身上，它一碰到血，即使只是擦破了一些皮肤，也会毒性发作，无论什么灵丹仙草，都不能挽救。我就去把剑尖蘸上这种烈性毒剂，只要我刺破他一点，就叫他送命。

国　　王　让我们再考虑考虑，看时间和机会能够给我们什么方便。要是这一个计策会失败，要是我们会在行动之间露出破

And that our drift look through our bad performance,

'Twere better not assayed. Therefore this project

Should have a back or second that might hold,

If this did blast in proof; soft, let me see,

We'll make a solemn wager on your cunnings,

I ha' t! When in your motion you are hot and dry,

As make your bouts more violent to that end,

And that he calls for drink, I'll have preferred him

A chalice for the nonce, whereon but sipping,

If he by chance escape your venomed stuck,

Our purpose may hold there. But stay, what noise?

  [*Enter the Queen.*]

QUEEN One woe doth tread upon another's heel,

So fast they follow; your sister's drowned, Laertes.

LAERTES Drowned! O, where?

QUEEN There is a willow grows askant the brook,

That shows his hoar leaves in the glassy stream,

Therewith fantastic garlands did she make

Of crow-flowers, nettles, daisies, and long purples

That liberal shepherds give a grosser name,

But our cold maids do dead men's fingers call them.

There on the pendent boughs her crownet weeds

Clamb' ring to hang, an envious sliver broke,

When down her weedy trophies and herself

Fell in the weeping brook. Her clothes spread wide,

And mermaid-like awhile they bore her up,

Which time she chanted snatches of old lauds,

As one incapable of her own distress,

绽，那么还是不要尝试的好。为了预防失败起见，我们应该另外再想一个万全之计。且慢！让我想来：我们可以对你们两人的胜负打赌；啊，有了：你在跟他交手的时候，必须使出你全副的精神，使他疲于奔命，等他口干烦躁，要讨水喝的当儿，我就为他预备好一杯毒计，万一他逃过了你的毒剑，只要他让酒沾唇，我们的目的也就同样达到了。且慢！什么声音？

（王后上。）

啊，亲爱的王后！

王　　　后　一桩祸事刚刚到来，又有一桩接踵而至。雷欧提斯，你的妹妹掉在水里淹死了。

雷 欧 提 斯　淹死了！啊！在哪儿？

王　　　后　在小溪之旁，斜生着一株杨柳，它的毵毵的枝叶倒映在明镜一样的水流之中；她编了几个奇异的花环来到那里，用的是毛茛、荨麻、雏菊和长颈兰——正派的姑娘管这种花叫死人指头，说粗话的牧人却给它起了另一个不雅的名字。——她爬上一根横垂的树枝，想要把她的花冠挂在上面；就在这时候，一根心怀恶意的树枝折断了，她就连人带花一起落下呜咽的溪水里。她的衣服四散展开，使她暂

Or like a creature native and indued

Unto that elemant. But long it could not be

Till that her garments, heavy, with their drink,

Pulled the poor wretch from her melodious lay

To muddy death.

LAERTES   Alas then, she is drowned?

QUEEN   Drowned, drowned.

LAERTES   Too much of water hast thou, poor Ophelia,

And therefore I forbid my tears; but yet

It is our trick, nature her custom holds,

Let shame say what it will; when these are gone,

The woman will be out. Adieu, my lord!

I have a speech o' fire that fain would blaze,

But that this folly douts it   [*Exit.*]

KING   Let's follow, Gertrude.

How much I had to do to calm his rage!

Now fear I this will give it start again,

Therefore let's follow.   [*Exeunt.*]

时像人鱼一样飘浮水上；她嘴里还断断续续唱着古老的谣曲，好像一点不感觉到她处境的险恶，又好像她本来就是生长在水中一般。可是不多一会儿，她的衣服给水浸得重起来了，这可怜的人歌儿还没有唱完，就已经沉到泥里去了。

雷欧提斯　唉！那么她淹死了吗？

王　　后　淹死了，淹死了！

雷欧提斯　太多的水淹没了你的身体，可怜的奥菲利娅，所以我必须忍住我的眼泪。可是人类的常情是不能遏阻的，我掩饰不了心中的悲哀，只好顾不得惭愧了；当我们的眼泪干了以后，我们的妇人之仁也会随着消失的。再会，陛下！我有一段炎炎欲焚的烈火般的话，可是我的傻气的眼泪把它浇熄了。（下。）

国　　王　让我们跟上去，乔特鲁德；我好容易才把他的怒气平息了一下，现在我怕又要把它挑起来了。快让我们跟上去吧。（同下。）

ACT 5　SCENE 1

A churchyard

[*Enter two Clowns with spades.*]

1 CLOWN　Is she to be buried in Christian burial when she wilfully seeks her own salvation?

2 CLOWN　I tell thee she is, therefore make her grave straight. The crowner hath sat on her, and finds it Christian burial.

1 CLOWN　How can that be, unless she drowned herself in her own defence ?

2 CLOWN　Why, ' tis found so.

1 CLOWN　It must be ' se offendendo', it cannot be else. For here lies the point, if I drown myself wittingly, it argues an act, and an act hath three branches, it is to act, to do, and to perform; argal, she drowned herself wittingly.

2 CLOWN　Nay, but hear you, goodman delver——

1 CLOWN　Give me leave. Here lies the water; good: here stands the man; good: if the man go to this water and drown himself, it is, will he nill he, he goes, mark you that. But if the water come to him, and drown him, he drowns not himself. Argal, he that is not guilty of his own death, shortens not his own life.

2 CLOWN　But is this law?

1 CLOWN　Ay, marry is't, crowner's quest law.

2 CLOWN　Will you ha' the truth an' t? If this had not been a

第 五 幕

第一场 墓 地

（二小丑携锄锹等上。）

小 丑 甲　她真心自己脱离人世，却要照基督徒的仪式下葬吗？

小 丑 乙　我对你说是的，所以你赶快把她的坟掘好吧；验尸官已经
　　　　　验明她的死状，宣布应该按照基督徒的仪式把她下葬。

小 丑 甲　这可奇了，难道她是因为自卫而跳下水里的吗？

小 丑 乙　他们验明是这样的。

小 丑 甲　那一定是为了自毁，不可能有别的原因。因为问题是这样
　　　　　的：要是我有意投水自杀，那必须成立一个行为；一个行
　　　　　为可以分为三部分，那就是干、行、做；所以，她是有意
　　　　　投水自杀的。

小 丑 乙　嗳，你听我说——

小 丑 甲　让我说完。这儿是水；好，这儿站着人；好，要是这个人
　　　　　跑到这个水里，把他自己淹死了，那么，不管他自己愿不
　　　　　愿意，总是他自己跑下去的；你听见了没有？可是要是那
　　　　　水来到他的身上把他淹死了，那就不是他自己把自己淹
　　　　　死；所以，对于他自己的死无罪的人，并没有缩短他自己
　　　　　的生命。

小 丑 乙　法律上是这样说的吗？

小 丑 甲　嗯，是的，这是验尸官的验尸法。

小 丑 乙　说一句老实话，要是死的不是一位贵家女子，他们决不会

gentlewoman, she should have been buried out a Christian burial.

1 CLOWN　Why, there thou say'st, and the more pity that great folk should have countenance in this world to drown or hang themselves more than their even Christen. Come, my spade! there is no ancient gentlemen but gardeners, ditchers and grave-makers; they hold up Adam's profession.

2 CLOWN　Was he a gentleman?

1 CLOWN　He was the first that ever bore arms.

2 CLOWN　Why, he had none.

1 CLOWN　What, art a heathen? How dost thou understand the Scripture? the Scripture says Adam digged; could he dig without arms? I'll put another question to thee. If thou answerest me not to the purpose, confess thyself —

2 CLOWN　Goto.

1 CLOWN　What is he that builds stronger than either the mason, the shipwright, or the carpenter?

2 CLOWN　The gallows-maker, for that frame outlives a thousand tenants.

1 CLOWN　I like thy wit well in good faith, the gallows does well; but how does it well? It does well to those that do ill. Now thou dost ill to say the gallows is built stronger than the church: argal, the gallows may do well to thee. To't again, come.

2 CLOWN　'who builds stronger than a mason, a shipwright, or a carpenter?'

1 CLOWN　Ay, tell me that, and unyoke.

2 CLOWN　Marry, now I can tell.

1 CLOWN　To't.

按照基督徒的仪式把她下葬的。

| 小　丑　甲 | 对了，你说得有理；有财有势的人，就是要投河上吊，比起他们同教的基督徒来也可以格外通融，世上的事情真是太不公平了！来，我的锄头。要讲家世最悠久的人，就得数种地的、开沟的和掘坟的；他们继承着亚当的行业。 |

小　丑　乙　亚当也算世家吗?

小　丑　甲　自然要算，他在创立家业方面很有两手呢。

小　丑　乙　他有什么两手?

小　丑　甲　怎么？你是个异教徒吗？你的《圣经》是怎么念的？《圣经》上说亚当掘地；没有两手，能够掘地吗？让我再问你一个问题；要是你回答得不对，那么你就承认你自己——

小　丑　乙　你问吧。

小　丑　甲　谁造出东西来比泥水匠、船匠或是木匠更坚固?

小　丑　乙　造绞架的人；因为一千个寄寓在上面的人都已经先后死去，它还是站在那儿动都不动。

小　丑　甲　我很喜欢你的聪明，真的。绞架是很合适的；可是它怎么是合适的？它对于那些有罪的人是合适的。你说绞架造得比教堂还坚固，说这样的话是罪过的；所以，绞架对于你是合适的。来，重新说过。

小　丑　乙　谁造出东西来比泥水匠、船匠或是木匠更坚固?

小　丑　甲　嗯，你回答了这个问题，我就让你下工。

小　丑　乙　呃，现在我知道了。

小　丑　甲　说吧。

2 **CLOWN**   Mass, I cannot tell.

[*Enter Hamlet and Horatio, at distance.*]

1 **CLOWN**   Cudgel thy brains no more about it, for your dull ass will
not mend his pace with beating. And when you are asked
this question next, say 'a grave-maker'. The houses he
makes lasts till doomsday. Co, get thee to Yanghan, and
fetch me a stoup of liquor.   [*Exit 2 Clown.*]

[1 *Clown digs and sings*]

In youth when I did love, did love,

Methought it was very sweet,

To contract o' the time for a my behove,

O, methought there a was nothing a meet.

HAMLET   Has this fellow no feeling of his business that he sings in
grave-making?

HORATIO   Custom hath made it in him a property of easiness.

HAMLET   'Tis e' en so, the hand of little employment hath the daintier sense.

1 **CLOWN**   [*Sings*] *But age with his stealing steps*

Hath clawed me in his clutch,

And hath shipped me intil the land,

As if I had never been such.

[*He throws up a skull.*]

HAMLET   That skull had a tongue in it, and conld sing once! How
the knave jowls it to the ground, as if ' twere Cain's jawbone, that did the first murder! This might be the pate of a
politician, which this ass now o' er-reaches; one that would
circumvent God, might it not?

哈姆莱特
Hamlet

小 丑 乙 真的，我可回答不出来。

（哈姆莱特及霍拉旭上，立远处。）

小 丑 甲 别尽绞你的脑汁了，懒驴子是打死也走不快的；下回有人问你这个问题的时候，你就对他说，"掘坟的人，"因为他造的房子是可以一直住到世界末日的。去，到约翰的面店里去给我倒一杯酒来。（小丑乙下。小丑甲且掘且歌）

年轻时候最爱偷情，

觉得那事很有趣味；

规规矩矩学做好人，

在我看来太无意义。

哈 姆 莱 特 这家伙难道对于他的工作一点没有什么感觉，在掘坟的时候还会唱歌吗？

霍 拉 旭 他做惯了这种事，所以不以为意。

哈 姆 莱 特 正是；不大劳动的手，它的感觉要比较灵敏一些。

小 丑 甲 （唱）

谁料如今岁月潜移，

老景催人急于星火，

两腿挺直，一命归西，

世上原来不曾有我。（掷起一骷髅。）

哈 姆 莱 特 那个骷髅里面曾经有一条舌头，它也会唱歌哩；瞧这家伙把它摔在地上，好像它是第一个杀人凶手该隐的颚骨似的！它也许是一个政客的头颅，现在却让这蠢货把它丢来踢去；也许他生前是个偷天换日的好手，你看是不是？

HORATIO	It might, my lord.
HAMLET	Or of a courtier, which could say ' Good morrow, sweet lord! How dost thou, good lord? ' This might be my lord such-a- one, that praised my lord such-a-one's horse, when he meant to beg it, might it not?
HORATIO	Ay, my lord.
HAMLET	Why, e'en so, and now my Lady Worm's, chopless and knocked about the mazzard with a sexton' s spade; here' s fine revolution an we had the trick to See't! Did these bones cost no more the breeding, but to play at loggats with them? Mine ache to think on't.
1 CLOWN	[*Sings*]*A pick-axe, and a spade, a spade,*
	For and a shrouding sheet,
	O, a pit of clay for to be made
	For such a guest is meet.
	[*He throws up a second skuu.*]
HAMLET	There's another. Why may not that be the skull of a law-yer? Where be his quiddities now, his quillities, his ca-ses, his tenures, and his tricks ? Why does he suffer this rude knave now to knock him about the sconce with a dirty shovel, and will not tell him of his action of battery? Hum ! This fellow might be in's time a great buyer of land, with his statutes, his recognizances, his fines, his double vouchers, his recoveries: is this the fine of his fines, and the recovery of his recoveries, to have his fine pate full of fine dirt? Will his vouchers vouch him no more of his pur-chases, anddouble ones too, than the length and breadth of a pair of indentures ? The very conveyances of his lands will

霍 拉 旭	也许是的，殿下。
哈 姆 莱 特	也许是一个朝臣，他会说，"早安，大人！您好，大人！"也许他就是某大人，嘴里称赞某大人的马好，心里却想把它讨了来，你看是不是？
霍 拉 旭	是，殿下。
哈 姆 莱 特	啊，正是；现在却让蛆虫伴寝，他的下巴也脱掉了，一柄工役的锄头可以在他头上敲来敲去。从这种变化上，我们大可看透了生命的无常。难道这些枯骨生前受了那么多的教养，死后却只好给人家当木块一般抛着玩吗？想起来真是怪不好受的。
小 丑 甲	（唱） 锄头一柄，铁铲一把， 殓衾一方掩面遮身； 挖松泥土深深掘下， 掘了个坑招待客人。（掷起另一骷髅。）
哈 姆 莱 特	又是一个；谁知道那不会是一个律师的骷髅？他的玩弄刀笔的手段，颠倒黑白的雄辩，现在都到哪儿去了？为什么他让这个放肆的家伙用龌龊的铁铲敲他的脑壳，不去控告他一个殴打罪？哼！这家伙生前也许曾经买下许多地产，开口闭口用那些条文、具结、罚款、双重保证、赔偿一类的名词吓人；现在他的脑壳里塞满了泥土，这就算是他所取得的罚款和最后的赔偿了吗？他的双重保证人难道不能保他再多买点地皮？，只给他留下和那种一式二份的契约同样大小的一块地面吗？这个小木头匣子，原来要装他土地的字

scarcely lie in this box, and must th' inheritor himseff have no more, ha?

HORATIO　Not a jot more, my lord.

HAMLET　Is not parchment made of sheep-skins?

HORATIO　Ay, my lord, and of calves'-skins too.

HAMLET　They are sheep and calves which seek out assurance in that. I will speak to this fellow. Whose grave's this, sirrah?

1 CLOWN　Mine, sir

(O, a pit of clay for to be made

For such a guest is meet.)

HAMLET　I think it be thine, indeed, for thou hest in't.

1 CLOWN　You lie out on' t sir, and therefore 'tis not yours; for my part I do not lie in't, and yet it is mine.

HAMLET　Thou dost lie in' t, to be in' t and say it is thine. 'Tis for the dead, not for the quick, therefore thou liest.

1 CLOWN　'Tis a quick lie, sir, ' twill away again from me to you.

HAMLET　What man dost thou dig it for?

1 CLOWN　For no man, sir.

HAMLET　What woman then?

1 CLOWN　For none neither.

HAMLET　Who is to be buried in' t?

1 CLOWN　One that was a woman, sir, but rest her soul she's dead.

HAMLET　How absolute the knave is! We must speak by the card or equivocation will undo us. By the Lord, Horatio, this three years I have took note of it, the age is grown so picked, that the toe of the peasant comes so near the heel of the courtier he galla his kibe. How long hast thou been grave-maker?

据都恐怕装不下，如今地主本人却也只能有这么一点地盘，哈？

霍 拉 旭　不能比这再多一点了，殿下。

哈 姆 莱 特　契约纸不是用羊皮作的吗？

霍 拉 旭　是的，殿下，也有用牛皮作的。

哈 姆 莱 特　我看痴心指靠那些玩意儿的人，比牲口聪明不了多少。我要去跟这家伙谈谈。大哥，这是谁的坟？

小 丑 甲　我的，先生——

（挖松泥土深深掘下，掘了个坑招待客人。）

哈 姆 莱 特　我看也是你的，因为你在里头胡闹。

小 丑 甲　您在外头也不老实，先生，所以这坟不是您的；至于说我，我倒没有在里头胡闹，可是这坟的确是我的。

哈 姆 莱 特　你在里头，又说是你的，这就是"在里头胡闹"。因为挖坟是为死人，不是为会蹦会跳的活人，所以说你胡闹。

小 丑 甲　这套胡闹的话果然会蹦会跳，先生；等会儿又该从我这里跳到您那里去了。

哈 姆 莱 特　你是在给什么人挖坟？是个男人吗？

小 丑 甲　不是男人，先生。

哈 姆 莱 特　那么是个女人？

小 丑 甲　也不是女人。

哈 姆 莱 特　不是男人，也不是女人，那么谁葬在这里面？

小 丑 甲　先生，她本来是一个女人，可是上帝让她的灵魂得到安息，她已经死了。

哈 姆 莱 特　这混蛋倒会分辨得这样清楚！我们讲话可得字斟句酌，精心推敲，稍有含糊，就会出丑。凭着上帝发誓，霍拉旭，我觉得这三年来，人人都越变越精明，庄稼汉的脚指头已经挨近朝廷贵人的脚后跟，可以磨破那上面的冻疮了。——你做这掘墓的营生，已经多久了？

1 CLOWN	Of all the days i' th'year I came to' t that day that our last king Hamlet overcame Fortinbras.
HAMLET	How long is that since?
1 CLOWN	Cannot you tell that? Every fool can tell that. It was that very day that young Hamlet was born: he that is mad and sent into England.
HAMLET	Ay, marry, why was he sent into England?
1 CLOWN	Why, because he was mad: he shall recover his wits there, or if he do not, it's no great matter there.
HAMLET	Why?
1 CLOWN	'Twill not be seen in him there, there the men are as mad as he.
HAMLET	How came he mad?
1 CLOWN	Very strangely, they say.
HAMLET	How strangely?
1 CLOWN	Faith, e'en with losing his wits.
HAMLET	Upon what ground?
1 CLOWN	Why, here in Denmark? I have been sexton here man and boy thirty years.
HAMLET	How long will a man lie i'th' earth ere he rot?
1 CLOWN	Faith, if he be not rotten before he die——as we have many pocky corses nowadays that will scarce hold the laying in—— he will last you some eight year, or nine year. A tanner will last you nine year.
HAMLET	Why he more than another?
1 CLOWN	Why sir, his hide is so tanned with his trade, that he will keep out water a great while; and your water is a sore decayer of your whoreson dead body Here's a skull now. this skull

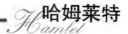

小　丑　甲	我开始干这营生，是在我们的老王爷哈姆莱特打败福丁布拉斯那一天。
哈 姆 莱 特	那是多久以前的事？
小　丑　甲	你不知道吗？每一个傻子都知道的；那正是小哈姆莱特出世的那一天，就是那个发了疯给他们送到英国去的。
哈 姆 莱 特	嗯，对了；为什么他们叫他到英国去？
小　丑　甲	就是因为他发了疯呀；他到英国去，他的疯病就会好的，即使疯病不会好，在那边也没有什么关系。
哈 姆 莱 特	为什么？
小　丑　甲	英国人不会把他当作疯子；他们都跟他一样疯。
哈 姆 莱 特	他怎么会发疯？
小　丑　甲	人家说得很奇怪。
哈 姆 莱 特	怎么奇怪？
小　丑　甲	他们说他神经有了毛病。
哈 姆 莱 特	从哪里来的？
小　丑　甲	还不就是从丹麦本地来的？我在本地干这掘墓的营生，从小到大，一共有三十年了。
哈 姆 莱 特	一个人埋在地下，要经过多少时候才会腐烂？
小　丑　甲	假如他不是在未死以前就已经腐烂——就如现在有的是害杨梅疮死去的尸体，简直抬都抬不下去——他大概可以过八九年。一个硝皮匠在九年以内不会腐烂。
哈 姆 莱 特	为什么他要比别人长久一些？
小　丑　甲	因为，先生，他的皮硝得比人家的硬，可以长久不透水；倒霉的尸体一碰到水，是最会腐烂的。这儿又是一个骷

hath lien you i' th'earth three and twenty years.

HAMLET	Whose was it?
1 CLOWN	A whoreson mad fellow's it was, whose do you think it was?
HAMLET	Nay, I know not.
1 CLOWN	A pestilence on him for a mad rogue! He poured a flagon of Rhenish on my head once; this same skull, sir, was sir Yorick' s skull, the king' s jester.
HAMLET	This?
1 CLOWN	E' en that.
HAMLET	Let me see. [*He takes the skull*] Alas, poor Yorick ! I knew him, Horatio, a fellow of infinite jest, of most excellent fancy. He hath borne me on his bask a thousand times, and now how abhorred in my imagination it is! My gorge rises at it. Here hung those lips that I have kissed I know not how oft, Where be your gibes now? Your gambols, your songs, your flashes of merriment, that were wont to set the table on a roar? Not one now to mock your own grinning? Quite chop fallen? Now get you to my lady's chamber, and tell her, let her paint an inch thick, to this favour she must come. Make her laugh at that. Prithee, Horatio, tell me one thing.
HORATIO	What's that, my lord.
HAMLET	Dost thou think Alexander looked o' this fashion i' th' earth?
HORATIO	E' en so.
HAMLET	And smelt so? Pah! [*He sets down the skull.*]
HORATIO	E'en so, my lord.
HAMLET	To what base uses we may return, Horatio! Why may not imagination trace the noble dust of Alexander, till he find it stopping a bung-hole?

髅；这骷髅已经埋在地下二十三年了。

哈姆莱特　它是谁的骷髅？

小丑甲　是个婊子养的疯小子；你猜是谁？

哈姆莱特　不，我猜不出。

小丑甲　这个遭瘟的疯小子！他有一次把一瓶葡萄酒倒在我的头上。这一个骷髅，先生，是国王的弄人郁利克的骷髅。

哈姆莱特　这就是他！

小丑甲　正是他。

哈姆莱特　让我看。（取骷髅）唉，可怜的郁利克！霍拉旭，我认识他；他是一个最会开玩笑、非常富于想象力的家伙。他曾经把我负在背上一千次；现在我一想起来，却忍不住胸头作恶。这儿本来有两片嘴唇，我不知吻过它们多少次。——现在你还会挖苦人吗？你还会蹦蹦跳跳，逗人发笑吗？你还会唱歌吗？你还会随口编造一些笑话，说得满座捧腹吗？你没有留下一个笑话，讥笑你自己吗？这样垂头丧气了吗？现在你给我到小姐的闺房里去，对她说，凭她脸上的脂粉搽得一寸厚，到后来总要变成这个样子的；你用这样的话告诉她，看她笑不笑吧。霍拉旭，请你告诉我一件事情。

霍拉旭　什么事情，殿下？

哈姆莱特　你想亚历山大在地下也是这副形状吗？

霍拉旭　也是这样。

哈姆莱特　也有同样的臭味吗？呸！（掷下骷髅。）

霍拉旭　也有同样的臭味，殿下。

哈姆莱特　谁知道我们将来会变成一些什么下贱的东西，霍拉旭！要是我们用想象推测下去，谁知道亚历山大的高贵的尸体，不就是塞在酒桶口上的泥土？

HORATIO	'Twere to consider too curiously, to consider so.
HAMLET	No, faith, not a jot, but to follow him thither with modesty e-

nough, and likelihood to lead it; as thus. Alexander died, Al-
exander was buried, Alexander returneth to dust, the dust is
earth, of earth we make loam, and why of that loam whereto
he was converted might they not stop a beer-barrel?
Imperious Caesar, dead and turned to clay,
Might stop a hole to keep the wind away.
O, that that earth, which kept the world in awe,
Should patch a wall t'expel the winter's flaw!
But soft, but soft, awhile; here comes the king,
The queen, the courtiers.

　　[*A procession enters the graveyard: the corpse of Ophelia in
an open coffin, with Laertes, the King, the Queen, courtiers
and a Doctor of Divinity in cassock and gown following.*]
Who is this they follow?
And with such maimed rites? This doth betoken
The corse they follow did with desperate hand
Fordo it own life. 'Twas of some estate.
Couch we awhile, and mark.
　　[*Retiring with Horatio.*]

LAERTES	What ceremony else?
HAMLET	That is Laertes, a very noble youth; mark.
LAERTES	What ceremony else?
PRIEST	Her obsequies have been as far enlarged

As we have warranty. Her death was doubtful,
And but that great o' ersways the order,
She should in ground unsanctified have lodged

霍 拉 旭	那未免太想入非非了。
哈姆莱特	不，一点不，我们可以不作怪论、合情合理地推想他怎样会到那个地步；比方说吧：亚历山大死了；亚历山大埋葬了；亚历山大化为尘土；人们把尘土做成烂泥；那么为什么亚历山大所变成的烂泥，不会被人家拿来塞在酒瓶桶的口上呢？

恺撒死了，你尊严的尸体

也许变了泥把破墙填砌；

啊！他从前是何等的英雄，

现在只好替人挡雨遮风！

可是不要作声！不要作声！站开；国王来了。

  （教士等列队上；众舁奥菲利娅尸体前行；雷欧提斯及诸送葬者、国王、王后及侍从等随后。）

王后和朝臣们也都来了；他们是送什么人下葬呢？仪式又是这样草率的？瞧上去好像他们所送葬的那个人，是自杀而死的，同时又是个很有身份的人。让我们躲在一旁瞧瞧他们。（与霍拉旭退后。）

雷欧提斯	还有些什么仪式？
哈姆莱特	（向霍拉旭旁白）那是雷欧提斯，一个很高贵的青年；听着。
雷欧提斯	还有些什么仪式？
教 士 甲	她的葬礼已经超过了她所应得的名分。她的死状很是可疑；倘不是因为我们迫于权力，按例就该把她安葬在圣

Till the last trumpet: for charitable prayers,

Shards, flints and pebbles should be thrown on her:

Yet here she is allowed her virgin crants,

Her maiden strewments, and the bringing home

Of bell and burial.

LAERTES　　Must there no more be done?

PRIEST　　No more be done!

We should profane the service of the dead

To sing sage requiem and such rest to her

As to peace-parted souls.

LAERTES　　lay her i' th' earth,

And from her fair and unpolluted flesh

May violets spring! I tell thee, churlish priest,

A minist' ring angel shall my sister be, When thou liest

howling.

HAMLET　　What, the fair Ophelia!

QUEEN　　Sweets to the sweet. Farewell!

I hoped thou shouldst have been my Hamlet's wife:

I thought thy bride-bed to have decked, sweet maid,

And not have strewed thy grave.

LAERTES　　O, treble wee fall ten times treble on that cursed head

Whose wicked deed thy most ingenious sense

Deprived thee of! Hold off the earth awhile,

Till I have caught her once more in mine arms:

　　[*Leaps in the grave*]

Now pile your dust upon the quick and dead,

Till of this flat a mountain you have made

T' o' ertop old Pelion, or the skyish head

地以外，直到最后审判的喇叭吹召她起来。我们不但不应该替她祷告，并且还要用砖瓦碎石丢在她坟上；可是现在我们已经允许给她处女的葬礼，用花圈盖在她的身上，替她散播鲜花，鸣钟送她入土，这还不够吗？

雷欧提斯 难道不能再有其他仪式了吗？

教　士　甲 不能再有其他仪式了；要是我们为她唱安魂曲，就像对于一般平安死去的灵魂一样，那就要亵渎了教规。

雷欧提斯 把她放下泥土里去；愿她的娇美无瑕的肉体上，生出芬芳馥郁的紫罗兰来！我告诉你，你这下贱的教士，我的妹妹将要做一个天使，你死了却要在地狱里呼号。

哈姆莱特 什么！美丽的奥菲利娅吗？

王　　后 好花是应当散在美人身上的；永别了！（散花）我本来希望你做我的哈姆莱特的妻子；这些鲜花本来要铺在你的新床上，亲爱的女郎，谁想得到我要把它们散在你的坟上！

雷欧提斯 啊！但愿千百重的灾祸，降临在害得你精神错乱的那个该死的恶人的头上！等一等，不要就把泥土盖上去，让我再拥抱她一次。（跳下墓中）现在把你们的泥土倒下来，把死的和活的一起掩埋了吧；让这块平地上堆起一座高山，那古老的丕利恩和苍秀插天的俄林吗？你会绝食

Of blue Olympus.

HAMLET　[*advancing*] What is he whose grief

Bears such an emphasis? whose phrase of sorrow

Conjures the wand'ring stars, and makes them stand

Like wonder-wounded hearers? This is I,

Hamlet the Dane.　　　　　[*Leaps in after Iaertes.*]

LAERTES　The devil take thy soul ! [*Grappling with him.*]

HAMLET　Thou pray' st not well. I prithee take thy fingers from my

throat,

For though I am not splenitive and rash,

Yet have I in me something dangerous,

Which let thy wiseness fear; hold off thy hand.

KING　Pluck them asunder.

QUEEN　Hamlet, Hamlet!

ALL　Gentlemen!

HORATIO　Good my lord, be quiet.

　　[*Attendants part them, and they come up out of the*
grave.]

HAMLET　Why, I will fight with him upon this theme

Until my eyelids will no longer wag.

QUEEN　O my son, what theme?

HAMLET　I loved Ophelia, forty thousand brothers

Could not with all their quantity of love

Make up my sum. What wilt thou do for her?

KING　O he is mad, laertes.

QUEEN　For love of God, forbear him.

HAMLET　'Swounds, show me what thou't do.

Woo' t weep Woo't fight? Woo' t fast? Woo't tear thyself?

Woo't drink up eisel? Eat a crocodile?

波斯都要俯伏在它的足下。

哈 姆 莱 特　（上前）哪一个人的心里装载得下这样沉重的悲伤？哪一个人的哀恸的词句，可以使天上的行星惊疑止步？那是我，丹麦王子哈姆莱特！（跳下墓中。）

雷 欧 提 斯　魔鬼抓了你的灵魂去！（将哈姆莱特揪住。）

哈 姆 莱 特　你祷告错了。请你不要掐住我的头颈；因为我虽然不是一个暴躁易怒的人，可是我的火性发作起来，是很危险的，你还是不要激恼我吧。放开你的手！

国　　　王　把他们扯开！

王　　　后　哈姆莱特！哈姆莱特！

众　　　人　殿下，公子——

霍　拉　旭　好殿下，安静点儿。（侍从等分开二人，二人自墓中出。）

哈 姆 莱 特　嘿，我愿意为了这个题目跟他决斗，直到我的眼皮不再眨动。

王　　　后　啊，我的孩子！什么题目？

哈 姆 莱 特　我爱奥菲利娅；四万个兄弟的爱合起来，还抵不过我对她的爱。你愿意为她干些什么事情？

国　　　王　啊！他是个疯人，雷欧提斯。

王　　　后　看在上帝的情分上，不要跟他认真。

哈 姆 莱 特　哼，让我瞧瞧你会干些什么事。你会哭吗？你会打架吗？你会撕破你自己的身体吗？你会喝一大缸醋吗？你会吃一

I'll do't. Dost thou come here to whine?

To outface me with leaping in her grave?

Be buried quick with her, and so will I.

And if thou prate of mountains, let them throw

Millions of acres on us, fill our ground,

Singeing his pate against the burning zone,

Make Ossa like a wart! Nay, an thou'lt mouth,

I'll rant as well as thou.

QUEEN　This is mere madness,

And thus awhile the fit will work on him.

Anon as patient as the female dove

When that her golden couplets are disclosed

His silence will sit drooping.

HAMLET　Hear you, sir,

What is the reason that you use me thus?

I loved you ever, but it is no matter,

Let Hercules himself do what he may,

The cat will mow, and dog will have his day. [*Exit.*]

KING　I pray thee, good Horatio, wait upon him. [*Exit Horati-*

o.] [*To Laertes*] strengthen your patience in our

last night's

speech,

We'll put the matter to the present push.

Good Gertrude, set some watch over your son.

This grave shall have a living monument;

An hour of quiet shortly shall we see,

Till then, in patience our proceeding be.　　　[*Exeunt.*]

条鳄鱼吗？我都做得到。你是到这儿来哭泣的吗？你跳下她的坟墓里，是要当面羞辱我吗？你跟她活埋在一起，我也会跟她活埋在一起；要是你还要夸说什么高山大岭，那么让他们把几百万亩的泥土堆在我们身上，直到把我们的地面堆得高到可以被"烈火天"烧焦，让巍峨的奥萨山在相形之下变得只像一个瘤那么大吧！嘿，你会吹，我就不会吹吗？

王　　后　这不过是他一时的疯话。他的疯病一发作起来，总是这个样子的；可是等一会儿他就会安静下来，正像母鸽孵育它那一双金羽的雏鸽的时候一样温和了。

哈姆莱特　听我说，老兄；你为什么这样对待我？我一向是爱你的。可是这些都不用说了，有本领的，随他干什么事吧；猫总是要叫，狗总是要闹的。（下。）

国　　王　好霍拉旭，请你跟住他。（霍拉旭下。向雷欧提斯）记住我们昨天晚上所说的话，格外忍耐点儿吧；我们马上就可以实行我们的办法。好乔特鲁德，叫几个人好好看守你的儿子。这一个坟上要有个活生生的纪念物，平静的时间不久就会到来；现在我们必须耐着心把一切安排。（同下。）

SCENE 2

A hall in the castle

[*Enter Hamlet and Horatio.*]

HAMLET	So much for this, sir, now shall you see the other.
	You do remember all the circumstance?
HORATIO	Remember it, my lord!
HAMLET	Sir, in my heart there was a kind of fighting
	That would not let me sleep; methought I lay
	Worse than the murines in the bilboes. Rashly,
	And praised be rashness for it. Let us know
	Our indiscretion sometime serves us well,
	When our deep plots do pall, and that should learn us
	There's a divinity that shapes our ends,
	Rough-hew them how we will —
HORATIO	That is most certain.
	Up from my cabin, my sea-gown scarfed about me, in the dark,
	Groped I to fred out them, had my desire,
	Fingered their packet, and in fine withdrew
	To mine own room again, making so bold,
	My fears forgetting manners, to unseal
	Their grand commission; where I found, Horatio——
	Ah, royal knavery——an exact command,
	Larded with many several sorts of reasons,
	Importing Denmark's health and England's too,
	With, ho! such bags and goblins in my life,

第二场　城堡中的厅堂

（哈姆莱特及霍拉旭上。）

哈 姆 莱 特　这个题目已经讲完，现在我可以让你知道另外一段事情。你还记得当初的一切经过情形吗？

霍 拉 旭　记得，殿下！

哈 姆 莱 特　当时在我的心里有一种战争，使我不能睡眠；我觉得我的处境比锁在脚镣里的叛变的水手还要难堪。我就鲁莽行事。——结果倒鲁莽对了，我们应该承认，有时候一时孟浪，往往反而可以做出一些为我们的深谋密虑所做不成功的事；从这一点上，我们可以看出来，无论我们怎样辛苦图谋，我们的结果却早已有一种冥冥中的力量把它布置好了。

霍 拉 旭　这是无可置疑的。

哈 姆 莱 特　我从舱里起来，把一件航海的宽衣罩在我的身上，在黑暗之中摸索着找寻那封公文，果然给我达到目的，摸到了他们的包裹；我拿着它回到我自己的地方，疑心使我忘记了礼貌，我大胆地拆开了他们的公文，在那里面，霍拉旭——啊，堂皇的诡计！——我发现一道严厉的命令，借了许多好听的理由为名，说是为了丹麦和英国双方的利益，决不能让我这个险恶的人物逃脱，接到公文之后，必须不

That on the supervise, no leisure bated,

No, not to stay the grinding of the axe,

My head should be struck off.

HORATIO   Is' t possible?

HAMLET   Here's the commission, read it at more leisure.

But wilt thou hear now how I did proceed?

HORATIO   I beseech you.

HAMLET   Being thus be-netted round with villainies,

Or I could make a prologue to my brains

They had begun the play. I sat me down,

Devised a new commission, wrote it fair,

I once did hold it, as our statists do,

A baseness to write fair, and laboured much

How to forget that learning, but, sir, now

It did me yeoman's service. Wilt thou know

Th'effect of what I wrote?

HORATIO   Ay, good my lord.

HAMLET   An earnest conjuration from the king,

As England was his faithful tributary,

As love between them like the pahlm might flourish,

As peace should still her wheaten garland wear

And stand a com comma' tween their amities,

And many such like as' es of great charge,

That on the view and knowing of these contents

Without debatement further, more or less,

He should those beavers put to sudden death,

Not shriving-time allowed.

HORATIO   How was this sealed?

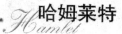
等磨好利斧，立即枭下我的首级。

霍 拉 旭　有这等事？

哈姆莱特　这一封就是原来的国书；你有空的时候可以仔细读一下。可是你愿意听我告诉你后来我怎么办吗？

霍 拉 旭　请您告诉我。

哈姆莱特　在这样重重诡计的包围之中，我的脑筋不等我定下心来思索，就开始活动起来了；我坐下来另外写了一通国书，字迹清清楚楚。从前我曾经抱着跟我们那些政治家们同样的意见，认为字体端正是一件有失体面的事，总是想竭力忘记这一种技能，可是现在它却对我有了大大的用处。你知道我写些什么话吗？

霍 拉 旭　嗯，殿下。

哈姆莱特　我用国王的名义，向英王提出恳切的要求，因为英国是他忠心的藩属，因为两国之间的友谊，必须让它像棕榈树一样发荣繁茂，因为和平的女神必须永远戴着她的荣冠，沟通彼此的情感，以及许许多多诸如此类的重要理由，请他在读完这一封信以后，不要有任何的迟延，立刻把那两个传书的来使处死，不让他们有从容忏悔的时间。

霍 拉 旭　可是国书上没有盖印，那怎么办呢？

HAMLET	Why, even in that was heaven ordinant,
	I had my father's signet in my purse,
	Which was the model of that Danish seal,
	Folded the writ up in the form of th'other,
	Subscribed it, gave' t th' impression, placed it safely,
	The changeling never known: now, the next day
	Was our sea-fight, and what to this was sequent
	Thou knowest already.
HORATIO	So Guildenstern and Rosencrantz go to't.
	Why, man, they did make love to this employment,
	They are not near my conscience, their defeat
	Does by their own insinuation grow.
	'Tis dangerous when the baser nature comes
	Between the pass and fell incensed points
	Of mighty opposites.
HORATIO	Why, what a king is this!
HAMLET	Does it not, think thee, stand me now upon —
	He that hath killed my king, and whored my mother,
	Popped in between th' election and my hopes,
	Thrown out his angle for my proper life,
	And with such cozenage; is' t not perfect conscience
	To quit him with this arm? And is' t not to be damned,
	To let this canker of our nature come
	In further evil?
HORATIO	It must be shortly known to him from England
	What is the issue of the business there.
HAMLET	It will be short, the interim is mine,
	And a man's life's no more than to say ' one'.

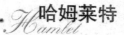
哈 姆 莱 特	啊，就在这件事上，也可以看出一切都是上天预先注定。我的衣袋里恰巧藏着我父亲的私印，它跟丹麦的国玺是一个式样的；我把伪造的国书照着原来的样子折好，签上名字，盖上印玺，把它小心封好，归还原处，一点没有露出破绽。下一天就遇见了海盗，那以后的情形，你早已知道了。
霍 拉 旭	这样说来，吉尔登斯吞和罗森格兰兹是去送死的了。
哈 姆 莱 特	哎，朋友，他们本来是自己钻求这件差使的；我在良心上没有对不起他们的地方，是他们自己的阿谀献媚断送了他们的生命。两个强敌猛烈争斗的时候，不自量力的微弱之辈，却去插身在他们的刀剑中间，这样的事情是最危险不过的。
霍 拉 旭	想不到竟是这样一个国王！
哈 姆 莱 特	你想，我是不是应该——他杀死了我的父王，奸污了我的母亲，篡夺了我的嗣位的权利，用这种诡计谋害我的生命，凭良心说我是不是应该亲手向他复仇雪恨？如果我不去剪除这一个戕害天性的蟊贼，让他继续为非作恶，岂不是该受天谴吗？
霍 拉 旭	他不久就会从英国得到消息，知道这一回事情产生了怎样的结果。
哈 姆 莱 特	时间虽然很局促，可是我已经抓住眼前这一刻工夫；一个人的生命可以在说一个"一"字的一刹那之间了结。可

莎士比亚经典戏剧

But I am very sorry, good Horatio,

That to Laertes I forgot myself;

For by the image of my cause I see

The portraiture of his; I'll court his favours:

But sure the bravery of his grief did put me

Into a towering passion.

HORATIO Peace, who comes here?

[*Enter Osric.*]

OSRIC *Your lordship is right welcome back to Denmark.*

HAMLET [*Aside to Horatio*] I humbly thank you, sir. Dost know this water-fly?

HORATIO [*Aside to Hamlet*] No, my good lord.

HAMLET [*Aside to Horatio*] Thy state is the more gracious, for 'tis a vice to know him. He hath much land, and fertile: let a beast be lord of beasts, and his crib shall stand at the king's mess. 'Tis a chough, but——as I say——spacious in the possession of dirt.

OSRIC Sweet lord, if your lordship were at leisure, I should impart a thing to you from his majesty.

HAMLET I will receive it, sir, with all diligence of spirit. Put your bonnet to his right use, 'tis for the head.

OSRIC I thank your lordship, it is very hot.

No, believe me, 'tis very cold, the wind is northerly.

OSRIC It is indifferent cold, my lord, indeed.

HAMLET But yet, methinks, it is very sultry and hot for my complexion.

OSRIC Exceedingly, my lord, it is very sultry, as 'twere I cannot

是我很后悔，好霍拉旭，不该在雷欧提斯之前失去了自制；因为他所遭遇的惨痛，正是我自己的怨愤的影子。我要取得他的好感。可是他倘不是那样夸大他的悲哀，我也决不会动起那么大的火性来的。

霍　拉　旭　不要作声！谁来了？

　　　　　　（奥斯里克上。）

奥斯里克　殿下，欢迎您回到丹麦来！

哈姆莱特　谢谢您，先生。（向霍拉旭旁白）你认识这只水苍蝇吗？

霍　拉　旭　（向哈姆莱特旁白）不，殿下。

哈姆莱特　（向霍拉旭旁白）那是你的运气，因为认识他是一件丢脸的事。他有许多肥田美壤；一头畜生要是作了一群畜生的主子，就有资格把食槽搬到国王的席上来了。他"咯咯"叫起来简直没个完，可是——我方才也说了——他拥有大批粪土。

奥斯里克　殿下，您要是有空的话，我奉陛下之命，要来告诉您一件事情。

哈姆莱特　先生，我愿意恭聆大教。您的帽子是应该戴在头上的，您还是戴上去吧。

奥斯里克　谢谢殿下，天气真热。

哈姆莱特　不，相信我，天冷得很，在刮北风哩。

奥斯里克　真的有点儿冷，殿下。

哈姆莱特　可是对于像我这样的体质，我觉得这一种天气却是闷热得厉害。

奥斯里克　对了，殿下；真是说不出来的闷热。可是，殿下，陛下叫

tell how. But, my lord, his majesty bade me signify to you
that he has laid a great wager on your head. Sir, this is the
matter.

HAMLET I beseech you remember. [*again moves him to put on his hat*]

OSRIC Nay, good my lord, for mine ease, in good faith. Sir, here
is newly come to court Laertes, believe me, an absolute
gentleman, full of most excellent differences, of very soft
society, and great showing: indeed, to speak sellingly of
him, he is the card or calendar of gentry; for you shall find
in him the continent of what parts a gentleman would see.

HAMLET Sir, his definement suffers no perdition in you, though I
know to divide him inventorially would dizzy th' arithmetic
of memory, and yet but yaw neither in respect of his quick
sail, but in the verity of extolment I take him to be a soul of
great article, and his infusion of such dearth and rareness,
as to make true diction of him his semblable is his mirror,
and who else would trace him? his umbrage, nothing more.

OSRIC Your lordship speaks most infallibly of him.

HAMLET The concernancy, sir? Why do we wrap the gentleman in
our more rawer breath?

OSRIC Sir?

HORATIO Is' t not possible to understand in another tongue? You will
to't, sir, really.

HAMLET What imports the nomination of this gentleman?

OSRIC Of Laertes?

HORATIO His purse is empty already, all's golden words are spent.

HAMLET Of him, sir.

我来通知您一声，他已经为您下了一个很大的赌注了。殿下，事情是这样的——

哈姆莱特	请您不要这样多礼。（促奥斯里克戴上帽子。）
奥斯里克	不，殿下，我还是这样舒服些，真的。殿下，雷欧提斯新近到我们的宫廷里来；相信我，他是一位完善的绅士，充满着最卓越的特点，他的态度非常温雅，他的仪表非常英俊；说一句发自衷心的话，他是上流社会的指南针，因为在他身上可以找到一个绅士所应有的品质的总汇。
哈姆莱特	先生，他对于您这一番描写，的确可以当之无愧；虽然我知道，要是把他的好处一件一件列举出来，不但我们的记忆将要因此而淆乱，交不出一个正确的账目来，而且他这一艘满帆的快船，也决不是我们失舵之舟所能追及；可是，凭着真诚的赞美而言，我认为他是一个才德优异的人，他的高超的禀赋是那样稀有而罕见，说一句真心的话，除了在他的镜子里以外，再也找不到第二个跟他同样的人，纷纷追踪求迹之辈，不过是他的影子而已。
奥斯里克	殿下把他说得一点不错。
哈姆莱特	您的用意呢？为什么我们要用尘俗的呼吸，嘘在这位绅士的身上呢？
奥斯里克	殿下？
霍拉旭	自己所用的语言，到了别人嘴里，就听不懂了吗？早晚你会懂的，先生。
哈姆莱特	您向我提起这位绅士的名字，是什么意思？
奥斯里克	雷欧提斯吗？
霍拉旭	他的嘴里已经变得空空洞洞，因为他的那些好听话都说完了。
哈姆莱特	正是雷欧提斯。

OSRIC	I know you are not ignorant —
HAMLET	I would you did, sir, yet in faith if you did, it would not much approve me. well, sir?
OSRIC	You are not ignorant of what excellence Laertes is —
HAMLET	I dare not confess that, lest I should compare with him in excellence, but to know a nan well were to know himself.
OSRIC	I mean, sir, for his weapon, but in the imputation laid on him by them in his meed, he's unfellowed.
HAMLET	What' s his weapon?
OSRIC	Rapier and dagger.
HAMLET	That' s two of his weapons; but, well.
OSRIC	The king, sir, hath wagered with him six Barbary horses, against the which he has iropawned, as I take it, six French rapiers and poniards, with their assigns, as girdle, hangers, and so. Three of the carriages in faith are very dear to fancy, very responsive to the hilts, most delicate carriages, and of very liberal conceit.
HAMLET	What call you the carriages?
HORATIO	I knew you must be edified by the margent ere you had done.
OSRIC	The carriages, sir, are the hangers.
HAMLET	The phrase would be more germane to the matter, if we could carry a cannon by our sides; I would it might be hangers till then. But on! Six Barbary horses against six French swords, their assigns, and three liberal-conceited carriages, that's the French bet against the Danish. Why is this all ' impawned' as you call it?
OSRIC	The king, sir, hath laid, sir, that in a dozen passes between yourself and him he shall not exceed you three hits.

奥斯里克　我知道您不是不明白——

哈姆莱特　您真能知道我这人不是不明白，那倒很好；可是，说老实话，即使你知道我是明白人，对我也不是什么光彩的事。好，您怎么说？

奥斯里克　我是说，您不是不明白雷欧提斯有些什么特长——

哈姆莱特　那我可不敢说，因为也许人家会疑心我有意跟他比拼高下；可是要知道一个人的底细，应该先知道他自己。

奥斯里克　殿下，我的意思是说他的武艺；人家都称赞他的本领一时无两。

哈姆莱特　他会使些什么武器？

奥斯里克　长剑和短刀。

哈姆莱特　他会使这两种武器吗？很好。

奥斯里克　殿下，王上已经用六匹巴巴里的骏马跟他打赌；在他的一方面，照我所知道的，押的是六柄法国的宝剑和好刀，连同一切鞘带钩子之类的附件，其中有三柄的挂机尤其珍奇可爱，跟剑柄配得非常合式，式样非常精致，花纹非常富丽。

哈姆莱特　您所说的挂机是什么东西？

霍　拉　旭　我知道您要听懂他的话，非得翻查一下注解不可。

奥斯里克　殿下，挂机就是钩子。

哈姆莱特　要是我们腰间挂着大炮，用这个名词倒还合适；在那一天没有来到以前，我看还是就叫它钩子吧。好，说下去；六匹巴巴里骏马对六柄法国宝剑，附件在内，外加三个花纹富丽的挂机；法国产品对丹麦产品。可是，用你的话来说，这样"押"是为了什么呢？

奥斯里克　殿下，王上跟他打赌，要是你们两人交起手来，在十二个回合之中，他至多不过多赢您三着；可是他却觉得他可以

He hath laid on twelve for nine. And it would come to immediate trial, if your lordship would vouchsafe the answer.

HAMLET   How if I answer 'no'?

OSRIC   I mean, my lord, the opposition of your person in trial.

HAMLET   Sir, I will walk here in the hall, if it please his majesty. It is the breathing time of day with me. Let the foils be brought, the gentleman willing, and the king hold his purpose, I will win for him an I can, if not I will gain nothing but my shame and the odd hits.

OSRIC   Shall I re-deliver you e'en so?

HAMLET   To this effect, sir, after what flourish your nature will.

OSRIC   I commend my duty to your lordship.   [*Exit Osric.*]

HAMLET   Yours, yours.

He does well to commend it himself, there are no tongues else for's turn.

HORATIO   This lapwing runs away with the shell on his head.

HAMLET   He did comply, sir, with his dug before he sucked it. Thus has he and many more of the same bevy that I know the drossy age dotes on, only got the tune of the time and, out of an habit of encounter, a kind of yeasty collection, which carries them through and through the most profound and winnowed opinions, and do but blow them to their trial, the bubbles are out.

[*Enter a Lord.*]

LORD   My lord, his majesty commended him to you by young Osric, who brings back to him that you attend him in the hall. He sends to know if your pleasure hold to play with Laertes, or that you will take longer time.

稳赢九个回合。殿下要是答应的话，马上就可以试一试。

哈 姆 莱 特　要是我答应个"不"字呢？

奥 斯 里 克　殿下，我的意思是说，您答应跟他当面比较高低。

哈 姆 莱 特　先生，我还要在这儿厅堂里散散步。您去回陛下说，现在是我一天之中休息的时间。叫他们把比赛用的钝剑预备好了，要是这位绅士愿意，王上也不改变他的意见的话，我愿意尽力为他博取一次胜利；万一不幸失败，那我也不过丢了一次脸，给他多剁了两下。

奥 斯 里 克　我就照这样去回话吗？

哈 姆 莱 特　您就照这个意思去说，随便您再加上一些什么新颖辞藻都行。

奥 斯 里 克　我保证为殿下效劳。

哈 姆 莱 特　不敢，不敢。（奥斯里克下。）多亏他自己保证，别人谁也不会替他张口的。

霍 拉 旭　这一只小鸭子顶着壳儿逃走了。

哈 姆 莱 特　他在母亲怀抱里的时候，也要先把他母亲的奶头恭维几句，然后吮吸。像他这一类靠着一些繁文缛礼撑撑场面的家伙，正是愚妄的世人所醉心的；他们的浅薄的牙慧使傻瓜和聪明人同样受他们的欺骗，可是一经试验，他们的水泡就爆破了。

（一贵族上。）

贵　　　族　殿下，陛下刚才叫奥斯里克来向您传话，知道您在这儿厅上等候他的旨意；他叫我再来问您一声，您是不是仍旧愿意跟雷欧提斯比剑，还是慢慢再说。

HAMLET	I am constant to my purposes, they follow the king's pleasure. If his fitness speaks, mine is ready; now or whensoever, provided I be so able as now.
LORD	The king, and queen, and all are coming down.
HAMLET	In happy time.
LORD	The queen desires you to. use some gentle entertainment to laertes before you fall to play.
HAMLET	She well instructs me. [*Exit the Lord.*]
HORATIO	You will lose this wager, my lord.
HAMLET	I do not think so. Since he went into France, I have been in continual practice. I shall win at the odds; but thou wouldst not think how ill all's here about my heart: but it is no matter.
HORATIO	Nay, good my lord —
HAMLET	It is but foolery, but it is such a kind of gain-giving as would perhaps trouble a woman.
HORATIO	If your mind dislike , anything, obey it. I will forestall their repair hither, and say you are not fit.
HAMLET	Not a whit, we defy augury. There is special providence in the fall of a sparrow. If it be now, 'tis not to come: if it be not to come, it will be now: if it be not mow, yet it will come; the readiness is all. Since no man, of aught he leaves, knows what is' t to leave betimes. Let be.

[*Enter the King, and Queen, Laertes, Lords, Osric and Attendants with foil.*]

KING	Come, Hamlet, come and take this hand from me.

[*he puts the hand of Laertes into the hand of Hamlet.*]

HAMLET	Give me your pardon, sir. I have done you wrong,

哈 姆 莱 特　我没有改变我的初心，一切服从王上的旨意。现在也好，无论什么时候都好，只要他方便，我总是随时准备着，除非我丧失了现在所有的力气。

贵　　　族　王上、娘娘，跟其他的人都要到这儿来了。

哈 姆 莱 特　他们来得正好。

贵　　　族　娘娘请您在开始比赛以前，对雷欧提斯客气几句。

哈 姆 莱 特　我愿意服从她的教诲。（贵族下。）

霍 拉 旭　殿下，您在这一回打赌中间，多半要失败的。

哈 姆 莱 特　我想我不会失败。自从他到法国去以后，我练习得很勤；我一定可以把他打败。可是你不知道我的心里是多么不舒服；那也不用说了。

霍 拉 旭　啊，我的好殿下——

哈 姆 莱 特　那不过是一种傻气的心理；可是一个女人也许会因为这种莫名其妙的疑虑而惶惑。

霍 拉 旭　要是您心里不愿意做一件事，那么就不要做吧。我可以去通知他们不用到这儿来，说您现在不能比赛。

哈 姆 莱 特　不，我们不要害怕什么预兆；一只雀子的死生，都是命运预先注定的。注定在今天，就不会是明天，不是明天，就是今天；逃过了今天，明天还是逃不了，随时准备着就是了。一个人既然在离开世界的时候，只能一无所有，那么早早脱身而去，不是更好吗？随它去。

　　　　　（国王、王后、雷欧提斯、众贵族、奥斯里克及侍从等持钝剑等上。）

国　　　王　来，哈姆莱特，来，让我替你们两人和解和解。（牵雷欧提斯、哈姆莱特二人手使相握。）

哈 姆 莱 特　原谅我，雷欧提斯；我得罪了你，可是你是个堂堂男子，请

But pardon' t as you are a gentleman.

This presence knows, and you must needs have heard,

How I am punished with a sore distraction. What I have done

That might your nature; honour and exception

Roughly awake, I here proclaim was madness.

Was' t Hamlet wronged Laertes? Never Hamlet.

If Hamlet from himself be ta'en away,

And when he' s not himself does wrong Laertes,

Then Hamlet does it not, Hamlet denies it.

Who does it then? His madness. If't be so,

Hamlet is of the faction that is wronged,

His madness is poor Hamlet's enemy.

Sir, in this audience, let my disclaiming from a purposed evil

Free me so far in your most generous thoughts,

That I have shot my arrow o' er the house,

And hurt my brother.

LAERTES   I am satisfied in nature,

Whose motive in this case should stir me most

To my revenge, but in my terms of honour

I stand aloof; and will no reconcilement,

Till by some elder masters of known honour

I have a voice and precedent of peace,

To keep my name ungored. but till that time,

I do receive your offered love like love,

And will not wrong it.

HAMLET   I embrace it freely,

And will this brother's wager frankly paly.

Give us the foils, come on.

你原谅我吧。这儿在场的众人都知道，你也一定听见人家说过，我是怎样被疯狂害苦了。凡是我的所作所为，足以伤害你的感情和荣誉、激起你的愤怒来的，我现在声明都是我在疯狂中犯下的过失。难道哈姆莱特会做对不起雷欧提斯的事吗？哈姆莱特决不会做这种事。要是哈姆莱特在丧失他自己的心神的时候，做了对不起雷欧提斯的事，那样的事不是哈姆莱特做的，哈姆莱特不能承认。那么是谁做的呢？是他的疯狂。既然是这样，那么哈姆莱特也是属于受害的一方，他的疯狂是可怜的哈姆莱特的敌人。当着在座众人之前，我承认我在无心中射出的箭，误伤了我的兄弟；我现在要向他请求大度包涵，宽恕我的不是出于故意的罪恶。

雷欧提斯　按理讲，对这件事情，我的感情应该是激动我复仇的主要力量，现在我在感情上总算满意了；但是另外还有荣誉这一关，除非有什么为众人所敬仰的长者，告诉我可以跟你捐除宿怨，指出这样的事是有前例可援的，不至于损害我的名誉，那时我才可以跟你言归于好。目前我且先接受你友好的表示，并且保证决不会辜负你的盛情。

哈姆莱特　我绝对信任你的诚意，愿意奉陪你举行这一次友谊的比赛。把钝剑给我们。来。

LAERTES	Come, one for me.
HAMLET	I'll be your foil, Laertes. In mine ignorance
	Your skill shall like a star i' th' darkest night
	Stick fiery off indeed.
LAERTES	You mock me, sir.
HAMLET	No, by, this hand.
KING	Give them the foils, young Osric.
	Cousin Hamlet, you know the wager?
HAMLET	Very well, my lord.
	Your grace has hid the odds o' th' weaker side.
KING	I do not fear it, I have seen you both:
	But since he is bettered, we have therefore odds.
LAERTES	This is too heavy: let me see another.
HAMLET	This likes me well. These foils have all a length?
OSRIC	Ay, my good lord.
KING	Set me the stoups of wine upon that table.
	If Hamlet give the first or second hit,
	Or quit in answer of the third exchange,
	Let all the battlements their ordnance fire.
	The king shall drink to Hamlet's better breath,
	And in the cup an union shall he throw,
	Richer than that which four successive kings
	In Denmark's crown have worn: give me the cups,
	And let the kettle to the trumpet speak,
	The trumpet to the cannoneer without,
	The cannons to the heavens, the heaven to earth,
	'Now the king drinks to Hamlet.' Come, begin,
	And you, the judges, bear a wary eye.

哈姆莱特

Hamlet

雷欧提斯	来，给我一柄。
哈姆莱特	雷欧提斯，我的剑术荒疏已久，只能给你帮场；正像最黑暗的夜里一颗吐耀的明星一般，彼此相形之下，一定更显得你的本领的高强。
雷欧提斯	殿下不要取笑。
哈姆莱特	不，我可以举手起誓，这不是取笑。
国　王	奥斯里克，把钝剑分给他们。哈姆莱特侄儿，你知道我们怎样打赌吗？
哈姆莱特	我知道，陛下；您把赌注下在实力较弱的一方了。
国　王	我想我的判断不会有错。你们两人的技术我都领教过；但是后来他又有了进步，所以才规定他必须多赢几着。
雷欧提斯	这一柄太重了；换一柄给我。
哈姆莱特	这一柄我很满意。这些钝剑都是同样长短的吗？
奥斯里克	是，殿下。（二人准备比剑。）
国　王	替我在那桌子上斟下几杯酒。要是哈姆莱特击中了第一剑或是第二剑，或者在第三次交面的时候争得上风，让所有的碉堡上一起鸣起炮来；国王将要饮酒慰劳哈姆莱特，他还要拿一颗比丹麦四代国王戴在王冠上的更贵重的珍珠丢在酒杯里。把杯子给我；鼓声一起，喇叭就接着吹响，通知外面的炮手，让炮声震彻天地，报告这一个消息，"现在国王为哈姆莱特祝饮了！"来，开始比赛吧；你们在场裁判的都要留心看着。

HAMLET	Come on, sir.
LAERTES	Come, my lord,
	[*They play.*]
HAMLET	One!
LAERTES	No.
HAMLET	Judgment?
OSRIC	A hit, a very palpable hit.
LAERTES	Well, again.
KING	Stay, give me drink. Hamlet, this pearl is thine.
	Here's to thy health!
	[*Trumpets sound, and cannon shot off within*]
	Give him the cup.
HAMLET	I'll play this bout first, set it by a while. Come. [*They play.*]
	Another hit! What say you?
LAERTES	A touch, a touch, I do confess' t.
KING	Our son shall win.
QUEEN	He' s fat, and scant of breath.
	Here, Hamlet, take my napkin, rub thy brows.
	The queen carouses to thy fortune, Hamlet.
HAMLET	Good madam!
KING	Gertrude, do not drink.
QUEEN	I will, my lord, I pray you pardon me.
KING	[*Aside*] It is the poisoned cup, it is too late!
HAMLET	I dare not drink yet, madam, by and by.
QUEEN	Come, let me wipe thy face.
LAERTES	My lord, I'll hit him now.
KING	I do not think't.
LAERTES	[*Aside*] And yet 'tis almost 'gainst my conscience.

哈姆莱特

Hamlet

哈 姆 莱 特　请了。

雷 欧 提 斯　请了，殿下。（二人比剑。）

哈 姆 莱 特　一剑。

雷 欧 提 斯　不，没有击中。

哈 姆 莱 特　请裁判员公断。

奥 斯 里 克　中了，很明显的一剑。

雷 欧 提 斯　好；再来。

国　　　王　且慢；拿酒来。哈姆莱特，这一颗珍珠是你的；祝你健
康！把这一杯酒给他。（喇叭起奏。内鸣炮。）

哈 姆 莱 特　让我先赛完这一局；暂时把它放在一旁。来。（二人比
剑。）又是一剑；你怎么说？

雷 欧 提 斯　我承认给你碰着了。

国　　　王　我们的孩子一定会胜利。

王　　　后　他身体太胖，有些喘不过气来。来，哈姆莱特，把我的手
巾拿去，揩干你额上的汗。王后为你饮下这一杯酒，祝你
的胜利了，哈姆莱特。

哈 姆 莱 特　好妈妈！

国　　　王　乔特鲁德，不要喝。

王　　　后　我要喝的，陛下；请您原谅我。

国　　　王　（旁白）这一杯酒里有毒；太迟了！

哈 姆 莱 特　母亲，我现在还不敢喝酒；等一等再喝吧。

王　　　后　来，让我擦干你的脸。

雷 欧 提 斯　陛下，现在我一定要击中他了。

国　　　王　我怕你击不中他。

雷 欧 提 斯　（旁白）可是我的良心却不赞成我干这件事。

莎士比亚经典戏剧

HAMLET	Come, for the third, Laertes. You do but dally,
	I pray you pass with your best violence.
	I am afeard you make a wanton of me.
LAERTES	Say you so? Come on.
	[*They play.*]
OSRIC	Nothing neither way.
LAERTES	Have at you now!

[*He takes Hamlet off his guard and wounds him saghtly;
Hamlet enraged closes with him, and in scuffling they
change rapiers.*]

KING	Part them, they are incensed.
HAMLET	Nay, come again. [*The Queen falls.*]
OSRIC	Look to the queen there, ho!
HORATIO	They bleed on both sides! How is it, my lord?
OSRIC	How is' t, Laertes?
LAERTES	Why, as a woodcock to my own springe, Osric!
	I am justly killed with mine own teachery.
HAMLET	How does the queen?
KING	She swoons to see them bleed.
QUEEN	No, no, the drink, the drink — O my dear Hamlet,
	The drink, the drink! *I am poisoned!* [*She dies.*]
HAMLET	O villainy! Ho! Let the door be locked.
	Treachery! Seek it out. [*Laertes falls.*]
LAERTES	It is here, Hamlet. Hamlet! thou art slain,
	No medicine in the world do thee good,
	In thee there is not half an hour of life,
	The treacherous instrument is in thy hand,
	Unbated and envenomed. The foul practice

哈姆莱特
Hamlet

哈姆莱特	来，该第三个回合了，雷欧提斯。你怎么一点不起劲？请你使出你全身的本领来吧；我怕你在开我的玩笑哩。
雷欧提斯	你这样说吗？来。（二人比剑。）
奥斯里克	两边都没有中。
雷欧提斯	受我这一剑！（雷欧提斯挺剑刺伤哈姆莱特；二人在争夺中彼此手中之剑各为对方夺去，哈姆莱特以夺来之剑刺雷欧提斯，雷欧提斯亦受伤。）
国　　王	分开他们！他们动起火来了。
哈姆莱特	来，再试一下。（王后倒地。）
奥斯里克	哎哟，瞧王后怎么啦！
霍 拉 旭	他们两人都在流血。您怎么啦，殿下？
奥斯里克	您怎么啦，雷欧提斯？
雷欧提斯	唉，奥斯里克，正像一只自投罗网的山鹬，我用诡计害人，反而害了自己，这也是我应得的报应。
哈姆莱特	王后怎么啦？
国　　王	她看见他们流血，昏了过去了。
王　　后	不，不，那杯酒，那杯酒——啊，我的亲爱的哈姆莱特！那杯酒，那杯酒；我中毒了。（死。）
哈姆莱特	啊，奸恶的阴谋！喂！把门锁上！阴谋！查出来是哪一个人干的。（雷欧提斯倒地。）
雷欧提斯	凶手就在这儿，哈姆莱特。哈姆莱特，你已经不能活命了；世上没有一种药可以救治你，不到半小时，你就要死去。那杀人的凶器就在你的手里，它的锋利的刃上还涂着

Hath turned itself on me; lo, here I lie,

Neveer to rise again: thy mother's poisoned:

I can no more, the king, the king's to blame.

HAMLET The poim envenomed too! Then, venom, to thy work.

    [*He stabs the King.*]

ALL Treason! treason!

KING O, yet defend me, friends, I am but hurt.

HAMLET Here, thou incestuous, murderous, damned Dane,

    [*He forces him to drink.*]

Drink off this potion. Is thy union here? Follow my mother.

    [*The King dies.*]

LAERTES He is justly served, it is a poison tempered by himself.

Exchange forgiveness with me, noble Hamlet,

Mine and my father's death come not upon thee,

Nor thine on me!   [*He dies.*]

HAMLET Heaven make thee free of it, I follow thee.

I am dead, Horatio. Wretched queen, adieu!

You that look pale and tremble at this chance,

That are but mutes or audience to this act,

Had I but time, as this fell sergeant, Death,

Is strict in his arrest, O, I could tell you —

But let it be; Horatio, I am dead,

Thou livest, report me, and my cause aright

To the unsatisfied.

HORATIO Never believe it;

I am more an antique Roman than a Dane

Here's yet some liquor left.

HAMLET As thou'rt a man,

毒药。这奸恶的诡计已经回转来害了我自己；瞧！我躺在这儿，再也不会站起来了。你的母亲也中了毒。我说不下去了。国王——国王——都是他一个人的罪恶。

哈 姆 莱 特 锋利的刃上还涂着毒药！——好，毒药，发挥你的力量吧！（刺国王。）

众　　　人 反了！反了！

国　　　王 啊！帮帮我，朋友们；我不过受了点伤。

哈 姆 莱 特 好，你这败坏伦常、嗜杀贪淫、万恶不赦的丹麦奸王！喝干了这杯毒药——你那颗珍珠是在这儿吗？——跟我的母亲一道去吧！（国王死。）

雷 欧 提 斯 他死得应该；这毒药是他亲手调下的。尊贵的哈姆莱特，让我们互相宽恕；我不怪你杀死我和我的父亲，你也不要怪我杀死你！（死。）

哈 姆 莱 特 愿上天赦免你的错误！我也跟着你来了。我死了，霍拉旭。不幸的王后，别了！你们这些看见这一幕意外的惨变而战栗失色的无言的观众，倘不是因为死神的拘捕不给人片刻的停留，啊！我可以告诉你们——可是随它去吧。霍拉旭，我死了，你还活在世上；请你把我的行事的始末根由昭于世人，解除他们的疑惑。

霍 拉 旭 不，我虽然是个丹麦人，可是在精神上我却更是个古代的罗马人；这儿还留剩着一些毒药。

哈 姆 莱 特 你是个汉子，把那杯子给我；放手；凭着上天起誓，你

Give ne the cup, let go, by heaven I'll ha' t!

O God, Horatio, what a wounded name,

Things standing thus unknown, shall live behind me!

If thou didst ever hold me in thy heart,

Absent thee from felicity awhile,

And in this harsh world draw thy breath in pain.

To tell my story. [*March afar off, and shot within*]

What warlike noise is this?

OSRIC   Young Fortinbras, with conquest come from Poland,

To th' ambassadors of England gives

This warlike volley.

HAMLET   O, I die, Horatio, the potent poison quite o' er - crows my

spirit,

I cannot live to hear the news from England,

But I do prophesy th'election lights

On Fortinbras, he has my dying voice.

So tell him, with th'occurrents more and less

Which have solicited. The rest is silence.   [*Dies.*]

HORATIO   Now cracks a noble heart. Good night, sweet prince.

And flights of angels sing thee to thy rest. !

Why does the drum come hither?

[*Enter Fortinbras, the English Ambassadors, and others.*]

FORT'BRAS   Where is this sight?

HORATIO   What is it you would see?

If aught of woe or wonder cease your search

FORT' BRAS   This quarry cries on havoc. O proud death,

What feast is toward in thine eternal cell,

必须把它给我。啊，上帝！霍拉旭，我一死之后，要是世人不明白这一切事情的真相，我的名誉将要永远蒙着怎样的损伤！你倘然爱我，请你暂时牺牲一下天堂上的幸福，留在这一个冷酷的人间，替我传述我的故事吧。（内军队自远处行进及鸣炮声）这是哪儿来的战场上的声音？

奥斯里克 年轻的福丁布拉斯从波兰奏凯班师，这是他对英国来的钦使所发的礼炮。

哈姆莱特 啊！我死了，霍拉旭；猛烈的毒药已经克服了我的精神，我不能活着听见英国来的消息。可是我可以预言福丁布拉斯将被拥戴为王，他已经得到我这临死之人的同意；你可以把这儿所发生的一切事实告诉他。此外仅余沉默而已。（死。）

霍　拉　旭 一颗高贵的心现在碎裂了！晚安，亲爱的王子，愿成群的天使们用歌唱抚慰你安息！——为什么鼓声越来越近了？（内军队行进声。）

（福丁布拉斯、英国使臣及余人等上。）

福丁布拉斯 这一场比赛在什么地方举行？

霍　拉　旭 你们要看些什么？要是你们想知道一些惊人的惨事，那么不用再到别处去找了。

福丁布拉斯 好一场惊心动魄的屠杀！啊，骄傲的死神！你用这样残

That thou so many princes at a shot

So bloodily hast struck?

1 AMBASS　　The sight is dismal,

And our affairs from England come too late.

The ears are senseless that should give us hearing,

To tell him his commandment is fulfilled,

That Rosencrantz and Guildenstern are dead.

Where should we have our thanks?

HORATIO　　Not from his mouth

Had it th' ability of life to thank you;

He never gave commandment for their death;

But since, so jump upon this bloody question,

You from the Polack wars, and you from England,

Are here arrived, give order that these bodies

High on a stage be placed to the view,

And let me speak to th' yet unknowing world

How these things came about; so shall you hear

Of carnal, bloody and unnatural acts,

Of accidental judgments, casual slaughters,

Of deaths put on by cunning and forced cause,

And, in this upshot, purposes mistook

Fall'n on th'inventors' heads: all this can I truly deliver.

FORT'BRAS　　Let us haste to hear it,

And call the noblest to the audience.

For me, with sorrow I embrace my fortune.

I have some rights of memory in this kingdom,

Which now to claim my vantage doth invite me.

HORATIO　　Of that I shall have also cause to speak,

忍的手腕，一下子杀死了这许多王裔贵胄，在你的永久的幽窟里，将要有一席多么丰美的盛筵！

使臣甲 这一个景象太惨了。我们从英国奉命来此，本来是要回复这儿的王上，告诉他我们已经遵从他的命令，把罗森格兰兹和吉尔登斯吞两人处死；不幸我们来迟了一步，那应该听我们说话的耳朵已经没有知觉了，我们还希望从谁的嘴里得到一声感谢呢？

霍拉旭 即使他能够向你们开口说话，他也不会感谢你们；他从来不曾命令你们把他们处死。可是既然你们都来得这样凑巧，有的刚从波兰回来，有的刚从英国到来，恰好看见这一幕流血的惨剧，那么请你们叫人把这几个尸体抬起来放在高台上面，让大家可以看见，让我向那懵无所知的世人报告这些事情的发生经过；你们可以听到奸淫残杀、反常悖理的行为、冥冥中的判决、意外的屠戮、借手杀人的狡计，以及陷人自害的结局；这一切我都可以确确实实地告诉你们。

福丁布拉斯 让我们赶快听你说；所有最尊贵的人，都叫他们一起来吧。我在这一个国内本来也有继承王位的权利，现在国中无主，正是我要求这一个权利的机会；可是我虽然准备接受我的幸运，我的心里却充满了悲哀。

霍拉旭 关于那一点，我受死者的嘱托，也有一句话要说，他的

And from his mouth whose voice will draw on more.

But let this same be presently performed,

Even while men's minds are wild, lest more mischance

On plots and errors, happen.

FORT'BRAS   let four captains

Bear Hamlet like a soldier to the stage,

For he was likely, had he been put on,

To have proved most royal; and for his passage,

The soldiers' music and the rite of war

Speak loudly for him:

Take up the bodies; such a sight as this

Becomes the field, but here shows much amiss.

Go, bid the soldiers shoot.

　　[*A dead march. Exeunt, bearing off the dead bodies. after which a peal of ordnance is shot off.*]

意见是可以影响许多人的；可是在这人心惶惶的时候，让我还是先把这一切解释明白了，免得引起更多的不幸、阴谋和错误来。

福丁布拉斯 让四个将士把哈姆莱特像一个军人似的抬到台上，因为要是他能够践登王位，一定会成为一个贤明的君主的；为了表示对他的悲悼，我们要用军乐和战地的仪式，向他致敬。把这些尸体一起抬起来。这一种情形在战场上是不足为奇的，可是在宫廷之内，却是非常的变故。去，叫兵士放起炮来。（奏丧礼进行曲；众舁尸同下。内鸣炮。）